To Charlotte and Stern
From Jerusalem
with love
Ezra
Feb 27th 201?

ELNAKAM

EZRA YAKHIN

Translated by Herzlia Dobkin

D1529361

YAIR PUBLISHING HOUSE

TEL AVIV – 1992

© YAIR PUBLISHING HOUSE
PRINTED IN ISRAEL
SEPTEMBER 1992
HIDEKEL PRESS – TEL AVIV

THIS BOOK IS LOVINGLY DEDICATED
TO THE PARENTS OF THE
FIGHTERS

TABLE OF CONTENTS

Dr. Israel Eldad – Introduction to the book of a fighter
and a comrade   9

PART 1 – ON THY WALLS, O JERUSALEM!

In Blue Lettering   11
There was no King in Israel   14
Tale of a Snake   20
Itbach el Yahud! (Kill the Jews)   22
Down with the White Paper!   27
Bar Mitzva   29
A Telegram Boy in Jerusalem   32
How to Join the Underground   41
The High Commissioner is wounded   44
Blowing the Shofar at the Western Wall   45
Brith Hashmona'im   49
A Lehi Man am I   52
Conspiracy   54
The "Season"   59
Old Hillel   61
A Legend called Ya'ir   65
The Accused become Judges   71
Rebellion   74
The Ma'as (The Deed)   75
Tomorrow We meet at "X"   78
Ha'im is expelled from School   88
"A Girl's been looking for Me"   91
A Boy sleeps on the Stairs   95
The One Who refused to submit   99
One a Communist, One in the Hagana, One in the Etzel
and One in the Lehi   102
Brith Hashmona'im secedes from the Lehi   105
I'm a Petit Bourgeois   108
Every Corner in the City is an Ambush   113
A Tale of a Passport   121
A Punch in the Belly and a Kick in the Arse   127
What will I tell my Parents when they ask:
"Where is your Brother?"   128

PART II – MY COMRADES, SONS OF GLORY

In the Division	134
How to get a "Sick" Report	136
Off to the Course... and the Sea	142
Jerusalem seems Further and Further Away...	144
The Return Home	148
Mr. Khalil's Stick	152
Sans Home, Sans Family	155
"You're on Observation Duty this Evening"	158
"Datan, I envy You!..."	170
A Trap set at Night, during the Curfew	175
A Grenade between Two Hearts	182
The Target – MacMillan	184
"Canoodling behind the Rocks..."	187
"The General!"	190
The Center is silent	199
Where is the Boy?	202
"You are needed in the 'Youth' Division."	211
There's a Pasting in the Triangle this Evening	215
Elnakam	219
Ariella	222
"They hang Them..."	224
The Youngsters of Ra'anana	228

PART III – "OUR EYES ARE TURNED TOWARD ZION"

Let there be no Division!	235
The End of King George!	240
Let the Sabre speak!	244
Why I couldn't draw my Gun!	247
A Meeting in the Hospital	253
"When I shout 'Moshe!' You shout too!"	256
The Whole Land is a Frontier	249
The Slogan – A United Front	261
Islands of Hebrew Government	272
Grieve for the Jewish Quarter!	280
A State is declared in Tel-Aviv	282
May 15, 1948	284
Until the Arrival of the U.N.O.	292
This Night the Old City will be freed!	303

Dear Reader,

During the years which have passed since I wrote my book "THE STORY OF ELNAKAM", many underground comrades have given me additional details about the actual circumstances of the deeds in which they too were actively involved, and also other facts of actions which I had only heard about.

In writing this book I did not intend (nor do I now intend) to give the reader a detailed historical biography. I wanted to tell my own story, but in the nature of things it is also the story of the youth of my generation who joined the underground movements.

If I have inadvertantly left out or forgotten those comrades who took part in the same actions as I – I ask their pardon. I am especially sorry if I have done an injustice to those close comrades whose vital actions should have been, but were not recorded; this was because of the injunction of the leaders of the underground which prohibited publication of certain actions and insisted that the heroes of those events remain anonymous – even to us, the fighters.

However, I do particularly want to mention my comrade-in-arms Zvi Frunin who, only days after this book was written, did his history become known to me. Zvi, who worked side by side with Yair and was the leader of underground cells in Haifa and Tel Aviv, never surrendered. The British never succeeded in capturing him even though his picture appeared in all the newspapers with a price on his head. And this during the black days after the murder of Yair when many of the best of our fighters were arrested or gave themselves up.

Ezra Yakhin.

Some Remarks on the Book of a Freedom Fighter and a Friend

At first glance it would seem that there is no shortage of books dealing with the underground: historical books, personal reminiscences, political and ideological analyses, and the literature of the underground itself such as proclamations, pamphlets etc. Yet there is still something lacking no less important than all of these, an element that would bring those days and, even more so the nights, alive for the contemporary reader, make him participate in the fighters' experiences, their moods and emotions, sense what the Jews were feeling in the street, at home, in the synagogue day after day, night after night, feel the reality behind the newspaper headlines, beyond the thunder of explosions, watch and listen with them, know their longings and fears, sense the flesh-and-blood reality of the underground and its peculiar environment. To do all this it seems there must be poets and artists, dramatists and interpreters skilled in the art and craft of representation. All these will come in time, who can doubt it, even though they have held back till now for reasons not to be discussed here. There is no subject under the sun too lowly to serve as material for their writing, sculpting and painting; all has been grist to their mill but for this unique treasure of dramatic experience – a treasure assiduously ignored as if relegated to oblivion by force. Is this a manifestation of self-abnegation, an attempt to escape from ourselves? One Arab's death in the '48 war, another's suffering at the hands of the Israeli 'oppressor' – these are "interpreted", considered worthy of dramatization. But for two or three exceptions, has any attempt been made to create an epic, an educational model out of the heroism and self-sacrifice of the men who died on the scaffold, of the youth caught putting up proclamations and tortured to death by a minion of the Empire?

They are still to come, these artists, and future generations will yet be nurtured by the song, story and drama of those days of glory, just as we, in our time were nurtured on the tales of Dvora the Prophetess, of Samson, of the Holy Temples and the Ten Victims of Tyranny. But what in the meantime?

In the interim it is most important to prepare documentary material, a living testimony not only in the form of catalogs and descriptions of operations or collections of proclamations and speeches but living evidence in its most literal form and meaning, facts of life of the underground, the living cells, their formation, their cohesion into a fabric palpitating and glowing, often to go up in flames – the testimony of the rank and file.

Such a testimony in offered is this book, showing how a Hebrew youth found his way to the underground movement. The stress is laid not on the technical ways and means of the process but rather on the emotional development leading to such a step; what he read, heard, felt before taking the crucial step. We not only find here the mechanics of pasting proclamations on the walls but see his emotional involvement with the deed, an involvement investing those proclamations with a power not less than that of the written words, a power that was transmitted the following morning to all those who read them. We read how a decent, honest boy is driven to deceive not just the British policeman but his own father and mother, motivated by a love so deep that it sanctifies his behaviour, makes it acceptable and even compulsory. The authenticity and scope of the book are deepened and widened by the considerations of state to be found in it and also by the manifestations of love and hatred with which it abounds. For it is only the pseudo-intellectual eunuchs who mock the "emotionalism" of the underground, those whose inability to feel makes them hate anything imbued with emotion.

This book is a revelation of the inner feelings of a youth in the underground. It has the additional grace of being imbued with the very atmosphere of Jerusalem. Jerusalem is not only the scene of the action, with the stress placed on the battle for the city, but we get an insight into the lives of the Jerusalem suburbs where patriotism and faith go hand in hand. This is a stylised reconstruction of actions and experiences and also a fighter's lament for the liberty of Israel, rising from the very roots of the people and their faith, roots going back for generations. The dominant characteristic of this testimony is its authenticity. Without the help of such a testimony no historian, let alone a poet, may hope to understand that generation and its struggle, sense the flesh-and-blood reality of waging a war in the underground. This war is seen here through the eye of the writer, symbolically enough an eye that was wounded and turned to bleeding flesh during the battle for the Old City. It is fitting that this war, this city and even the reality of today and our struggle should thus be regarded: with love and pain, with love in spite of pain. From being just another testimonial to the past, this book is transmuted by the power of love into a link in the continuous chain of the struggle for liberty and complete salvation.

Israel Eldad

PART 1

ON THY WALLS, O JERUSALEM

In Blue Lettering

February, 1, 1944, the last year of World War II

It was just another cold winter morning when I set out for work at the Jaffa Road Central Post Office. Lightly running down the steps of our house in the Machane Yehuda Quarter, I left Tachkimoni Lane and turned into Jaffa Road, which was at that hour humming with children, some carrying school bags and others, like me, hurrying to their places of work.

A quick flick of the hand to brush my uniform – the dark blue suit of a messenger boy in the Postal Service of the Government of Palestine (*Eretz Israel*), a pat along the scarlet piping running down the length of my pants, a final adjusting of my cap to the desired angle – and I was all set for the office from which, riding a red bike, I would begin my day's work.

A large crowd pressing around the billboard beside Oplatka's Pharmacy caught my eye, their breath steaming in the cold morning air as they stood reading a large placard. Curious, I pushed my way among them, eager to get a look at the notice that seemed to have been printed in blue-colored ink. It said:

To the Hebrew youth of Zion!
A Temporary Hebrew government must be proclaimed immediately...
Raise a Hebrew army... admit the Jews of Europe into Israel...
Damn all traitors and down with the cowards... do not obey any orders
issued by the foreign government – break them and swear to obey
Hebrew rule alone!

The Words seared my brain: "The insurgents will not be deterred... blood and suffering... we will fight... every Jew in the homeland will fight..." Suddenly realizing I was late for work, I

11

lengthened my stride, my pulse beating to the rhythm of the slogans I had just read: "will submit to Hebrew rule alone... Damn the traitors, down with the cowards... Every Jew in the homeland will fight..." Was I imagining things or had the dreams I had dreamt since childhood finally become reality?

The mass demonstrations against the White Paper, held when I was just eleven years old, came to my mind. At that time unbelievable rumors of the devastation of European Jewry had begun filtering through to us, becoming progressively more terrifying as the truth began to emerge, and the cold indifference of the British, adamant in their refusal to admit more than a handful of the survivors into the country, was more than flesh and blood could bear. With the beginning of the demonstrations I had hoped that the people would rise and rebel against the tyrants, just as they had done in the glorious days of Yehuda the Maccabbee and Bar Kochba, driving the alien rulers from the land. All the kids in our quarter, myself included, were quick to join these demonstrations, shouting slogans with the grown-ups: "Down with the White Paper! Free immigration! A Jewish State!" till we could shout no more, and surrounded by British policemen, reiterated: "We will not give in, we will not give in!"

That was four years ago, four years of frustration and a growing sense of helplessness. Jews were still being massacred wholesale in Europe but here the Jewish community went on as usual, quiet and passive, constantly avoiding any open confrontation with the British, not to say a declaration of war. But now? Would my compatriots still content themselves with high-sounding slogans printed in blue on the bill-boards, or was the proclamation I had just read the long awaited harbinger of rebellion? The bitterness of disappointment would have been so great that I daren't let myself hope at all.

Several days passed by when suddenly, out of the blue, the air was filled with the sound of explosion. Beginning with the Immigration Branches of the Criminal Investigation Department (C.I.D.) in Jerusalem, Tel-Aviv and Haifa, British Government buildings collapsed in ruins, buildings that had for so long symbolized the alien power, and their destruction bore witness to the fact that the blue printed proclamation had not let us down this time. The fight for freedom had seriously begun.

"Politics" held little interest for me at the time, nor was I especially attracted to any single party. It never occurred to me to ask who was responsible for these proclamations – enough that the struggle had begun, and I followed each development with breathless eagerness, my enthusiasm reaching its height whenever I read of an enemy casualty. War was war and no quarter must be given, a fact that I had been inculcated with since childhood when listening avidly to the many stories of our wars for freedom.

One morning the papers carried photographs of several men wanted by the Palestine Government, with liberal rewards offered to anyone supplying information about them. They were members of the *LEHI* movement (*Lohamei Herut Yisrael* – Fighters for the Liberation of Israel). I liked the name *Lehi* very much, it sounded just right for these fine, brave men, but I had always thought the movement fighting the British and covering the walls with anti-Government propaganda were called *ETZEL* (*Irgun Tzvai Leumi* – National Military Organization) and now there was this new group with a price on their heads. Every morning I would scan the wall for notices put up by the underground until finally I found a small stencilled sheet put out by *Lehi* which made the difference between the two organizations clear: *Lehi* made no bones about shooting down British soldiers and sought no moral justification for such contingencies, while the *Etzel*, on the other hand, limited itself to destroying buildings and confiscating arms and avoided killing, on the grounds that this might undermine the British war effort against the Germans at that time.

I was instinctively drawn to *Lehi* and it never occurred to me that these men I had so long admired were none other than the despised "Stern Group," a fact that was shortly brought home to *me by some members of the Shomer Hatzair.* There was a rumor* one day that a group of *Lehi* youths had tried to distribute some pamphlets at a *Shomer Hatzair* club where they were caught by the *Shomerniks* who held them by force and called for the police. One

---

* A Zionist-leftist party violently opposed to both the *Etzel* and the *Lehi*.

of the *Lehi* lads pulled out a revolver, fired a shot in the air and got away with all his friends in the ensuing panic. The angry *Shomerniks* threatened to take revenge, declaring. among other vilifications, that the members of *Lehi* were no less than some of the "Stern Gang," reverting to their usual evil doings.

To me this seemed no more than a blatant lie. An assiduous reader of wall pamphlets, I knew that the *Haganah* and the official National Institutions were in the habit of vilifying the *Etzel* and the, *Lehi*, not stopping short of any calumny. The connection between *Lehi* and the "Stern Gang", too, seemed to me trumped-up. It was inconceivable to me that these lads whom I admired so whole-heartedly, even though I didn't know a single one of them, would be no more than a notorious band of robbers whose daring coups had caused such a stir two years ago. Like all the law-abiding citizens at that time I had been pleased when the leader, Avraham Stern the 'Robber' was finally liquidated. I well remember how, that day, I walked into the house, the *Yediot Aharonoth* evening paper in my hand, and gladly announced that he was dead, killed by the police while trying to escape. Neither my friends, my parents or myself had the slightest intimation of the remorse that incident would cause us all in the years to come. How could we know when all the papers joined in describing him as a dangerous, mad dog, to be destroyed at any cost? It was some time before I came by a copy of *The Front*, the *Lehi* organ, giving the full story of the life and death of Ya'ir Avraham Stern.

There was no King in Israel

Before my fourteenth birthday I had to leave school and start contributing to the upkeep of the family. Till then, together with many of the poorer children of Jerusalem, I attended the Ratisbonne, a French-Catholic school which catered to the many not so prosperous parents desirous of giving their offspring a 'good European' education. Four languages were taught: French, English, Hebrew and Arabic. An added attraction were the low

14

school fees demanded, and the 350 pupil population was made up mostly of Jews, with a small minority of Christian and Moslem Arabs.

At 7:30 every morning the bell would ring and we would fall in line, class facing class. Monsieur Kamalle, who taught in the first grade and was in charge of general discipline, would inspect the rows, then march us all into the school rooms. For leaving the row or getting caught talking you had your hand slapped on the spot with Monsieur K's special rod, made for this specific purpose in the school workshop. Only after special monitors had gone through the class rooms and ensured perfect silence did the teachers finally enter. This ceremony of falling in line and marching into class was repeated after every break until all were released at four o'clock; all, that is, except for those unfortunates who were kept in and were *au piqúe*. But who is without sin among us? Hardly anyone was spared the dubious pleasure of being stood in the corner at least once a month, uncomfortably reading the book in his hands.

A list of the boys who had been unruly or downright disobedient was daily collected by the teachers and handed over to Monsieur K., who read it out for all to hear at the end-of-the-day assembly. Upon dismissal most of us would gladly rush out, leaving the unhappy sinners behind us, doomed to another hour of study behind the thick walls.

The punishments inflicted upon us at school were of a wondrous variety, with some, like the "Signal" being highly sophisticated. The "Signal" was, in fact, a square of plywood with a piece of string attached to it, and had to be passed from hand to hand during the day, all in accordance with certain rules. It was a convention at this school that only French and English should be spoken, and when anyone absent mindedly blurted out a word in Hebrew or Arabic he was immediately handed the "Signal" which could only be gotten rid of by catching another transgressor and thrusting it upon him. The unlucky possessor at the end of the day would be fined with an *au piqué*, put in the corner and subjected to the ridicule of his peers, who would cry: *"Le signal avec Chasson! Le signal avec Mizrachi!"* But there were times when esprit de corps and our innate loyalty to our native tongue, Hebrew, would overcome our fear and we would conspire to speak only Hebrew, come what may, and take the *au piqué* punishment in turn.

But being forced to use a foreign language in my own country was not our only humiliation – there was also the *chabass*, or solitary confinement, a first taste of which I was given after I had the misfortune to lose my French textbook which was owned jointly by my brother and myself. My father, who couldn't afford to buy one for each of us, was angry enough to go to the Principal to complain about our carelessness, and we were both duly warned that we would be punished should this happen again. All this took some time and when we arrived at our classes everybody was already in his seat, upon which the irritated teacher ordered us back to the Principal's office, telling me to shut up when I tried to explain.

This time the Principal was truly furious with the two boys causing so much trouble. Punishment was meted out forthwith and we were dispatched to the *chabass*, the territory of Pere Laniado the Convert. We were marched down into the cellar, little more than a narrow cell a meter and a half square, its only light a dim ray penetrating the tiny window, and there we sat for hours in complete isolation. As this was the time of the demonstrations frequently held against the White Paper, and schoolboys like us being naturally fervent patriots, the 'prison' became a symbol of oppression and we spent the time there shouting "Down with the White Paper!"

The teachers in this school were mainly priests of many nationalities, including native Arabs. Politics were seldom discussed, though I do recall one exception, a statement made by Pere Curtin: "It is perfectly clear to me why the High Commissioner refuses to admit European Jews to this country. After all, how can one tell if they're not spies?" – which earned him our eternal hatred. On the other hand there was Pere Buckley, an Irish priest whom we dearly loved for being so sparing with corporal punishment, evincing no signs of enjoyment when, as sometimes happened, he was forced to resort to it. Moreover, he was given to making derogatory remarks about the British, a

16

trait which endeared him to us even more.

The one teacher we really loved and whose lessons we enjoyed was Monsieur Pedro, the Bible teacher. When I sometimes met him in the Ohel Moshe quarter I would glow with happiness and it was an effort to greet him in a formal manner.

Hebrew was taught for one hour a day, first thing in the morning. The few Arab pupils were exempted from this lesson and arrived for the next one. Bible lessons were part of the Hebrew program, one hour weekly and we could hardly wait for Tuesday morning to arrive. Monsieur Pedro's class started off in such perfect quiet that even the monitors knew there was no need for class inspection before it, and when he entered, elegant, of medium size but exuding power, to greet us with his musical voice, a shudder seemed to pass through the class. As we waited expectantly he would open the book and read out a passage, then, using a simpler, more comprehensible vocabulary, paraphrase what he had just read. It was during the re-telling of the story that the room would sometimes seem to fill with giant figures from the Bible. First came the good Kings, honest and God-fearing, who built high walls for security, well-fortified with towers, enriched the Temple and gave no quarter to the idol-worshippers or their priests. Or there would be the bad, evil Kings, oppressing the orphans and the widows, robbing the poor. Interspersed among them would walk the Prophets in majesty, followed by the Zealots and Just Men advocating justice and fair trial. Feeling as though we were imprisoned in those high vaulted rooms, surrounded by high walls around the courtyard where the porter sat to prevent any child from leaving until school was officially over, we would be transported in our imagination to the far-away hills of Yehuda, all covered with vines, and to the green pastures of the Shomron. Such was the magic of Monsieur Pedro. When he spoke of Kings who had sinned I knew, without a shadow of doubt, that had I lived then I would have been among those fighting them to the death. As for the good, honest ones, I knew that I would have served them as long as there was breath in my body. How sad it seemed to me then that I had not been born in those wonderful times, the days when there was a King in Israel. Then, gradually returning to reality, I would consider the drabness of the world we lived in – no King so good all would flock to his banner, no, not even a bad King against whom one could take up arms.

My parents belonged to the Sephardic community, of well-born families boasting several famous Rabbis and wealty merchants. Mother was born and raised in Alexandria and Father, whose family came to Israel from Syria several generations ago, was born in Jerusalem. When a young man, Father went to America, seeking a livelihood, then returned on a visit to Jerusalem. In the course of his journey the ship anchored at Alexandria and he went ashore for a short respite and a visit to the local Jewish Community Center where, as was the custom in those days, a match was made for him with a respectable, well-born Jewish girl, a secretary in an office. Things went well from the very start – they liked each other and straight-away decided to make their home in Jerusalem.

Things did not perhaps go so smoothly as they appeared in the telling of the story. Father wanted to take his bride to America, the land of unlimited opportunity, but she wouldn't hear of it; it was too far away from her family in Egypt. They finally compromised and settled in Jerusalem.

Compared to Alexandria, which was at that time a bustling, modern city, Jerusalem was a provincial backwater – no roads, no taps in the houses and no electricity. It must have been difficult for a young woman brought up in the comforts of a city to adjust to the quiet, orthodox environment of Jerusalem. She missed the fun of swimming and the beach, the liveliness of a busy port, the well-paved roads. The cobbled streets hurt her feet that were shod in high-heeled shoes, and her newly aquired family, too, seemed strange at first. It must be remembered that at that time Jewish girls of even the best families were not given much education, nor were they supposed to make a living. She was therefore bored and lonely, particularly as there was much squabbling among the women in the family in which she couldn't help getting involved, try as she might to keep aloof.

But most of all she missed the sea-side, longing for it even after her first children were born. All in all Father decided it would be best to make our home in Jaffa, and the family went to Manshia, a suburb by the sea where eventually I was born. In spite of all their hopes things went against them and Mother was not destined to enjoy her new home for long. Business was bad in Jaffa and the children always ailing, especially with eye infections. Mother's love for the sea had to give way to other considerations and she agreed to return to Jerusalem.

Our first home, from which we eventually had to flee for our lives (as I shall describe later) was in the Yemin Moshe quarter, facing the walls of the Old City. From there we went to the Mahane Yehuda quarter, close to the fruit and vegetable market where we were still living at the time of this story.

Overlooking the courtyard of our house was a flight of steps on which I loved to sit with David, my brother, a great story teller. His tales were usually peopled with the heroic giants of our history and one day he told me about the Maccabees. This was a story I had long been familiar with, but David's version was somewhat different.

I had always been told that the Maccabee insurrection was caused by the insupportable tyranny of the Greeks; but, according to David, this wasn't so, "The Maccabees fought against a foreign conqueror; their object was freedom. Foreigners were ruling our country and controlling our Holy Places and the power had to be given back to the true masters of the land, the Jews."

Only ten at the time, I was too young to comprehend the significance of the problem, so simple yet so crucial: If the grown-ups are so full of admiration for the Maccabees who had fought for independence and succeeded in throwing off the foreign yoke – why don't they do anything to get rid of the British? True, we were in the minority, but the Maccabees, too, were few in number. If only we had a leader like Matithias! Fervently I hoped that one day there would rise such a one and, supported by his five sons, send forth the call: "He who is for God – come to me!"* But day followed day and no spectacular king or hero made his appearance. My only consolation was that with the passing of time

*Footnote (Ex: 32:26).

I would grow to manhood and, should he then appear I would no longer be a child but ready to take my place beside him.

A Tale of A Snake

Though I loved playing with other children and did my best to win at games, I was a bit diffident in the face of violence for its own sake and avoided the fights breaking out for no visible reason or provocation. Some of the more violent among my playmates were prone to a kind of primitive obstinacy which was incomprehensible to me, an avidity to win at any price, even at the risk of wounding themselves or their opponents. This harsh brutality revolted me and I would do my best to get out of a fight, even when I knew that with a little effort I could easily overcome them. But this did not prevent me from indulging in day dreams about all kinds of heroic deeds and acts of dauntless courage which I displayed for all the world to see, where I always acted for the good of all.

One day I heard some of the older boys at school boasting of how they had killed a snake with their bare hands. This made a deep impression on me. A few days later, as our class was going through physical training in the school yard, suddenly everybody began running in all directions, the teacher included. Not knowing the reason for the blind panic I ran with them; then, turning back for a moment, I caught sight of a medium sized speckled yellow snake crawling towards us on its belly. Without a moment's thought I ran back to the snake and crushed the head with the heel of my sandal, hitting again and again till the head fell away. Picking up the beheaded body I carried it proudly back to my mates who were huddled round the teacher. Fully expecting to be praised for my courage I could not understand why they seemed embarrassed and Monsieur Rolland, who was a well-known professional boxer ('boxer' being synonymous with 'hero' for us, at that age) barely managed to mumble something that sounded like "ßravo!" and remained silent. This reaction was highly confusing,

20

for in my innocence I never realized that they were jealous and ashamed of their own cowardice. Childishly enough I had expected them to show more respect for a boy who, with nothing but his sandal to help him, had crushed a poisonous snake.

A popular pastime often indulged in was that of stoning boys of other quarters. On Saturday mornings, Holy Days and during the summer vacation you could hear some of the kids, accompanied by friends from the Beit Yaakov quarter, calling for volunteers against the *Kurdim*. Right away a gang would be formed to be reinforced during the march by our allies in Beit Yaakov. Srulik, a tall, handsome stripling would lead them against the enemy at the Zichron Yossef quarter, mostly inhabited by Kurdish Jews, and the verbal provocation would begin. This quickly turned to fist fighting to be followed shortly by a hail of rocks and stones... Much later the wounded could be seen, proudly strutting through the quarter with bandaged hands and feet. There was one called Yehuda, I recall, whose head seemed to be bandaged most of the time.

My brother and I kept well away from these skirmishes and when called to join the gang would diplomatically retire to one of inner court-yards and play at *alamb oulic,* a game played with small wooden chips and a large stick with which we would tip them into the air, knocking them away as far as possible. Another game of ours was "five stones," or "knuckle bones."

I never could make out why the kids of our quarter hated the Kurds so much, always burning for a fight with them. I was no saint myself and would often join the gang in some exploit or other, even though my mother tried to keep me away from them, fearing their bad influence and doubtful morals. Sometimes we would hang around with them, mingling among the buyers in the market and badgering the Arab felaheen: *"Yah fellah, Bitu rach; chatu rassu, bil muftach."* (O, fellah, home he went, in the keyhole pushed his head.) When a Kurdish washerwoman passed by, crying *"Rassil, rassil"* (laundry) she would be greeted with: *"Kurdi, Kurdi, rass ichmar, diru, diru ma bindar!"* (Kurd, Kurd, ass's head, turning around – still doesn't work!) But the washerwoman had only to raise a threatening hand for the whole gang to disperse like birds at a shot – a far cry from stone throwing. I often asked myself, seeing the gang leaving for one of those interminable fights, why it was that we were fighting each other and not our common enemies.

Itbach el Yahud! (Kill the Jews)

In the "disturbances," sporadic or organized attacks by the Arabs on the Jews all over the country in the years 1936–1939, not a day passed but news came of Jews murdered by Arabs in the most horrifying ways. Something of the kind had happened to us too, while I was still an infant of six months, in 1929.

We lived then in the old Montifiore quarter (today Yemin Moshe) and our house lay on the slope of the hill, one in the outermost row of houses bordered by the Sultan's Pool opposite the walls of the Old City.

Like all the other small cottages in the quarter, the inhabitants of our house were lowly craftsmen, vendors and small merchants of modest means who had been encouraged by Lord Montifiore to leave the crowded, disease-ridden Old City. My father had a small haberdashery store there.

One day we heard rumors that the Jews in Zefat and Hebron were being massacred, and that there was much agitation among the Arabs of Jerusalem. Father hurriedly collected my brothers from the *Cheder* where they were studying and brought them home just as my mother was giving me a bath. Ordering her to take me out he quickly began to "fortify" the house, using heavy stones to support the ramshackle door. Before he had done, large crowds were heard approaching; tens to perhaps hundreds of *shabbab* (youth) were making their way to our houses, yelling and screeching: *"Aleyhum! Aleyhum!"* (have at them) while others chanted *"Idulla ma'na, wa'il Yahud Kalabna!* (the Government is with us, the Jews are dogs). Nearer and nearer came the screaming mob, shouting *"Idbach el Yahud!"* (kill the Jews) till they were just a few yards before our house, with a frail plywood door, reinforced by a few rocks that could easily be pushed aside with one kick, separating them from us. At this moment the baby (myself) began to wail, a wailing that still set my mother shuddering whenever she told the story many years later, reliving time and time again the terrible fear of that moment.

Realizing the effect an infant's cry would have on that bloodthirsty mob, they all tried to silence me, rocking and holding me tight. They even pressed a hand to my mouth but nothing would do, I continued to scream lustily. By this time the *Shabbab* were at the door, raining rocks upon the house. The women shut their eyes in terror, the men began to pray *vidu'y* (their death-bed confession) and it was then that the miracle took place, the first of many I was to experience in the future at my most difficult moments – one of the mob was badly hit in the head by a rock ricocheting from the wall and raised such a pandemonium that his companions had to carry him away, leaving us all unharmed.

We were reprieved, but not for long. Within a few hours the mob returned, this time accompanied by women and old men carrying sacks and all kinds of receptacles for the plunder they hoped to loot after killing us all. The women were wailing and singing war songs as they approached our door, ceaselessly bombarding us with stones. Then, just as they were about to break it down and enter, a second miracle occurred! There was an Arab whore with the mob who had had great plans for the looting. Looking around her she must have realized that there was little hope of finding jewels, money or gold in these humble cottages and was heard to call out:

"What do you expect to find here? Are you blind and can't see what miserable beggars live here? Come with me to Rehavia, where the rich ones live and we'll find jewels, money, gold, diamonds and beautiful white girls as well!"

Their imagination fired by the whore and brandishing wooden clubs and knives, they turned to follow her, leaving our house unharmed.

Ater they had gone we found that Father's shop had been looted, but who cared? This time we had all been spared, but the danger was by no means over. In fact, it might return at any moment. The inhabitants living on the periphery of the quarter retreated into the innermost part, and it was our lot to be sheltered in Chaham Ashriki's house, where about seventy people, among them women and children in a state of shock, were crowded into the small apartment. Gathering rocks the men carried them up to the roof to fend off the rioters should they decide to come again. It was only after four whole days spent crowded in the little rooms, that the British soldiers finally arrived, making a great show of being "in control." My grandmother on my father's side appeared at the same time as they did, determined to extricate us from this dangerous spot, and took us to her one single room in the Mahane Yehuda quarter. There we huddled like refugees, six of us crowded into that narrow space. Luckily a few months later a small, two-room apartment was vacated nearby and we moved in. At that time many other families besides my own left the Montifiore quarter, seeking a more secure neighbourhood, but some chose to remain, among them the beloved and respected teacher, Mizrahi, who refused to budge.

"I can speak their language and I can live with them in peace", he said. Not long afterwards he was murdered by the Arabs and his widow, Fanny, would sometimes visit us at our Mahane Yehuda home, sitting with my mother and bemoaning the naivete of the "dear departed" which had cost him his life.

Across the road from us there lived some relatives of the ill-starred Makleff family, their presence being the cause of much sympathetic speculation among us.

When they lived in Motza they kept many Arabs in their employ, letting them sleep and eat in the house, treating them warmly and with respect.

"Not", said my mother, "like the Arabs, who treat their servants like dogs, throwing them the left-overs at the end of the meal."

And, indeed, when the unrest among the Arabs began to spread, most of them left Motza, and only those working for the Makleffs stayed on as they were fully trusted by the family. Not many days later one of the Makleff children who was playing outside saw an angry mob approaching their home. In panic he hid with his sister behind a stone fence, from there to witness the horror. One of the laborers whom he knew by name and had regarded as almost part of his family, ran to the kitchen for a big bread knife, the very knife with which his benefactors had sliced his bread for him, and one by one the entire family was massacred: father, mother, sisters and brothers. Only the two hiding behind the stone wall managed to escape. The boy's name was Mordechai Makleff, a future Commander-in-Chief of the Israel Defence Forces.

For some reason, another case hardly so shocking impressed me very deeply at the time, perhaps because its protagonist was a boy of my own age and a pupil at my school. He was called Yoseph Bechar and was wounded by a piece of shrapnel from a bomb that went off near the Orion Cinema. There was his name in the headlines for all to see, together with the names of the other victims.

Growing up in such an atmosphere I always felt threatened by an Arab mob, imagining what I would do if they were to come at me that very moment. Once, standing on the balcony of the Ratisbonne building, whose balustrade was decorated with large pot-plants, I would say to myself:

'If they come now I'll grab these pots and throw them into the crowd!'

In time the conviction grew upon me that it was my duty to give the Arabs as good as they gave us. Since they threw bombs into crowded Jewish buses, I'd do the same. Since I had no bombs available, I decided stones would have to do instead. The first step was to raise an 'army' and Yehoshua my brother was the first conscript, followed by Yehuda and Shlomo, two skilled veterans in the art of stoning in the street, always foremost in the stick-and-stones skirmishes with the kids of the Kurdish quarter. Naturally they took the idea up very eagerly and in no time at all we sat down to plan our first foray. Zero hour was set for Saturday morning, a day on which there was no school and only Arab buses driving in the streets. Privately owned Jewish cars were a rarity in those days, particularly on the Sabbath, so there was no danger there either.

We made our way, therefore, to Jaffa Road, crossing it at the empty lot where the *arbengis*, or coach drivers used to gather. This lot, adjacent to the street leading to the Machane Yehuda market, was close to a bus stop, and buses always stopped at it as there were always people coming or going about their shopping. What better target for our missiles?

First the ammunition had to be collected, an operation that had caused us some anxiety, but the passers-by paid us scant attention as we went about our work. Just some kids playing with stones! A bus was not long in coming and as soon as it stopped it was showered with stones coming from all directions. The passengers began screaming, and to our surprise a Jewish policeman leapt from the bus to give chase. We began to run away but he kept after us, sticking especially to me as I twisted and turned in and out of the courtyards and lanes. My only conscious thought at the time was that my partners in crime would all get away and, even if one of them was caught, would keep his mouth shut and deny taking part in the incident. Any other course seemed to me unthinkable.

I was wrong. At the corner of our street stood my parents, their faces cold and angry. It later transpired that the policeman had first got hold of Shlomo, and the "prisoner," without much ado, gave him the names and even led him to my parents' house. They, in their turn, decided that this Shlomo had been the moving spirit of the whole affair and forbade my playing with such hooligans again, for who knows what influence they might have on me. It never occurred to them that their quiet, gentle Zuri had been the one actually responsible. For my part I gladly accepted the ban. How could I ever play with Shlomo, who had betrayed us, again? He was nothing but a base informer (this miserable informer being all of eight years old at the time).

Several months later a "similar" incident took place with consequences far more tragic. A youngster named Shlomo ben Yoseph, together with some friends from the *Betar* movement, attacked an Arab bus near Rosh Pina. He was sentenced to death, the first of many Jews to be hanged by the British in the Land of Israel.

Down with the White Paper!

This paper was published by the Government of the British Mandate at the end of the thirties just before the second world war and Hitler's march of death through Europe. In it Britain denied any obligation whatsoever to assist in the building of a Jewish National Homeland in Palestine, and drastically limited all immigration of Jews into the country, as well as their right to buy land in Arab zones.

At this time some ships carrying helpless Jewish refugees to Palestine in the hope of entering illegally were callously sunk at sea, abandoned by the whole civilized world. The Jewish community in Israel marched into the streets in stormy demonstrations. In Jerusalem thousands marched towards the police stations and Government offices, demanding free immigration and a Jewish State.

Only ten years old at the time, I was convinced that the times of the Maccabees had returned and that great changes were in store. I remember a great crowd in long rows confronting the Mahane Yehuda Police Station and shouting "Down with the Government!" rows of alert British policemen facing them tensely. The shouting intensified: "Down with Chamberlain! Down with the White Paper!"

Electrified at the sight I watched from a distance, eager for every new development. Suddenly a fire engine materialized from nowhere, spraying the demonstrators with strong jets of water. Some, drenched to the skin, left quickly, but others, mainly young boys, snatched up some stones in the near-by empty lots and began stoning the police. It was all very exciting and I ran to school to tell my brother all about it.

Next day the kids at school were all agog with the latest developments. Some bravely declared that this was war and the British would be taught a lesson. During the lunch break we were told that members of various youth movements were gathering for a demonstration near the Chorev School and when we got there we saw crowds of boys and girls streaming in from all parts of town. Forming rows, they marched towards the town center, chanting "Down with the Government! Free immigration!"

Some of them tired after a while and left but we kids stuck it out as long as it lasted. I don't remember returning to school that day at all. Later on we heard that not all the demonstrators had returned peaceably home but some had proceeded to destroy some pill boxes and telephone booths.

Anti-British feeling was growing high, fed by a deepening sense of injustice, and betrayal. Every time Father, a great admirer of Ze'ev Jabotinsky, picked up a newspaper he would exclaim:

"Hypocrites! Pure as the untrodden snow, all they do is keep law and order! When Jabotinsky began to organize a defence force to save our people from massacre, did they encourage him? No indeed! He was arrested and banished from the country. And if a Jew, by some miracle, manages to get out of Europe and reach Israel, how do they welcome him? By pronouncing him 'illegal' and putting him in prison!"

In their attempts to prevent "illegal" immigration the British spared no effort to block the unbelievable hulks that somehow managed to reach our shores. Each day brought more terrifying revelations about the true function of the concentration camps and the gas chambers. Hitler's speeches were explicit about the Nazi doctrine of the "Master" race and the extermination of the Jewish people. In Germany it was Hitler, in Israel the British, hunting down the "illegals" like animals and torpedoing their ships at sea.

"These demonstrations are only the beginning," we all thought. "Next time they'll throw bombs, burn cars and destroy police stations."

One day my cousin, Avraham Pinto, came home with his head wounded, all covered with blood. My aunt forbade him to leave the house for fear he would be arrested, but in our eyes, what a hero!

The demonstrations seemed to become an almost daily fixture. I remember one occasion when we came up against a mass of British policemen, helmeted and brandishing bludgeons and shields. The mass of demonstrators halted, the two camps stood facing each other, almost palpable tension growing between them. Suddenly I was being pressed to suffocation, bumped and pushed on every side. Stones began to fly through the air, the orderly rows disintegrated and everywhere people were running, disappearing into the narrow streets. But the children and the youngsters who had been following the adults jumped behind the fences and went on stoning the British. I thought it was great – here we were fighting the enemy and forcing them to relinquish their White Paper. Surely they will realize that if they persist in their perfidy it will lead to a war of liberation, the end of which would be as inevitable as was the end of the war of the Hasmoneans – complete victory for us. In my fantasy I saw myself hiding in the mountains, living in caves, lying in ambush and throwing grenades – exactly as the Maccabbeans, the sons of Matithias had done in their time.

Yet with time everything calmed down. The youths who had demonstrated in the streets and thrown stones in protest were now called upon by our National Institutions to don British uniforms and join the British Forces. My brothers, too, joined up and I was forced to admit that the greatest evil and our arch enemy were the Nazis, who must be fought first. Still, it pained me to see my brothers wearing that hated uniform of an enemy who did not hesitate to drive desperate refugees from Europe back to the hell from which they had managed to escape.

Bar Mitzva

After my thirteenth birthday my life took a strange turn. At that time the sons of good, orthodox families generally began to grow away from their religion, and only rarely would a boy revert at this age to orthodoxy. I myself have never heard of such a case but that's how it was with me. My parents, whose forebears numbered some Rabbis of renown were, like all our friends and neighbours, conventional in their way of life. No fire or light was lit on the Sabbath and our food was strictly *Kosher* – indeed it would never have occurred to anyone of us to behave otherwise. But all this was done largely as a matter of habit. My parents were not overly religious, going to the synagogue only on the High Holy Days or special occasions. At my *Bar Mitzva* ceremony I laid *Tefillin* like all the others and went up to read the *Torah* before the Ark, and it was while standing there I suddenly realized as of that moment, I was no longer a child but a full-grown man, fully responsible for my own actions and no longer able to shield myself from every crisis by hiding behind my father's back. From now on I would be judged on my own merits.

Religiously I began to observe the precepts of the *Torah*, pledging myself never to desecrate the Sabbath and to pray every day.

It was during these daily prayer sessions that I realized that I was the son of a people with a great mission, my part of which was to fulfill my personal obligation by studying the *Torah* and observing its commands, and in this way to bring about the ultimate salvation of Zion and the building of the Third Temple. Overlying this newly awakened conviction was my desperate desire to help my parents in every possible way. Long forgotten memories came to my mind of the trouble I had caused them when, still an infant, I was subject to fainting fits, making them fear for my life. My heart overflowed with love for them and I knew that I must find a way to ease their burden.

When I was four years old, I remember, a new quarter was going up near us, Mekor Baruch, and my brother David went to play there with his friends. I began nagging him to let me join them, the 'older' guys, but he wouldn't hear of it and tried to get away from me. Fearing to be left behind, I started to follow him, making my precarious way between piles of building materials and pits filled with quicklime. Suddenly I tumbled into one of those pits and, were it not for an Arab laborer who saw what had happened, I would have been drowned then and there. He managed to pull me out, washed my face in a barrel of dirty water on the site and told my brother to take me home immediately. For three days I lay in bed, unable to open my eyes. On the fourth I could only open my left one, the right one being terribly swollen and inflamed. Every day Father had to carry me to the doctor pushing me along in my sister Margalit's baby carriage, and the walk from our home in Mahane Yehuda to the Opthalmological

Hospital in Abu Tor was long and hard. Today this building houses Arts and Crafts exhibitions, but I am still moved whenever I see the well-remembered iron railing which has been preserved.

Another time my parents would not let me join my brothers who were going to a movie and I wept bitterly in my disappointment, crying for hours on end until the right eye became inflamed once more, a strange white dot appearing near the pupil.

Once more poor Father had to cart me to the St. John's Hospital at Abu Tor, pushing hard all the way. At that time I had no idea what a chore it was to push a grown boy for several kilometers in a rickety baby carriage through the steep streets of Jerusalem. Now, having reached my *Bar Mitzva,* I became aware of many things, among them the pain and trouble I had caused my parents, and I felt that there was nothing I wouldn't do for them in return. I used to fantasize that I was very rich, buying them their every heart's desire and surprising them with things they never dreamt of.

Actually we were quite poor but the children were never conscious of lacking anything that other, more privileged children could afford, nor were we ever envious of our peers. Our apartment had belonged to my grandmother and was in some respects better that the general run of apartments in the quarter. There were only eight of us in three rooms. Like all the others we had no bathroom and washed in a tin tub. The toilet was no more than an outhouse, boasting no water flusher, little more than a hole in the ground. But we did have water on tap in the yard, saving us the trouble of raising it from the well, as our neighbours had to do, or, in times of drought having recourse to the good services of Azaria, owner of the neighbourhood water supply, who charged two mils per tin of water.

Our house was not wired for electricity until I was twelve years old and we could only afford this luxury when one of my brothers got a job as messenger boy in the Schwartz general store. Till then homework had to be done by the light of an oil lamp, but this in no way meant that we felt inferior to or less respectable than any other family in the quarter.

After my *Bar Mitzva* I had only a few months to go before graduating from the eighth grade at Ratisbonne. I knew that I would have to start working right afterwards and was already feeling apprehensive about finding a job after graduation. I applied to various Government offices, among them the Postal Service, and right in the middle of the school year, was called there for an interview with a Mr. Mehudar.

A Telegram Boy in Jerusalem

There were other boys already waiting when I arrived at Mr. Mehudar's office. He opened the interview by asking why I wanted to work. I explained that I wished to help my parents. After testing my English, which appeared satisfactory, he informed me that I had been accepted, provided I began immediately, a month before my graduation. Jobs were hard to come by in those times and I had no choice but to accept. With me there were two other newcomers, both Arabs.

The Principal of Ratisbonne was generous enough to give me a written confirmation that I had completed my course of studies. Mother, who thought I would be able to continue my studies at night school, didn't mind too much that I had missed graduating so narrowly. But as it happened I had to give up the idea of night school because I was often called to deliver telegrams evenings and even nights.

For the first six months I was on probation and distributed the express mail and telegrams on foot. My districts were the *Ballad* (the city) and the *Bar* (outlying areas). In the *Ballad* mail was delivered by regular postmen for its tortuous alleys could daunt the best bicycle rider, and the *Bar* was served by regular post boys too. In a group of forty Arabs there were just three Jewish lads, myself and two others. The Postal Service preferred Arabs for making its deliveries, as they were ready to take their weekly day off any day of the week, regardless of their Sabbath or Holy Days.

Mr. Channania, one of those in charge of the Telegram Department, provided me with a guide to instruct me at the initial stages – an Arab boy of my own age called Ma'atuf. Going with me on my rounds, he explained the division of labor among the various postmen, the identification of the endless alleys and how to master their names most of which were not to be found in any known map. Ma'atuf also pointed out the addresses of important people and institutions with a large daily post and, because of his guidance, I found myself able to get around alone within a few days. Unlike the other lads I preferred to work in the "Ballad" rather than the "Bar".

Every morning I would leave the Post Office by the back entrance in Storrs St., cross into Jaffa Road to gaze at the souvenir shops, deliver my telegrams and turn towards the Jaffa Gate. Not a Friday went by but I would visit the *'Suk el Jum'ah'*, the Friday market, watching the merchants offering their animals for sale in the market square, near the Sultan's Pool. It was fascinating to watch the sheep and donkey merchants lauding their wares in rhyme, praising them to the skies. Mules would be described as beautiful, modest, pious and possessed of lovely eyes – like perfect brides. My Arab friends informed me that it was the practice of these merchants to place some grains of pepper in the rectums of these stolid beasts, causing them to appear restless and full of 'pep'. At first I didn't believe them but now I had the evidence of my own eyes. I would have loitered there willingly all day, gaping at one strange sight after another, but duty called and I would tear myself away and walk back into the Old City proper.

The first thing to strike one on entering the *Ballad* was the masses of people milling around, pushing to stare at something or other – a weeping child or a screaming woman – shouting, advising, cajoling, pushing, cursing or praising something to the skies.

On the verge of every crowd there would be boys carrying trays and loudly proclaiming their wares, sometimes in song: *Ke'ach ubeid* (rings of sesame-covered bread and eggs)... *Ke'ach uza'atr.... suss** and *tamar hindi...*** Crashing their cymbals they

---

*   Suss: a drink made from the dried, crushed seedlings of the Suss plant growing in the Jordan Valley and in the area of the Suez Canal. Probably named after the plant.

** Tamar Hindi: 'Indian dates' a name of a species of date and the drink made from it.

would invite the parched and the thirsty to partake of the cool drinks in their copper containers with their long, narrow spouts. After use the cup was rinsed with water from a smaller container carried on their backs.

Entering Jaffa Gate I would be surrounded by the burly Hebron porters, crouched on the ground, their backs loaded with heavy mattresses like pack animals. Pushing with the best of them I would make my way through the packed crowds, colliding with the daintily stepping donkeys picking their way through the narrow lanes, or with the porters loaded with huge pyramids of cartons or tins on their backs, looking neither to right or left and crying monotonously *Heuh, hueh* to warn passers-by of their coming.

I enjoyed watching the *Kobaz*-clad vendors loudly proclaiming their wares, the *suss, charuv** and *tamar-hindi* sellers on every side rattling their copper and glass jars, some of which were embellished with blue-painted verses from the Koran for protection against the evil eye. How I longed for some of the ice cubes floating around on top of the black liquid in the jars surrounded by copper saucers, set rattling by the vendor to attract the tired and thirsty.

And the Arab restaurants... I sometimes had to pinch my nostrils to avoid the sharp odours of the strange, exotic spices they used in their food.

On entering one of the courtyards I would be greeted with gratifying respect. A telegram meant news, good or bad, and upon receiving one, people would fearfully murmur: *"Kher inshalla, kher inshalla..."* (Good news, God willing).

My next stop at the Jewish Quarter was like stepping into a different world. After the stench of the Moslem and Christian quarters I would now be met by the smell of soapy water used to scrub the floors inside and the courtyards outside. The air was filled with a babel of languages: Yiddish, Ladino, Arabic.... A telegram to a Jewish family was always rewarded by a cool drink from the earthen jar and a cookie.

---

* Charuv: a drink made from the fruit of the carob tree.

In the alleys I would often come upon a certain Moroccan Jew, tall and bandy-legged, carrying a large wooden tray loaded with loaves of bread that seemed to dance as he stepped upon the crooked cobble stones. It was said that he had arrived all alone from Morocco many years ago and, being a bull of a man, had been given a job at a printer's where he served as a living dynamo for the printing press, turning the enormous wheel that worked it. That was how he made his living for many years until, civilization having finally penetrated the cobbled lanes of the Old City, the human dynamo had to give way to one run by electricity. The solitary Mugrabbi was left without a job.

A kind-hearted baker took pity on him and employed him as a porter, letting him sleep on top of the oven, provided he undertook to see to it that the fire did not go out at night. This arrangement suited the Mugrabbi very well. Weekdays he distributed bread at the customers' houses and on Shabbat he would deliver the hot bowls of *cholent* placed in the oven by the Jewish housewives on the preceding Friday.

One day I met him, a giant of a man, shambling sadly through some alley, no tray of bread loaves on his shoulder. "Is it a holiday today that you're not working?" He was silent, refusing to answer. But a woman to whom I had just delivered a telegram readily explained why he was hanging around, unemployed.

It seems that, being so lonely on Friday nights, he would lie down early in his corner at the bakery and, as a result, wake up very early on Saturday morning with a healthy appetite. By then the air in the bakery was redolent with the delicious smell of the *cholent:* well-browned potatoes, stuffed cabbage, jellied calf's foot, mutton in rice and beans... Half crazed by the delicious odours he couldn't resist prying up a lid or two and helping himself to a potato here, a spoonful of rice there.... just a small pinch from every pot. This satisfied his hunger, leaving him contented and the housewives innocent of the fact that they had a 'sleeping partner' at their Sabbath meal.

This convenient arrangement could have gone on forever, but one Saturday a feast in honor of the bridegroom was held at one of the more well-to-do homes in the Old City, and in preparing for it the lady of the house had stuffed the bakery oven that Friday with all manner of casseroles, one more delicious than the other. The following Sabbath, as soon as all the guests were properly seated, she proudly announced her *tour de force,* a special surprise prepared with her own hands in honor of the bridegroom. With great ceremony the casserole was opened when lo and behold – all it contained were some grains of rice and a few miserable lentils... the pigeons stuffed with pine nuts and raisins had disappeared as if they had never been.

That evening, right after the *Havdalla* prayer consummating the Sabbath, the lady confronted the baker with her just complaint:

"Where are the stuffed pigeons I put in the oven in honor of the groom?"

The seeds of suspicion were planted.

The following Saturday the baker decided to catch the voracious porter red-handed. No sooner had he fallen asleep when the baker hid himself in an obscure corner of the bakery, prepared to keep watch all night. Just before sunrise the porter rose from his bed and, in the subdued light of the oven, began to take his tithe from each and every one of the casseroles.

Being at heart a good man, the baker decided to spare his hapless employee such a shock on the Sabbath and kept his counsel till the sun had set, at which time the Mugrabbi was out on his ear.

The messenger boys had no end of wonderful stories to tell about Selma, a black-skinned whore I still remembered from my childhood days, when I had been visiting Yemin Moshe. I heard some kids chanting "Selma's coming, Selma's coming!" and saw that the cause of the merriment was a young negress of about twenty. Of medium height, she wore a red colored dress slit high at the sides and accenting her curves and breasts... The boys were all around her, touching and even pinching her, and when I begged them to tell me who she was they informed me that she could be seen every day hanging around the King David Hotel, where British soldiers could always be found to invite her to the 'Koffria', a small wood lying between the hotel and the quarter. "Come and hide with us behind the trees," they generously

36

offered, "and you'll get an eyeful, 'cinema balash'." (a movie for free).

And here I was seeing her almost every day, usually followed by a bevy of burly Hebron porters, some just showing off to assert their virility and others intent on winning her graces. Her regular beat was Jaffa Road, mincing along in her perrenial red dress or seated on a bench with the usual groups of men and boys somewhere in the background. One day she accosted me as I was passing by on my bike:

"Come with me", she called, "You're so nice and you want to don't you?" "I'm busy," I retorted, but she was ready to wait until I completed my rounds.

My probation period at work soon being over I was promoted and awarded permanency. I became a privileged messenger on wheels, pedalling on my bike up and down the steep roads of Jerusalem, familiarizing myself with every obscure corner of the beautiful city and learning to love it. I went into the homes of Jews of every tribe and sect, discovering a wealth of cultures and ways of life the existence of which I had never before suspected. There were the exotic Bukharian Jews, calm and stately in their long velvet robes worn even on week days, well sheltered from the outside world behind the high walls of their court-yards; the volatile, lovable Yemenite Jews; the stocky Hungarians of the Ungaren Houses – a complex quarter with many confusing entrances, so that once inside I could never find my way out again. Amused by my confusion would be the tall, buxom women, black stockinged, their heads bound so tightly by their silk scarves that not a hair could escape. Fair complexioned girls with tangled golden hair would point me out to each other, giggling, and ask me in enchanting, musical voices who it was I was looking for. Young men in white stockings shoved into their black trousers would glance at me with contempt, curling their long side locks as they walked purposefully away. Another source of enjoyment were *Yekes,* the stiff, buttoned-up German Jews whose door-bell I sometimes had to ring between one and three in the afternoon, in spite of the written injunction on the door not to do so. Behind the door I could hear the *Yekes* grumbling about the rude

"Asiatics" who disturbed the rest of respectable people... Then there were the pretty, tranquil cottages and the sweet pure air of Beith Hakerem, where the houses seemed to grow out of the rocks together with the pine trees, while everywhere could be heard the song of the birds. Or, on the other side of town, there was the heady ride to Mount Scopus from whose top I had a clear view of Shu'afat Village in all its surroundings as well as the Holy Mount. Sometimes I would stand there, imagining an endless line of Jews, beginning somewhere in the hills beyond the horizon and streaming towards the Temple on the Holy Mount of Moriah. It was like the continuation of a recurring dream I used to have in my childhood where we would be going down the steps leading to the Wall, part of an enormous crowd, when suddenly, there was my father! "Where are we going?" I would ask him, and the answer was always the same: "To the Temple!"

Yet it was hard work. Climbing the steep hills with which Jerusalem abounded I would be covered with sweat even in winter as I pushed my bike along. Out in the rain and the cold, fierce storms, I would envy those more fortunate who worked in heated houses or drove buses or closed cars. I had another cause for envy at the time – my friends who managed both to work and attend evening classes. When I had started to work I planned to do the same but what with frequent night deliveries of telegrams and having to be on duty from three to ten at night for two weeks of every month, all my plans for study had to be shelved.

Ever since that morning when I saw the proclamation opposite the Oplatka Pharmacy I was a zealous reader of these stencilled sheets, and in my perambulations all over the city, seeking out this or that address, I would peek into the letter boxes in the entrance halls, hoping that some unseen hand had deposited one of them there. If I was fortunate enough to find one I would read it fervently, identifying myself with the words completely. The proclamations urged the declaration of a state of war, something I myself had felt was unavoidable. In my imagination I saw myself, rifle in hand, attacking the enemy, Arab or British, under the leadership of a Jewish officer, a modern Yehuda Hamaccabee.

A leaflet I happened to find one day disturbed me very much. It reported an attempt to broadcast from the Government Broadcasting Station in Ramallah. The station was captured but the Etzel refrained from destroying it as this would have harmed the war effort against Germany. I wasn't very clear about the connection between the Ramallah Broadcasting Station and the war against the Nazis in Germany but this in no way marred my pleasure at the fact the Jews in the underground were capable of capturing the broadcasting station of a great power such as England. The war, I believed, would shortly be over, and then we would show them! At the end of the leaflet I read that a freedom fighter had been wounded, and once again I asked myself what I was doing about it while others were fighting and sacrificing themselves. Although I had known for some time that one day I would become a freedom fighter, I suddenly became aware of the immediacy of the problem. I was still only a lad and no one had ever asked me to join up, so that I didn't feel too guilty about not doing my share and enjoyed reading about "acts of hostility". But now it suddenly struck me that people could get hurt while taking part in these attacks, and who was I to feel glad when young men were being wounded?

At first there was no urgency about it and I felt sure that when the time came I, too, would give up my freedom and perhaps my life. The question was "when?" Could it be that the time had come? No, I assuaged my conscience, no one has approached me or asked me to join. But if they should do so, what would my answer be? What about my parents, wouldn't they be the first to suffer? The answer came, loud and clear: these men, fighting and wounded alike, also have parents who love them, worry about them. Every member of the underground had a father and mother just as I had, and who was I to make an exception of myself.

I well remember the day when riding my bike in the Ben Maimon Boulevard, I tried hard to weigh the pros and cons of the situation, well aware of the fact that my life was not solely mine, to do with as I pleased. On the one hand I was deeply in debt to my parents; on the other I had a duty to my people. All my instincts cried out to join the underground, but the dilemma was still there – which of my debts was greater? Then and there I cut

39

the Gordian knot in favor of the underground. If they failed to approach me I would find some way of contacting them. The decision brought me a profound relief and it became imperative that I lose no time in joining up. I had no clear idea how this was to be done as I didn't know anyone who was an active member, and with this stumbling block I was again assailed by doubts. If I found a way to reach them now, this minute, would I ask them to accept me, would I join them if they wanted me? But surely they would never take the first step – they would consider me too young. Yet, say they did, what then? Would a quiet type like me, never one for the wild escapades of my friends, fit into an underground existence of fighting and violence? But again, was this the time to huddle behind the protective walls of home? I was back where I had started, struggling on the horns of my dilemma.

The only real block that stood between me and the underground was my parents, whom I loved and felt I owed a deep debt of gratitude. Well aware of all the pain and trouble I had caused them in the past I felt I had no right to aggravate their sufferings and cause them such a shock. But, I asked myself, did they have to find out? Would I be too young and inexperienced to keep my activities secret from them?

I was regarded by everybody as 'a good lad,' a 'mother's boy.' Every morning I would get up while it was still dark, right after father who left for work even earlier. I would find mother already bustling around between the dining room and the outside kitchen, preparing food on the noisy Primus stove and by the time I finished my morning prayers and laid *tefillin,* there was an omelet and a cup of hot cocoa waiting for me. My older brothers, Berto and Dudu, were by then serving with the British army, but Yehoshua and Margalit, my sister, breakfasted without saying any prayers. Mother would serve us all, then, seated with us at the table, would watch us with delight enjoying our food.

There was another aspect of my dilemma I hadn't thought of before. Ever since I began working at the Post Office I had completely neglected all my friends and indulged in very few social activities, so tiring was the work. My parents were used to seeing me always at home and if I were to start disappearing at all hours their suspicions would certainly be aroused and they might even forbid it. Was I prepared to disobey them? But, I repeated to myself, *ad nauseam,* the men who took the broadcasting station had mothers and fathers too, and what gave me the right to give mine preferrential treatment while theirs were made to suffer?

The deep relief I felt when finally I swept all my doubts away turned slowly to excitement, overcoming all my former feelings of depression and guilt. Proudly I told myself that my final and irrevocable decision had not stemmed from mere love of adventure, so typical of many boys of my age, but had been reached by seriously weighing all of the aspects of the problem. The thought of my parents still gave me pain but now I knew that my joining up was inevitable.

How to Join the Underground?

There was just the one snag – how was I to contact these people whose safety lay in their complete anonymity? When delivering telegrams in the evening on my bike I always kept an eye open for anyone distributing leaflets but, though I often discovered that new ones had been put up on the walls, the paste still wet behind them, I could never catch a glimpse of the unknown hands that had put them there. As time passed my frustration began to grow at my inability to get in touch with even a single member but, in a way, this caused me a deep satisfaction too – if I couldn't do it neither could the British.

In any case I began telling the family at home that I might often be absent in the future, and at improbable hours. My story was that I had been offered some over-time work at the office, which would mean extra pay. This I would collect from the tips usually offered at every delivery and which, till then, I had steadfastly refused.

We were always short of money at home and all my earnings went into the kitty. Father's affairs had at that time deteriorated and he had become involved in an inheritance case which claimed all his time and energy so that he couldn't keep a steady job. It all began when my paternal grandfather died and left three properties to his sons and nephews: the one in which we lived in Mahane Yehuda, one in the Yemin Moshe quarter and the third in Nachlat Shiv'a. One of grandfather's legatees had lived for many years in Mexico so, with my grandmother's permission, my father collected the rents and used them to support his family: But one day this relative returned and demanded that the whole sum consisting of his part of those rents be returned in full and immediately. This father could not do of course. So began an endless round of lawyers and law-suits, involving great expense and time. Mother had to sell all her jewels, paid for by her earnings before she married father in Egypt. My older brothers, Avraham and David, who were serving with the British army, would sometimes make a contribution out of their meagre pay and the sale of the cigarettes which they were alloted. My own wages went to my father, down to the last penny.

★

Weeks went by and I could still find no way to join the underground. I began to feel doubtful I would ever make it and in the meantime I indulged in all kinds of fantasies about what I would do if certain situations arose. I would imagine myself following a British policeman in the street and suddenly grabbing his gun. If I had a gun, I thought, I would show them, once and for all... In reality I certainly did not look the part, a skinny, rather weak stripling, and the only gun I had ever fired was a Purim pop-gun, giving a bang to frighten the passers by. So what? I could attack an Englishman with a knife too, couldn't I?.... But, if I failed in the attempt it would mean prison or perhaps the death sentence, and that before I had made the slightest contribution to the welfare of my people...

In those days any object that came into my hands was carefully inspected for its potential use as a weapon. I remember getting a thick carpenter's pencil one day and had the idea of writing slogans on the walls of the entries into the houses. The slogans would be similar to the ones with which the *Etzel* covered the outer street walls, like "Freedom or Death," "Death to the Enemy" and so on. No sooner said than done! Carefully inspecting the "terrain" I would look around to make sure all was clear, pull out my pencil and quickly write the appropriate slogan. As my confidence grew so did my enthusiasm, and not a house at which I made a delivery passed without my "writing on the wall."

One day, walking into the building of the Central Post Office, my place of work, I took a quick look around and seeing nobody in sight and a freshly whitewashed wall before me I covered it quickly with giant lead letters saying "Freedom or Death." Only after I had finished did it strike me how flagrantly careless I had been to risk it in a place daily used by hundreds of employees, many of them British, with not a few Jews among them who were not exactly sympathetic to my cause. Being caught would have meant many months in prison, months which might have been used to much better purpose. I told myself firmly that this practice had better stop, but somehow I couldn't give it up entirely and "Freedom or Death" would still appear wherever I deemed it safe enough to risk it.

Returning one day from my rounds I met Joseph Brichner at the Central Office and was told that some detectives had come to look for the perpetrator of the wall literature. He himself had already been interrogated and they had asked him to print the alphabet on a sheet of paper. Then they asked him about me and the Jewish messenger boys and when we were due to return to the office, as they wanted to question us. Pretending to know nothing about the whole affair I waited till he was on his way then hurried to an empty lot in Shamai street, where I buried my precious weapon in a small hole I dug out with my hands. Only then did I return to the office where I was told that some detectives were waiting to talk to me. There were two of them and their questions were many: Did I belong to any youth movement? Had I ever been a member of *Betar?* Who were my friends and how did I spend my free time? Because I told them the truth my replies sounded innocent enough. I had never belonged to any movement, working from dawn to dusk and meeting nobody outside my own family. They went on to tell me to print the alphabet. Luckily, when writing on the walls, I had camouflaged my real handwriting, using a sharp and angular script, and all I had to do now was produce my usual rounded lettering. Still, I was very tense, thinking that a trained graphologist would have no difficulty in discovering that both had been written by the same hand. For many days after the interrogation I was in a state of tension, expecting to be arrested at any moment. It was a bit puzzling that the detectives had only been interested in young lads like myself, not questioning any of the other 200 adults there. Presumably they thought that no adult would risk his freedom for the sake of a few slogans, and only reckless youths would indulge in such games.

Afraid as I was of being arrested I felt that such a calamity would have its bright side as, once in prison, I would surely meet some bona fide members of the underground and thus become one of them. They might even include me in some daring plan of escape... But what if they refused me? After all, how could anybody trust someone too irresponsible to observe the most elementary rules of caution?

The High Commissioner is Wounded

One day, while making deliveries in Beith Hakerem, I saw an unusual sight: hundreds of British policemen were spread out in the empty lots surrounding the Diskin Home for the Blind, cautiously advancing towards the Giv'at Sha'ul quarter. I soon learnt the reason for this police action, as the news spread like wild-fire through the city – an attempt had been made on the life of the Chief High Commissioner, Sir Harold MacMichael, on his way to Jaffa from his mansion in Jerusalem. His wife and driver had both been wounded while he himself escaped with some light scratches on his hand. Looking at the scene I little guessed that some years later my friends and I would be hunted in much the same fashion in that very vicinity – for an attempt to kill General MacMillan, Commander in Chief of the British Forces in Palestine and what was then Trans-Jordan.

An assault on the high Commissioner was an unheard of event. Unknown forces, doubtless members of the underground, had dared to go straight for the viper's head. What a great pity that they had failed, but surely they would have better luck next time. The main thing was that a beginning had been made, the enemy made to feel vulnerable, getting a taste of its own medicine. No bombardment of mere stones and rocks this time, but the real thing. I felt instinctively that this was the work of *Lehi* and I fervently prayed that they would get away unscatched. Yet my own reaction was a feeling of deep frustration. What was I doing, pedalling on my bike with "their" telegrams, serving the enemy, with the struggle accelerating all around me while all I did was observe it passively. It was getting insupportable and something must happen soon to show me the way to join them, but I still hadn't a clue how it was to be done.

In the first month of the Jewish year, *Tishrei,* a notice was put up by the *Etzel* warning the British not to interfere with the rite of blowing the *shofar,* the ram's horn, at the Western Wall at the close of the Day of Atonement service, this being an ancient custom marking the end of the Day of Awe. The warning was issued that any policeman preventing this would be severely punished. For me this meant one thing only: there would be members of the *Etzel* at the Wall when the time came for blowing the shofar on the eve of the Day of Atonement, and this was the opprtunity I had been seeking. On *Yom Kippur,* right after the evening prayer, I told my father that I felt like praying *Ne'illa* (the final service) at another synagogue. I had found a means of contacting the underground!

Blowing the Shofar at the Western Wall

Father had already caught me several times as I was deeply immersed in illegal underground literature, and with Mother's spirited backing he made a terrible row about keeping such dangerous stuff on me. Like me, he had read the proclamation, issued by *Etzel,* about blowing the shofar at the Western Wall and when he heard that I wasn't going to the synagogue with him that day his suspicion was immediately aroused. He went off to consult Mother who, in a state of agitation, begged me not to go to the *Kottel* (Western Wall) but join my father at the service, as a good son should. She pleaded so earnestly that I gave in, promising to do as she asked. This was my first conscious lie to my parents – making a promise I didn't intend to keep.

Conferring with Yehoshua, my brother, whom I had decided some time before to take with me should I find a way of contacting the underground, I asked him to go with me to the *Kottel,* and as soon as our parents' attention was diverted we sneaked out and made our way to the Old City.

I couldn't shake off a feeling of gloom, imagining their pain when they realized that not only had I broken my promise but I had also drawn young 'Salvo' (as Yehoshua was nicknamed) with me. I shuddered when I thought of their suffering if I were to join the underground and they found out. Yet torn as I was by my love for them and my desire to join the *Lehi,* there was by now no doubt in my mind as to my future course of action, at whatever the cost.

When we arrived at the *Kottel* the space before it was crowded with worshippers, but as *Ne'illa,* the closing prayer drew near, most of them began to slip away, fearful of what was to come. No more than thirty young people were left in the square, practically surrounded by British Police who were all carrying the regulation bludgeons used for dispersing demonstrators.

As the service continued one could sense the rise in tension, and the policemen with their bludgeons brought a long forgotten incident to my mind, when my father came home once, his arms bruised black and blue, choking back his groans so as not to frighten the little ones. He told us that when he was passing through the market place, looking for some bananas, a British policeman appeared suddenly, hitting the Jews right and left and cursing "Bloody Jews! Fuckin' Jews!" It later transpired that a Jew had been killed and some of our people, angered by the murder, had retaliated by overturning an Arab vegetable truck. This beating up of innocent people at random in the market place was just another example of how the "keepers of the peace" fulfilled their duty.

Here they were again, those same bludgeons, ready to descend upon the heads of Jews, and the picture of my wounded father seemed, somehow, to justify my decision to join the underground, not in a quest for revenge or adventure but out of a conviction that the time had come to free my people of such needless humiliation and suffering.

It was almost sunset, the time for blowing the ram's horn, and the tension was palpably rising. The cantor concluded the *Ne'illa* prayer and we all stood waiting expectantly for the familiar sound, which failed to come for some reason. A moment passed and then another... out of the corner of my eye I saw a youth drawing out a horn from his shirt and passing it out quickly to his companion, whom I recognized to my astonishment as one of the Ezra brothers, a Ratisbonne pupil two grades above me. Just as I was thinking that these brothers were *Betar* members, the boy raised the *Shofar* and gave a loud blast. The police burst into the circle of worshippers, trying to reach him, but the blowing stopped, the *shofar* disappeared, only to be heard once more from an entirely different direction. This happened several times, the police turning around wildly, pushing everyone brutally and striking right and left, wild with frustration. The crowd took up the prayer once more, praying with feeling as if inspired, completely oblivious of the British policemen rampaging all around them, going on to the very end of the service, when the worshippers fell into rows and marched back to the New City, singing *Betar* songs interspersed with anti-British slogans. Yehoshua and I joined them and we were all singing lustily when someone noticed a strange face among us, a face that was out of place that didn't belong with us. I heard the lads around me whispering "careful! a detective!" The man seemed intent on sticking to me and I began racking my brains for the reason. Could he have been following me since the business of the slogans on the walls of the Central Post Office? In that case I had better put off any attempt to get in touch with an underground member for fear I might get myself arrested and put others in danger.

Finally we were in town, having forgotten, in all the excitement, that we had been fasting all day. I was especially elated for now I knew one underground member for certain – Eliyahu Ezra, a boy I used to see often. As soon as I met him next time, I would ask him to recommend me, I thought. But I never saw him again, although I looked for him everywhere. He simply disappeared. Some years later I heard that he had been arrested and exiled to a prison camp in Africa. One of the African guards killed him and Sha'ul Haglili of *Lehi* as well.

Reaching home we found our parents quiet and restrained, as if thankful that we had returned safe and sound. But that night and for many nights that followed they never ceased begging us to give up that dangerous nonsense... Days passed, weeks... not a sign was there of Ezra, and any contact with the underground remained as elusive as ever. I racked my brains to find a way and finally decided that as Ezra had been a *Betar* member there must be some connection between this youth movement and the underground. I decided to find out.

There was a *Betar* club near the Abyssinian Monastery, and one day I went there and applied for membership. I learnt that most of the club's activities were held on Shabbat and Saturday nights – another problem of what to say to my parents. They were perfectly aware that I never worked Saturday nights, nor indeed did I ever leave home at all in the evenings since the day I left school. They would have to be told something, so I concocted a story about Joshua (who had joined *Betar* with me) and myself having decided to attend an *Oneg Shabbat* (Shabbat evening service) at the synagogue. When they asked suspiciously which synagogue, I named one that I used to pass every morning on my way to work, the "Truth and Faith" Temple. Since it never occurred to them that I could lie to them they believed me. After all I was a very devout boy and my parents, who were not very particular about these things themselves, considered me a good influence on my brother Joshua. Mother couldn't resist bragging about me to her friend and neighbour Esther, particularly about this new club I had joined, and the latter, no whit less zealous than my own mother about her sons' moral wellbeing, began to goad them to follow my example and join as well. Esther was particularly insistent about this with her son Israel who at first, would have nothing to do with the idea but finally gave in and asked me to let him go along with me to the *Oneg Shabbat* service. Time and time again I avoided taking him, inventing all sorts of excuses, until there was nothing for it but to let him into the secret and I offered to take him with us to the *Betar* club, provided he didn't tell a soul about where we were really going.

That very night he blurted out the story to his parents and they rushed to tell mine. Thus began a campaign to stop me from going to the *Betar* club, beginning with persuasion and reasonable arguments that quickly changed to blatant threats. I felt I was at the end of my tether and, after a three weeks' membership, stopped going there, consoling myself that after all the club had little more to offer than some folk dancing and singing. It was also a well known fact that *Betar* members were all under police surveillance so it was just risking arrest before having done anything worth while. But I was left restless and frustrated for I was just as determined as ever to find my way to the underground even though I hadn't a clue how this could be done.

Brith Hashmona'im

A chance rumor reached me about a new movement of religious youth called *Brith Hashmona'im* which had underground men among its members and was located somewhere among the labyrinthian alleys of the Bukhara quarter. Before I could go there I had to find someone to introduce me, as one couldn't just show up and be accepted as a member. Either you had a friend who was already a member or they asked you to join. Otherwise you would arouse the suspicion of those connected with the underground.

Luck was with me. As I was walking along in the Bukharan quarter, trying to solve my problem, I saw a notice announcing a lecture about Ze'ev Jabotinsky, scheduled to be given in the courtyard of the club. Eureka! What excuse could be better.

Punctual to the minute I arrived there but paid the lecture itself very little attention, being intent on getting into conversation with one of the twenty or so youths there. I examined them one by one, searching for a familiar face, when suddenly I recognized Itzhak Aharonov, a boy I knew from school. At the end of the lecture I approached him, asking him if he was a member of the club or had just come to hear about Jabotinsky like me. Imagine my satisfaction when he told me that he was a member and went on to introduce me to Shimeon Barmatz, who told me he would be very pleased to accept me as a member of *Brith Hashmona'im*.

I thought my mother would be pleased to hear that I had joined a religious youth movement but she was smart enough to realize the connection between the Hashmona'im of old and the contemporary underground movements. She didn't like the idea at all and said that it was probably a terrorist organization. The more vehement my denials, the stronger was her opposition, but this time I was adamant and wouldn't let her stop me.

From the day I started working I had lost all contact with my friends at school and even those in the neighbourhood. The work was very tiring and I was forced to rest a lot. This constant feeling of fatigue worried me sometimes as I feared it might be a handicap in underground work. But now I became a changed person, flying on my bike up and down the steep streets of Jerusalem as if I had grown wings. Not only was I never tired, forced to take a break, but I felt light-hearted and happy, a feeling I had rarely known before. I had new friends now, boys who thought and felt as I did, and what was more important still, I was confident that any day now I would be recruited into the underground. There were stories circulating round the club about a Moishe David, one of the instructors who had been arrested while putting up proclamations, and exiled to Africa just before I had become a member.

In order to come to the notice of those interested in new recruits, I would freely express my opinions about the underground while within the confines of the club, and not a day passed but that I expected to be approached. One day, on the ninth of the month of *Av* (anniversary of the destruction of the Temple) a group of us went to the *Kottel* for prayers. After the service we sang the *Hatikva,* despite the British prohibition to sing the anthem there, and two of us were arrested for interrogation. On the way home we noticed our instructor, Bonaventura, whispering to one of the boys, Eliezer Greiber, and I felt sure he was recruiting him there and then. I decided to bide my time patiently, hoping that before long I, too, would be called.

And my turn came. "I'd like a word with you," said Aharon Levitan. I understood immediately and we went outside, on a leisurely walk through the streets of Jerusalem that lasted for hours. Aharon began by asking all sorts of questions: How did I find my job? What did I think of the situation generally? What was my opinion of the chances to drive the British out of the country and how was this to be done. The answers I gave were careful and considered. There was too much at stake for me to let my tongue run away with me or let myself be passed over as unworthy.

My replies appeared to be satisfactory and Aharon began telling me of the necessity to fight the British. Realizing that I had passed the test successfully I waited with bated breath for the end of his lecture and the fateful question I had been waiting for so many months. But he went on and on and the more he talked the more depressed I became till it slowly dawned on me that he might think me unfit to join the *Lehi.* Who knows when I might get such a chance again? Suddenly I felt that this talking round and round the point was more than I could bear and blurted out "I want to join the underground! I've been looking for a contact for a long time now but couldn't find one. If you can be my contact, please tell me so." Everything was now clear. "I suggest that you join the Fighters for the Freedom of Israel-*Lehi,*" he said.

I wanted to thank him, to tell him how much this meant to me, but was choked with excitement and couldn't bring out a word. Thank God, my dream had finally materialized and I stood trembling like a child, completely overcome. What would Aharon think of me? Would he think I was afraid? I tried again to speak, to explain, but to my shame was again unable to say a word for my throat was choked with tears, now coursing down my cheeks. Who knows what he would think of me now, I thought. Would he understand that these were tears of joy and not of fear; would he believe me if I told him? As for me I had never believed that a person could weep and tremble with happiness.

A Lehi Man am I!

Our talk went on for many more hours and we strolled through the Bukharim quarter, crossing Ge'ula Street and Kerem Avraham time and time again until many things that had been obscure were made clear to me and all my questions answered.

As I walked with Aharon through the darkened streets (this was the time of the Second World War) no street lights were lit and all the windows were heavily draped with dark curtains. The passers-by looked like shadows but even so they seemed to be cheering me soundlessly, pleased with this youth setting out to fight the foreign tyrant and bring liberty to his people, freedom from slavery and torture. For too long had this freedom been denied them, and here was I, barely sixteen, not armed with gun or bullet or bomb but with the consciousness of their crying need and the courage to fight for it. Yes, here it was at last, finally and irrevocably true – I was a *Lehi* man!

Our walk continued – King David Street, King Solomon Street – evoking the ancient kings of Israel. Here was the meeting place of the fighter king and his son, the builder, and we walk their streets, murmuring their names. But are we not more than just passers-by? Do we not symbolize the courageous battle for the freedom of Israel, the promise that it would surely come?

We finally part and Aharon promises to arrange a meeting with my 'man in charge' the following day. "This," he explained, "is what we call the group leader, for in *Lehi* there are no officers or ranks but a division into cells, each headed by a custodian who instructs its members and serves as a liaison between them and the center." *Lehi* members were sent on their various missions according to their suitability by nature or profession and there was no single man at the top but a 'Center,' a small group organizing all the activities, choosing the targets and the methods of operation. Their names and identities were a highly guarded secret, it went without saying, but it never occurred to me to try and find out who they were. After all, what did the names their parents had given them at birth matter? Enough that they were fighters directing the battle.

Just before we finally parted I consulted Aharon about my dilemma – my parents, hoping, perhaps, that he would have some advice on how I could calm them down and still their fears when they found out, as they were bound to, that I was an active member of the underground. Was there some way, I asked him, of convincing them of the need for my clandestine activities, of reconciling them to the way I had chosen?

Aharon regarded me sadly. He, too, had parents, he admitted, who were constantly worried about him. No one, he quipped, was immune from the sorrows of raising parents.... But, joking apart, this was the highest price a freedom fighter had to pay for the privilege of dedicating himself to his people. One could get used to all sorts of persecution but never to the grief you were causing your loved ones, to the awareness that they lived in constant fear of losing their beloved son. This was the greatest sorrow of all, the ultimate torture.

Next day, as planned, I met Aharon once more at the *Brith Hashmona'im* club and learnt that the following week I was to wait at the corner of Ge'ula and Tahkemoni Streets (today Malchei Israel Square), take off my beret and twirl it round my fingers while I was waiting. A man would then approach me and ask where the Russian Compound was. My answer would be: 'This is not the Russian Compound, it is the Syrian Orphanage.'*

Aharon asked me to be on time. "Punctuality," he said, "is compulsory in the underground. The man you're meeting may be under surveillance, by the police or some Jews who have volunteered for the dirty work of serving as hunting hounds. When these 'volunteers' catch sight of a young man loitering in the street

---

* Also called the Schneller Orphanage, founded by a German Christian Order at a period when Palestine was considered the southern zone of Syria – one of the Turkish provinces.

they hurry to sniff out if he is waiting for a friend or a girl or is, perhaps, keeping some clandestine appointment of the underground. The longer you hang around, the surer you are to arouse their suspicion. Not only must you never be late – you must see to it that you are not too early. If you feel you are being followed, change your route. Cross from one side of the street to the other and find out if you are really being tailed. If you are, avoid the meeting place until you have got rid of your tail."

Conspiracy

It is said that love can change the lover out of all recognition, turn him into an entirely different person. So it was with me when I joined the underground. Till then I had been a serious, introspective fellow, having little in common with boys of my own age. Now I became a convivial, happy chap, full of jokes and laughter, truly a strange metamorphosis.

Going to keep an appointment I made sure of leaving home in good time, so as not to be late, Heaven forbid! Nearing the spot I glanced at my watch, ten to seven, still too early to hang around there, but not to go too far away as that would make me late. To avoid arousing suspicion I walked around in the near-by alleys and at seven on the dot I was at the chosen spot, twirling my beret round my finger and examining every passing face, wandering about who it was I was supposed to meet. My eye fell on a slender Yemenite youth, with large brown eyes and a face reflecting too much suffering for one so young. As our eyes met he asked: "Where is the Russian Compound?" After having practiced the answer all through the night I gave it to him pat, to which he replied: "You're five minutes late. See that it never happens again!"

I felt awful. I had tried so hard to be on time. There was a large clock in the Schneller Camp but those wretches, the British who were stationed there, never saw to it that it should keep the correct time.

"Call me Eitan," he said, and explained that from then on I wasn't to use my given name and a cover name would be found for me. This was done in order to prevent the enemy from ever finding out my real name even if the boys I worked with were arrested. They would simply not know it.

Eitan wanted to know my motives for joining the underground and I said that I considered the struggle against the enemy to be both a national and a religious edict. "In that case," he pronounced, "We'll call you Datan." (Believer).

As he already knew that I was working at the Central Post Office, he explained what a great advantage it would be for the underground if I could let them have the contents of all telegrams sent to the British staff. He asked if I could supply him with copies but I told him that although I handled such telegrams every day, as they were sent from the British Foreign Office in London to the High Commissioner, to the Head Office and to the C.I.D., they were all in code, meaningless rows of numbers or letters. "Don't give it a thought," said Eitan. "We have someone who can take care of it."

*

After that first meeting there were many others, always in different places. Before parting we would make the next appointment, providing an alternative place in case of a change of plans. The bunch of telegram copies I aways brought with me to these rendevouz warmed me and made me feel lucky to be working where I was. I daresay I was the only messenger boy there who sincerely loved his work and not only did I carry out any odd job I was asked to do but I was always volunteering and 'doing favors' for the other messengers, delivering their letters and telegrams to the Head Office or to the High Commissioner at the King David Hotel. They hated going there because of a certain Mr. Major, a choleric official who took their deliveries. The first time I went there I knew nothing about this Mr. Major and his little ways. Entering his room I handed him the telegrams and asked him to sign the receipt. No sooner had I spoken than he started screaming at me and calling me names, his body contorted and his face blazing red, all the while fingering his ear as if I had bitten it. I froze there, thunderstruck, and it was some time before I realized that I had enraged him by daring to touch the edge of his desk!

I told my fellow messengers at the office about the treatment I had received and they confirmed that they, too, had been similarly treated. It seemed that the gentleman, when in a sour mood, regarded us all as uncouth louts intent on deliberately insulting the official representative of the British Empire, and that was why they were pleased to avoid making deliveries to 'the lion's den,' letting me do them so many 'favors.'

In time I learnt that Mr. Major had once been scheduled for kidnapping, in retribution for the kidnapping and murder of the youth Alexander Rubovich, but the attempt fell through and he was saved, for which, needless to say, I was sincerely sorry.

I went on meeting Eitan for some weeks more, always at street corners or in some obscure alley where we would walk along, holding lengthy conversations. I didn't know at the time that Eitan was a university student who would one day become a successful newspaper reporter, but I was deeply impressed by his clear thinking, his high ambitions and his expertise in all things military, for it seemed to me he talked like a Russian general. It was Eitan who taught me the elementary principles of undercover work, what we then called 'conspiracy.'

"You are going to a clandestine assignation – make sure you're not being followed! Your tail can be easily pinpointed because he's tied to you and can't afford to lose you at any price. The thing is to identify him out of all the passers-by filling the street, find out who's been sticking to you for a sizeable part of the way. This is how it's done: Look back and have a quick look around, 'photographing' all the faces behind you, then stop and stare at a pretty girl. Repeat this at intervals, 'photographing' as many faces as you can and keeping those who've been there before in your mind. There are all sorts of excuses for looking behind you – tying your shoe laces, looking in a shop window...

"If you're sure someone's following you, don't let him know it, it will only put him on his mettle. Try to lose him by disappearing casually in some court yard where you know there is an obscure exit to another street. Another trick is to get into lively conversation with some acquaintance in the street, even if he's not a particular friend of yours. The 'tail' will try to follow that friend, hoping to catch the whole gang, losing you completely in the meantime. In this way you've made him waste much time and man-power on a lot of useless information.

"Avoid being photographed and destroy any snaps or pictures that might give the enemy a lead to you or your comrades.

"Never join a crowd. Detectives are always interested in crowds. Take care never to break the law unwittingly, like not paying your rent on time or riding your bike without a light at night.

"Never get into arguments, not even with your friends. Avoid expressing extreme opinions or, conversely, embarrassing silences. If your friends know that you hold patriotic opinions, don't surprise them by changing radically overnight. That would really make you noticeable. You can even speak admiringly of the underground's courage, provided you give the impression that you yourself are too much of a coward to participate in such activities.

"When you meet someone eager to join the underground, don't even hint that you can help him. Give his name to your 'control' and he will be duly contacted in time. Even if he joins us there is no reason why he should know that you are a member as well.

"When you meet other members, don't ask any questions and avoid any personal contact over and above that which is neccessary, and tell them nothing about your private affairs that they don't have to know. The less you and they know about each other, the less there will be to tell, even under the pressure of torture.

"If you have to keep a note containing clandestine information, keep it where it can most easily be reached so that in case of accidental arrest or a sudden search it can be destroyed or swallowed on the spot.

"Clandestine meetings and activities must be code-named. Never use the real names.

"Avoid meeting anyone you know is a member of the underground."

Avraham Stern–Ya'ir

THE UNKNOWN SOLDIERS

We are soldiers unknown, uniforms we have none,
In death's shadow we march, in its terror
Volunteering to serve to the end of our days,
Only death from our duty can us sever.

    In days red with slaughter, destruction and blood,
    Endless nights black with pain and despair,
    Over village and town our flag we'll unfurl,
    Love and freedom the message 'twill bear.

Not like slaves brought to heel were we dragged to the fight,
In strange lands our life's blood to squander;
And if die we must our people to free,
'Tis our dream our lives to surrender.

    In days red with slaughter...

With obstacles rising to block every move,
By fate cruelly sent to entrap us,
Neither enemy, prison nor miserable spy
Will we ever permit to divert us.

    In days red with slaughter...

Should we happen to fall in some building or street,
To be furtively buried by night,
Many others by thousands will rise in our stead
To defend and continue to fight.

    In days red with slaughter...

With the tears of mothers bereaved of their young,
Sacred infant's blood wantonly spilt,
We'll cement the bricks of our bodies for walls
And our homeland will surely be built.

    In days red with slaughter...

The "Season"

What was I to do about my friends at the *Brith Hashmona'im?*
Sooner or later I would have to give up my membership there and
leave the club. This wasn't going to be as easy as it sounded for I
spent all my evenings there, from the moment I left work and took
off my blue uniform till I was due at my underground assignations.
At that time I was busy from morning till late at night yet never
felt tired, slept better than ever before, got up fresh in the
morning and had never felt better in my whole life. No longer did
I cuddle down into the bedclothes for "just one minute more" on
cold mornings, a habit that had plagued me ever since I could
remember.

I loved those hours at the *Brith Hashmona'im.* I knew that
many of the members were *Lehi* men, but there were some who
weren't and our clandestine activities were never mentioned, of
course.

Summer came, the war went on and on. By now the Allied
Forces had overrun Germany's villages and towns and there was
no room any more for doubt: all the rumors about the genocide of
the Jewish people in the death factories were true. Each day
brought new revelations of the destruction of European Jewry,
more horrifying than the last. It was a fearful holocaust – a whole
tree of life had been cut down and uprooted. Fathers, mothers,
brothers, sisters, sons and daughters, uncles and aunts – a whole
nation had gone up in smoke.

And what was the main preoccupation of the Jewish community
in Palestine while this was going on that kept the press busy? The
major and most troublesome problem seemed to be the final
liquidation of the "terrorist movements."

That winter representatives of all the Jewish Agency controlled
youth movements, were exhorted to identify themselves with the
campaign against the "terrorist movements" and assist it actively.
Ben-Gurion, whose passionate rhetoric against the British
Government was never backed by serious action, was more than
ready to fight the underground organizations to the death. He
called upon all *Histadruth* (General Federation of Labor)

members as well as the community at large to mobilize against these 'charlatans' and 'maniacs' whose only objectives were 'murder, robbery, stealing and corruption.' Moshe Shertock (later Sharett) cried out to fight with 'any means' at their disposal and save the nation from the plague of terrorism. Special units were created to infiltrate the underground, kidnap and torture its members and finally hand them over to the British. This unholy war was named the 'Season,' based on the various British hunting seasons.

We knew that not all those participating in the 'Season' were wholehearted about it. Some were even opposed to it but were acting under orders. However, there was one group that truly derived enjoyment from the hunt and were completely identified with the ideas behind the orders: the *Hashomer Hatza'ir* members who regarded themselves as 'the men of the future.' They accepted the spiritual leadership of Stalin while at the same time classed themselves as Zionists, unwilling to admit that these last were reactionaries in the communist world, partners of the hated bourgeois imperialism which Stalin considered anathema. The *kibbutzim* (collective farms) of the *Hashomer Hatza'ir* volunteered to provide prison quarters for the kidnapped members of the underground, to torture them there until they told everything they knew, after which they would be handed to the British.

Neither did the younger members of the *Hashomer Hatza'ir* disgrace their elders. Refusing to be satisfied with spying for the *Hagana* they used their own initiative to widen the scope of their activities to include school rooms and playgrounds in every district. With indescribable enthusiasm and devotion they set out to catch any youth whose behavior was in any way suspicious and opinions unconventional, handing him over to their leaders, there to receive suitable treatment.

Old Hillel

Eitan asked me to go to Hillel's room one day – my first visit to an actual underground place indoors. I followed him through the maze of alleys comprising the Beith Israel quarter, tortuous narrow lanes in which only a local could find his bearings. A stranger, even if he had the exact address of the underground, would never get there. The place seemed to be ideal for undercover work and it must have been some "genius" who had discovered it. I had no idea at the time just how hard pressed our organization was for rented rooms nor could they pick and choose, as the choice was almost non-existent. They were undesirable tenants, to say the least, and if they somehow did manage to get a room, there was always the danger of some neighbours reporting them to the police the moment they got wind of the real nature of the new tenants. The only place where they sensed support and felt secure was in quarters such as these, among their own.

To get to the room we had to pass through an inhabited apartment. Once there, Eitan produced a written list of names and addresses. "We are about to publish *The Front,*" he told me. "This time it's going to be printed properly, not just mimeographed. The people on this list have expressed their national feelings and are also socially influential, so we want them to get it and understand our policies." I was instructed to familiarize myself with the addresses on the list, learn the exact location of the houses and the letter boxes in the entrances so that as soon as the booklets were available they could be distributed without any loss of time. I told Eitan that the reconnaissance was unneccessary as there wasn't a house I didn't know in Jerusalem because of my work as a telegram delivery boy. As I was talking Eitan suddenly made a sign for me to be quiet. I stopped talking and in the ensuing silence we heard a Yemenite cantor somewhere outside trilling an air from the prayer service, Yemenite style.

As we stood there in silence I wondered what could have happened and if the British were on to us. But the only sound was that of the cantor, singing loud and clear. Suddenly the melody changed and Eitan exhaled in relief, taking up the conversation exactly where it had stopped before the interruption. There was someone keeping watch outside, he explained, and if anyone approached the room while we were there he would warn us by praying a Yemenite chant. The "all clear" would be given as a melody sung in a completely different style.

I got to know the singer in time – Old Hillel, head of a family with many children and the beadle of a local synagogue. He boasted a reddish beard, reminding me of another Yemenite boy who had once told me that the Messiah, son of David, would be a Yemenite. I hadn't believed him then as it was inconceivable to me that the Yemenites were descendants of David for they were all dark-skinned and dark eyed, while everyone knew that King David was "red-haired with bright eyes (Sam. 16:12)." But the sight of Hillel's red hair made me change my mind. Perhaps the Messiah would indeed be a Yemenite!

In giving the organization a room in his home, permitting it to be turned into an arsenal, Hillel was endangering his own life and that of his children. Not satisfied with that, he requested and received many other assignments from us, ranging from collecting information, reconnoitering the area and keeping watch for us while we were conferring inside, to the more dangerous task of transferring arms from one cache to another whenever searches were going on for freedom fighters hiding in the labyrinthian quarters and their cached ammunition.

Old Hillel and all he stood for warmed our hearts and stimulated our imagination. In appearance he was just another undersized, dark-skinned old Yemenite, a mite of a man. Who could believe that this small, gentle person was actually a terrorist, nay, an arch-terrorist!

Not only had Hillel's home long been serving as a storehouse of illegal arms and ammunition but so had the synagogue he worked in. His apartment was a safe house to which underground members would repair after an operation, with the police hot on their heels. Needless to say, such safe houses were few and far between at the time, and people like Hillel rarer still. His very existence seemed miraculous to us, putting himself and his family at risk for our sakes, and we trusted him implicitly. It was awesome and rather frightening how convinced we all were that this man would withstand censure, arrest and torture without ever breathing a word to inform on us.

In the course of my work at the Post Office I often saw letters marked "Opened by Censor" I now inaugurated a new censorship, that of the underground. A letter from the London Central Office or, indeed, any other letter that seemed of any importance, would find its way to the underground censor, something I found highly gratifying. But I wanted to participate in some real fighting operation, like the grown-ups, or, if not, then at least to be allowed to paste the wall proclamations, like the other youngsters. Weeks had gone by since Eitan told me about *The Front* in Old Hillel's house, and I was eager to see it, the articles and notices for once in bright, legible print instead of the usual blurred typing on the yellow stencilled sheets. But according to Eitan "there was a hitch or two" and the publication was being delayed.

Eitan and I still met regularly and sometimes I would be given an assignment. My work in the Post Office had made me a real find for the organization and I now belonged to Section 6 – the *Lehi* information service.

One assignment he gave me was to follow a young couple, an English detective and his Jewish mistress who used to frequent the Reviah café near the Zion cinema. Never before had I ever sat in a café and only went in to deliver a telegram or an express letter and I feared that I would stick out like a sore thumb. Then I remembered that long ago my parents had taken my brother and me to one called 'Ginati' for ice cream. Thus encouraged I went in, sat down and ordered coffee and cake. To my confusion the waiter placed a plate containing not one but three cakes before me. I said nothing as perhaps he hadn't heard my order properly and I didn't want to appear a greenhorn in matters of café behavior. Chewing slowly and carefully to draw out the time, I demolished all the cakes. But my Englishman had failed to show up and I didn't know what to do. I waited for what seemed an interminable time then gave up and left.

When I reported all this to Eitan he told me to be there again next day at the same time.

The minute I entered I saw that luck was with me. He was there in the company of a Jewish girl whom I identified at once from Eitan's description: "Black hair and a face covered with acne."

Taking a near-by table, I again ordered coffee and cake, this time stipulating that I meant one only. As before, the waiter presented me with three, but this time I had the courage to protest: "Sir, I ordered only one cake!" Very politely he explained that I need not eat all three of them, just the one I liked best.

I sat there, leafing through the illustrated magazines and trying hard to catch some of the conversation of the two, but there was nothing of interest, just some talk about a party. As a matter of fact, they didn't talk much at all, just sitting there, looking at each other. This went on for about two hours with me straining to catch a word here, an expression there, and they just sitting there, facing each other in silence. I almost fell asleep and it seemed to me that they had become stuck to their seats, becoming a part of them like statues. Dammit, how long was this to go on and what were they doing, sitting together if they had nothing to say to each other?

I had the bitter thought that if ever I suspected anyone of following me I would lead him to a café and just go on sitting there for hours and hours – till he exploded! Could it be they knew I was following them and had chosen this method to punish me?

Time crept along and in order to keep awake I began nibbling at the second cake. Only the fear that the waiter would think me a nut prevented me from eating the third one too.

Bored to death I went on turning the pages of the periodicals, now and then throwing a glance at my couple. At times I thought they were talking of leaving and hopefully prepared to follow them, but no, still sitting, stuck to their seats.

Another hour passed and I became hopelessly resigned to this aimless hanging around. Then suddenly he was on his feet! I was in a panic. By the time I paid the waiter I would probably lose them, and that would be the last straw... Hurriedly I called the waiter, asked for the bill, paid him and flew outside. But I hurried in vain, they hadn't left. There they were in their seats again, sitting...

64

Finding myself in the crowded street I met some acquaintances and got into conversation with them, keeping my eyes riveted on the Reviah café where my "friends" were calmly sipping their beer. What if they chose this moment to leave, disappearing while I was idly chatting away? I walked to the corner of the street from where watching would be easier. Finally they came out but, to my consternation, they decided to separate outside the café. The Englishman turned towards the direction of the Generali Building while the girl walked up Ben Yehuda Street. What was I to do and whom was I to follow? Eitan had not prepared me for such a contingency.

I decided to go after the girl. For twenty minutes I waited till she came out of a boutique and continued sauntering up Ben Yehuda, stopping to stare at every single shop window. At the corner of Hillel Street she stopped, as if unable to make up her mind whether to go into any more shops and then went into one of the houses, not coming out although I waited there for an hour. Deciding that this could be her home or that of friends who would detain her for a long time, I decided to go and report to Eitan. Imagine my chagrin when he upbraided me for letting her go. I should have gone on tailing her, he said, till I had learnt every significant detail about her – her address, the people she met with and so on.

A Legend Called Ya'ir

My meetings with Eitan continued. Gradually I learnt about "the black days and red nights," when the members of the underground were hunted like animals. Eitan told me about the tragedy at 30 Dizengoff Street in Tel-Aviv. There were four comrades sitting in the room when someone knocked on the door. As they were expecting a friend they opened it. Some British policemen rushed in, their guns at the ready and firing. Avraham Amper got three bullets in his stomach. Zelig Jacque was hit by three and Moshe Svora'i by two. Ya'acov Levstein (Eliav) managed to lock himself into the toilet and tried to climb down into the yard below by means of the sewage pipe but was wounded by some shots through the locked door. Even so, he managed to get down to the yard, but the police fell on him there, pulling his hair and beating him up, while upstairs their companions were having their fun with the three wounded men, hitting, kicking and spitting in their faces.

As justification for this massacre the British planted grenades and guns in the room, so that they later claimed it was a veritable arsenal of a terrorist movement.

A whole hour passed before they called an ambulance and the wounded were bandaged, but permission to take them to *Hadassah,* a Jewish hospital, was refused and they were taken to a Government hospital in Jaffa, where they were operated on. Jacque and Amper died there but before their death one of them said: "Perhaps the day will come when the Jewish community will realize that we were its anonymous soldiers – not Ya'ir's or the organization's but of the nation as a whole."

After five days they gave up their souls to their Maker.

I heard some hair-raising tales about the cruelty of the British who tortured our boys in the cellars of the C.I.D. (the Criminal Investigation Department) in Jerusalem, Jaffa and Acre. Eitan also told me about Jews informing on us for money, or out of sheer stupidity, and about our girl comrades wasting the best years of their lives in a women's prison in Bethlehem.

Then came the story about Ya'ir's last days, when he realized that the enemy was closing in and there was no way out. I could picture his quiet despair, resigned to the inevitable even though both the Revisionists and *Hagana* promised him shelter provided he gave up his campaign. Again and again I listened to how he went to his death, which was approaching with the inevitability of a Greek tragedy. A detective called Morton managed to break into the attic of a house at 2 Mizrahi Street, the home of a *Lehi* member named Tova Svora'i. The wanted man was found hiding in a closet. He was handcuffed and after Tova was sent out of the house he was shot in the back in cold blood. The man Ya'ir died, lonely, hunted and reviled. Many believed that no memory of him would remain.

66

The legend of Ya'ir was born bright, wondrous and shining. The few comrades remaining outside did their best to continue operations, but failed time and again. Those operations were carried out in areas where there were Jews, and try as they might not to harm them in the course of action, going so far as to endanger their own lives in order to spare the innocent, some Jews were hurt. Public opinion denounced the underground as dangerous adventurers and murderers, and all began howling for their blood. Backed by the National Institutions there began a crusade against the remnants of Ya'ir's group. Houses were festooned with their pictures, prizes offered for them "Dead or Alive" or for any help in apprehending them.

Some of the comrades were unable to withstand the pressure and gave themselves up, broken men. Others were arrested, helpless to fight back. There were hardly any freedom fighters left. The man in the street who knew nothing about "higher" politics believed his leaders and was incited by them. He found it convenient that Ya'ir, that "dangerous robber" had been finally got rid of, his "crazy companions" safe behind bars.

The wonderful image of Ya'ir filled me with pride and admiration. With all my heart I identified myself with the handsome, talented poet in his meticulous suit, the brilliant student with his great scholarly achievements. His teachers had predicted a great career for this gifted, sensitive man but not for him a life of success and personal glory. All he dreamt about was the founding of Israeli sovereignty in which he believed with all his heart.

Eitan gave me the details of the escape from the Latrun Detention Camp, accomplished by means of a tunnel dug under the guards' very noses. The whole thing sounded like a fairy tale bearing a message clear in its simplicity: no prison was strong enough or fence high enough to contain the spirit of the Hebrew freedom fighter or resist his statagems!

The prisoners spent many long months digging a tunnel that ran under the shacks of the camp, an operation involving much ingenuity in overcoming the enormous obstacles in their way. No tools for digging? They manufactured some out of kitchen knives and spoons. Impossible to hide such an activity and get rid of the waste earth brought up to the surface? A solution was found. No air in the deep tunnels? That, too, was solved. Keep the detectives from suspecting what was going on? They did. Tens of people were always milling around the shack above the tunnel yet this was the best-kept secret in the camp.

The night came when some twenty freedom fighters managed to get out through the tunnel, gaining the liberty to fight again. They were peerless men whose spirit could never be broken, not by imprisonment, torture and betrayal nor by assassination or lengthy incarceration. Their first task was to mend the torn network of the underground, restructure the force that was to fight for the freedom of Israel.

I learnt about their travails during the first days of freedom, when not one of them would part from his gun for any reason, day or night, so that no killer could catch them unarmed, their guard down. I heard of their wonderful devotion to each other and the unforgettable story of Baruch, (Joseph Rosenbaum) who, after having been shot in the belly by a bullet accidentally discharged from his own gun, still had the presence of mind to cover up all the blood stains, lower the shutters and do everything necessary to prevent the police from finding his comrades. In his last moments he managed to find a way for his friends to get away after they had arrived to rescue him. All the police found when they arrived was his dead body...

I was also told about Baruch's friends, Zion and Eliezer. Zion escaped, badly wounded, from the police station, and reached Eliezer's home in Yavne'el. When the police were informed they sent a large force and the house was surrounded. Eliezer, who was absent at the time, was found with the help of some neighbours and ordered to lead them to Zion. He broke into the room where his friend was hiding, determined to help him fight off the enemy. The British opened fire while the two tried to fend them off with only their small revolvers, continuing to shoot even after both were badly wounded. When there was no more ammunition they found a way out – a bullet in the mouth.

I was also told about Eliyahu Hakim and Eliyahu Beit Tzuri, the two who had just been hanged in Cairo.

PRINCIPLES OF THE REBIRTH

1) *THE NATION – The Jewish nation is unique in that it has given the world monotheism and the moral laws of the prophets. It is in the forefront of universal culture and is distinguished by its traditions, boundless faith, will to live and powers of resistance, its enlightment and confidence in salvation.*

2) *THE HOMELAND – This is the Land of Israel, the boundaries of which are explicitly stated in the Torah ('to your descendants I give this land from the River of Egypt to the Great River, the Euphrates...' Genesis 15, 18).*

3) *THE NATION AND ITS HOMELAND – The Land of Israel was conquered by the Israeli nation by means of the sword. It was here they became a nation and only here can they be reborn. Not only has Israel the right of ownership over the land but this ownership is absolute, nor has it ever been or can ever be rescinded.*

4) *DESTINY – The nation is dedicated to: 1. Redeeming the land. 2. Re-establishing our sovereignty. 3. Reviving the nation: there can be no sovereignty without redemption of the land and no national rebirth without renewing our sovereignty.*

The Roles of our Organization in the Struggle and Final Conquest

5) *EDUCATION – Fostering the love of freedom and a religious faith in the eternal values of the nation. Imbue the people with the concept that they are the masters of their fate. Renew their conviction that "the sword and the book came down intertwined from heaven".*

6) *UNITY – Unite the whole nation around the flag of the Hebrew Freedom Movement. Exploit the genius, status and power of individuals and direct the energy, devotion and enthusiasm of the masses towards a war of liberation.*

7) *TREATIES – Treaties will be signed with any power interested in the struggle of the Organization and willing to give direct assistance.*

8) *POWER – Strengthen the fighting forces and enhance their status both in the Homeland and the Diaspora, in the underground and in the barracks, until there emerges a Hebrew army of salvation with its own flag, arms and officers.*

9) *WAR – Wage constant war against those who would undermine this mission.*

10) *CONQUEST – The Promised Land, now in the hands of foreigners, will be conquered and held to the end of time.*

The Roles of the Movement in the Future, after Salvation has been Achieved and Our Domination Established

11) *MASTERY – Re-establishment of the rule of the Hebrews in the liberated land.*

12) *RULE OF JUSTICE – Creation of a social order founded on the morality of Israel and the justice of the prophets – an order where no man may be hungry or unemployed and all live in amity, mutual respect and friendship, setting an example to the whole world.*

13) *REPLANTING THE DESERTS – Rebuilding the ruins and replanting the ravished deserts in preparation for the arrival of millions and their offspring.*

14) *DEALING WITH ALIENS – This will be done by means of exchange of populations.*

15) *INGATHERING OF THE EXILES – Complete ingathering of Jews from all parts of the Diaspora in the State of Israel.*

16) *RULE – Strengthening the nation by developing it into a major military, political, cultural and economic power in the East and on the shores of the Mediterranean.*

17) *RENAISSANCE – Universal revival of the Hebrew language and of national and spiritual independence; refinement of the national character through the process of rebirth.*

18) *THE TEMPLE – A Third Temple will be built symbolizing complete salvation.*

'The *Principles of Rebirth*' appeared in the second publication of '*The Underground*', organ of the *Lehi*, Freedom Fighters of Israel. They were written by Ya'ir and members of the Central Command at the beginning of 1941.

The Accused become Judges

A new and unexpected front was opened against the enemy – the courtroom. *Lehi* men who were brought to trial in chains turned the judges into defendants, refusing to acknowledge the right of the British to sentence Jews for carrying weapons in Israel. Proud and radiating a matchless courage, their appearance aroused strong emotions in the Jewish community, their widespread intensity being no less harmful to the enemy than the bombs aimed at its fortresses.

New heroes were created every day in the court-rooms: Zvi Tabori, David Hame'iri, Anshel Shpielman, Khissia Shapira, Ya'acov Levstein, Moshe Svora'i and Matti Shmulevitz in this country, and the two Eliyahu's in Cairo.

Zvi Tabori was the first who refrained from trying to justify himself or deny his actions. On the contrary, he accepted all the facts presented by the court: He did own a gun and some ammunition, but it was wrong to say that he acted "without legal right or reasonable justification." "I was given the right to keep a gun by the only power I acknowlege in Israel, the Hebrew Freedom Fighters' Movement which is fighting to establish a Hebrew State in the Land of Israel." They tried to silence him, to frighten him by telling him that such talk was harmful to himself, inviting the severest sentence, but he persisted. "The whole trial is illegal, the judges are not proper judges and I refuse to recognize them for they represent a foreign power. I am duty bound to oppose such an authority."

The trial came as a shock to the community and many suddenly realized the true nature of the British Government. This was no longer an enlightened, friendly power under whose protection we would build a Jewish state in our historic homeland, but a foreign tyrant, alienated and hostile.

Then there was Matityahu Shmulevitz, unidentified when caught as he was carrying an identity card of one Rafi Birenbaum. When two policemen came to arrest him he shot one of them, fully aware that this entailed the death sentence. Appearing before the British court he was without fear and made the following proud declaration: He had reached Israel by a route declared by the British laws as illegel and his only regret was that thousands of other Jews had not done the same. If they had, they would have survived the death camps, and had he himself been a respecter of the law he would have perished with them... He then went on to confess his second crime: "My name is Matityhau Shmulevitz, not, as you think, Rafi Birenbaum. The name itself is not important but can serve as an indication of the mental capabilities of His Majesty's Police who murder people without knowing who they really are, arresting and putting them on trial..." Then he went on to add another crime to the list: "I participated in the escape from the Latrun Detention Camp... I was one of those who went on digging for weeks and months, shifting dirt and breaking rocks in order to be free! Why did we do it? To regain the pleasures of home, for fun? We left a quiet and relatively peaceful existence in Latrun in order to take up a life of danger and difficulty, to continue the struggle for liberty of the Hebrew nation..."

Turning from accused to accuser, Matti continued: "You say that my gun was illegal! My question is – what gives you the moral right? Are your guns legal? In justice they are not... Yours are the terrorist guns and mine is legal..." He concluded his astonishing statement with a chapter from the psalms that opens with the words: "To David – blessed is the Lord that teaches my hands to fight and my fingers to make war!" His sentence was not long in coming – death by hanging. Matti stood at attention and sang the *Hatikva*.

From the underground cellars of the *Lehi* rose the cry: *Freedom for Israel* – this time in many voices and in different forms. It was shouted from the proclamations on the house walls and by the heroes of the underground during their trials. It thundered in the sound of guns shooting boiling lead at the conquerors. *For the Freedom of Israel* – words that embarrassed our enemies and shook the hearts of our adherents. *For the Freedom of Israel* – and a nation that had been ground in the dust for two thousand years felt a renewed pride.

The second World War was nearing its termination, with Stalin entrenching his forces in Eastern Europe. In Greece the communists were getting impatient, unwilling to wait for the downfall of Hitler and, war within a war, bloody battles were fought between the communist rebels and the occupying British army that had taken the country. But what was permitted communist rebels in Greece was strictly forbidden to Jewish Freedom Fighters. The communists in Israel joined the unholy choir of hate against the insurgent underground movements with the excuse that their campaign was harmful to the war effort of the allies against Hitler...

The 8th of May, 1945. Germany capitulated and the whole world breathed a sigh of relief. In Israel too, crowds filled the streets, singing and dancing, celebrating the victory. Victory? Whose? Of the six million Jews, a third of the nation, annihilated by this war? Our "ally," Great Britain, never intervened in the holocaust waged against our people. True, it did not burn Jews, but neither did it agree to bomb the crematoria that did. It did not expel Jews – only forbade Jews to enter territories under its aegis, particularly Palestine which had been given in trust to Britain by an international mandate to turn it into a Jewish National Home.

At the same time, as the Jewish community here sent its young men to fight within the framework of the British Army, the British fleet busied itself with hunting refugee ships and returning them to the Nazi inferno.

The war was now over and victory achieved. Would the British government change its attitude and begin to show some remorse and compassion towards the surviving remnants, try to rehabilitate them before it was too late? Would the White Paper be cancelled?

True, Churchill, "our friend" had promised to do this as soon as the war was over and now he commanded a navy and military forces to do with as he liked. And he used them indeed. The British navy virtually blockaded the Israeli coast in order to prevent the refugees from entering by force, and the land forces entrenched themselves in preparation for putting down any form of rebellion.

Now that the true nature of the British was revealed for all to see, we hoped that the Jewish community would begin fighting against the White Paper, but our public leaders hesitated, waiting for the coming elections in England... The leaders of the British Labor Movement were much more radical than the socialist leaders in Israel. At one of their political conventions it was decided that the Arabs in Israel should be evacuated to other Arab states, to make room for all the Jews desiring to settle here...

When news reached Israel of the Labor victory in the British elections, the whole country celebrated. Everyone was wildly enthusiastic and the local labor leaders hurried to congratulate their "sister, mother of all democracies" – Britain. But Israel was due for a rude awakening. Ernest Bevin gave an anti-Zionist speech with deep anti-semitic undertones. He stressed that friendship towards the Arab nations had always been a British tradition and was now a necessity. These Jews, he said, "who were always pushing themselves to the head of the queue, must learn to accept the policies of the 'White Paper' and the quota of 1500 immigrants per month whether they like it or not."

Rebellion

The British had betrayed us openly, for all the world to see.

The Hebrew regiments volunteering the British army were of no avail. The "good behavior" during the war had been of no avail. "Marking time quietly" till the Labor came to power – that too, had been useless. Nothing had done any good!

The country was in turmoil. Members of the "organized" youth movements now refused to fight against their brothers who had taken up arms against the British. They, too. demanded war. The leaders realized that ignoring this demand would only turn their own youth against them. In this way the "Resistance Movement" came into being.

The underground movements had never wished to monopolize the struggle against the British; on the contrary, they regarded themselves as the spokesmen of the whole nation, always ready to cooperate with the *Hagana*, and ready to forget their persecutions of the past for the good of the common cause – the war against the British. Not so the official representatives of the community, who, it appeared, were not prepared to go so far. They hoped that by giving their younger members, who by now were thirsting for action, some opportunity of demonstrating their powers by launching an impressive operation, they would get them under firm control. Plans were therefore made for a prestigious series of actions to be carried out in various parts of the country.

The morning after the "Night of the Bridges" – work of the "Resistance Movement" – was one of exaltation for the whole community. Railway lines had been blown up, bridges went up in the air, planes were bombed, and radar stations demolished. Lord Gort, the new High Commissioner who had replaced MacMichael, resigned on the spot and left the country.

The Ma'as (The Deed)

All that time I had been impatiently waiting for *The Front* to appear in print as Eitan had promised. Seeing a group of people peering at something on the wall, I joined them and saw that they were reading *The Ma'as*. When I realized that the paper was a publication of the *Lehi,* there was no end to my satisfaction.

Unable to withstand the temptation I got as close as I could and read it from start to finish, knowing all the while that I was acting irresponsibly, going against all the laws of conspiracy I had been taught. But I couldn't resist it.

This time all the streets were well-covered with *The Ma'as* and what a fine sight it was! No wonder all the passers-by were deeply impressed. If only I had been given a chance to help with its distribution, our first major publication...

I decided to go to *Brith Hashmona'im*, and shortly after my arrival the club suddenly overflowed with many members, all filled with repressed excitement and greeting each other with the club's slogan: "With God is salvation!" Even though I had taken no part in the new publication, it was still a great day for me too.

When I next met Eitan it was the first time I had ever let him feel my resentment, and I was full of complaints: "Others take the risk of putting up the paper, and what about me?" I demanded angrily. "All I'm good for is following all kinds of characters and pinching mail for the 'censor'. It just isn't right or fair!" Eitan calmed me down, explaining that what I was doing was important and valuable and that, generally speaking, there was no important or unimportant work in the underground: "You don't understand... it's not every member who can supply us with the confidential telegrams sent by the Government of his Majesty, King George the Sixth to its administration in Israel... whereas anyone can paste proclamations..."

I got the point and blessed my good fortune for being in a position to supply the underground with vital information. But I was somewhat depressed by my suspicions that a smooth flow of information such as I supplied might be too important to the underground ever to let me take part in anything involving risk...

True, membership alone in the underground meant constant danger, and you could get caught just by being seen with a "suspect" or drawing the attention of an informer, but when an underground member goes out into the open whether to put up proclamations or as part of an attacking force – his chance of being seen by detectives, soldiers, policemen or informers among his own people is immeasurably greater. The risk of getting hurt or arrested is very real. All the underground members regarded this kind of activity, and the certain danger involved, as the height of fulfillment, the actual implementation of the objectives of the movement. I felt in no way different, but I had to acknowledge that those who were in the responsible posts were right in refusing to risk such a vital source of information. They would probably do anything to prevent putting me in a risky position, something that worried me deeply.

*

Eitan introduced me to Eli, an acquaintance of mine from *Brith Hashmona'im* – Eliezer Greiber by name – and told us that as of that moment we would be together at observation posts as well as in shadowing people. Good! This was much better than working alone, much, much pleasanter. You weren't so tense if you had someone to talk to, have a friendly chat with... But after a few days I was informed that I was to be attached to someone else, someone I would meet in Old Hillel's room.

There were three people in the room: Amos, who was "in charge," fair-haired and sturdy, with two boys sitting on each side of him, going by the code names of Ha'im and Israel. They looked younger than me and I was reminded of the time when, looking for a contact to the underground, I had felt so apprehensive about my youth.

I wondered what they were doing in the underground, thinking it might indicate the nature of my own future activities, but at that first meeting I had no opportunity of talking with my new friends. Only later did I learn that in spite of their youth they were veterans in the underground, their occupation being mainly that of pasting *The Front* and other material in the streets. They, too, were hoping that it wouldn't take too long before they were trained in the use of arms.

Israel was a handsome boy of medium build and, like many other observant boys at the time, wore a dark blue beret. He was a chap after my own heart, who knew how to keep his mouth shut.

Ha'im, in sharp contrast to Israel, looked like a dreamy sort of fellow, but as soon as he started talking he turned into burning lava. Whenever we met he would speak of his desire to confront the enemy of his people with gun in hand. His attitude to the British, a combination of derision and fury, was contagious. Again and again we would recall the bitter days of the "Season." Ha'im said that this was nothing new and it had been thus, brother against brother, the inferior against the superior, during the ancient Greek occupation and the Hellenists, a phenomenon that continued to this very day.

We also discussed the unification of all the underground

movements in the "Resistance Movement." Israeli youth was basically good, ready for sacrifice and struggle. The problem lay in the leaders and their decisions. Would they be prepared to fight? We found it hard to believe that those leaders who had always chosen to avoid confrontation, who had vilified the underground, would actually lead the people to war.

★

Israel and I spent many hours discussing the last "Season," of which the *Etzel* had been the main target. The *Lehi* group had remained virtually untouched – a fact hard to explain, as the "Season" had reached its worst climax after the execution of Lord Moyne, when the leaders of the "Organized Community" reacted with unbridled fury. As this execution had been the work of the *Lehi*, it was somewhat puzzling: Why was this fury now directed towards the *Etzel*, not the *Lehi*?

The explanation we got was that the *Lehi* had warned the Jewish Agency that it would punish its leaders if any *Lehi* man was harmed, and the warning had been well taken. The *Etzel*, conversely, let it be known that it would avoid an internecine war at any cost and refrain from harming the "Organized Community."

Tomorrow We Meet at "X"

Amos let me know about the meeting, "X" being the designation of a certain alley in the Akhva quarter. The time – four o'clock in the morning; the purpose – pasting *The Ma'as* (The Deed) on the street walls!

At four? What a time to choose? What excuse could I give my parents? It appeared that as soon as the blackout was cancelled with the cessation of hostilities, any passer-by could watch the boys putting up the proclamations of *The Ma'as* in the streets and even if there weren't any enemies or informers around at the time, there might be a friend with a loose tongue... At four in the morning the streets were quiet and almost empty – just the right time for such clandestine work. But how was I going to manage to leave the house so early?

There was a synagogue in our quarter, to which some laborers would go for prayers at five o'clock in the morning, before going to work. I made up my mind to tell my parents that I wanted to pray with them at the first, earlier service. I hoped that when I got up at half past three they wouldn't hear me at all, and if they did – why should they turn on the light to see the right time?

Ha'im and Israel, who were to join me in the pasting operation, had a different excuse. As they were high school students they told their parents that the Natural Science teacher had asked them to observe the stars before sunrise.

We separated in order to meet while it was still night. Happy though I was finally to be sent on the pasting assignment, I was terribly apprehensive that I wouldn't manage to wake up at the right time. Luckily I slept in a separate room, from which I could go out noiselessly, but how was I to ensure that I would wake up on time, when an alarm clock was out of the question? Thinking that the pressure on my bladder would wake me up, I skipped going to the toilet before going to bed at the early hour of ten p.m., my pyjamas over my clothes. But I was too keyed-up to sleep, twisting and turning for about two hours, dropping off for short naps, and waking in a panic... I was going to be late! It was too dark to see the time and I deeply envied those fortunate enough to have luminous watches. When I finally dared to turn on the light I saw it was only 2 a.m. I turned it off and returned to bed, congratulating myself that I hadn't awakened the whole household. After half an hour the story repeated itself, and this time I sprang out of bed feeling I had slept for hours; but it was only a quarter past three. Going back to bed was out of the question – I might fall asleep again and not awaken in time. I couldn't get up and go out into the street, attracting undesirable attention, so I just sat there on a chair, waiting for the time to pass.

After a quarter of an hour I stripped off my pyjamas, tucked my prayer shawl and *tefillin* under my arm and, raising my voice, called out: "Shalom, I'm going to the synagogue." If my parents were awake, they wouldn't be surprised to hear the creaking of the door as I left.

It was wonderful outside! The old quarters of Jerusalem before morning in summer are bathed in a contented tranquility, the chirping of the waking birds, or the occasional rooster proclaiming the dawn, being the only sounds you hear as you go on your way. All your senses are alerted as you breathe in the pure, sweet air. No words can describe this wonderful sensation of walking alone in the byways of Jerusalem early on a summer morning, feeling you are the sole master of its beautiful vistas, beloved by the whole world. Not even a poet can do it justice.

I walked along in my city, prayer shawl and *tefillin* under my arm. If I encountered a police ambush, I would say that I'm on my way to the synagogue. In the distance a man appears, walking slowly – probably delivering the morning papers.

I was fifteen minutes too early at "X", our rendevouz spot. Slowing my pace I turned towards the Kerem quarter, which began behind the Tachkimoni School. The quarter was small, and whenever I went there with my bag of telegrams I would find myself surrounded by tens of children, all eager to find out who I was looking for and what I had brought for them – what the news was...

It was here that Eliezer Feinstein lived, the same man who used to keep a grocery store beneath our balcony when I was a child. I remember being sorry when he left us to live with his family in the Kerem quarter. His children were friendly by nature and we used to play together often, though his son, Meir, was my favorite. It was this Meir who, together with his friend and cell-mate Moshe Barazani, achieved immortality by their courageous act of self-immolation in their prison-cell in Jerusalem just a few moments before they were due to be hanged.

Amos, armed with a tin of glue and a pile of *The Ma'as* (The Deed), was already there before me and we were soon joined by Ha'im and Israel. The task of look-outs was given to Amos and Israel, I was to spread the glue on the walls and Ha'im to put up the sheets.

Amos walked ahead of us, surveying the terrain. I pushed my prayer shawl and *tefillin* into my shirt and tightened my belt so they wouldn't fall out. With the tin of glue in one hand and a sticky rag in the other, I covered the wall surfaces for Ha'im, who quickly pulled out a sheet from under his arm, smoothing it out on the prepared space. Israel kept up the rear, some disance behind us.

We had a warning system for every emergency based on whistling a particular melody. There was one tune warning us of the approach of the British, another sounding the all-clear. Thus we moved from one wall to the other, from one quarter to the next – left hand holding the glue, right hand dunking the rag in the sticky mess. As soon as I had smeared the wall, Ha'im would put up the sheet and we would both steal a quick look of satisfaction at it. It was a quick look indeed, and we would run along in the footsteps of Amos, picking out a suitable wall to be quickly smeared and covered with living, breathing words. Ha'im and I felt as if we were talking to our people for needless to say – this was the only way we could communicate with them.

"We are talking by means of the wall, while the heads of the National Institutions are talking to the wall..." quipped Ha'im. How right he was! That was just how Golda Meirson (later Meir) sounded, when, on meeting with the High Commissioner, she asked him to change his immigration policy or she would be helpless to curb terrorism...

Ha'im sounded so bitter that I reminded him we were now living in a new era. The nation was now united in its struggle with the British, in the common front of the Rebellion Movement, and hopefully the ugly sight of brother against brother would become a thing of the past.

"You don't know them," he replied. "If I wasn't in secrecy bound I'd tell you something that has just happened which would prove that they haven't changed one iota. Why, even today, with Bevin declaring that 'the Jews are always pushing themselves to the head of the queue,' their actions prove just how deeply they hate us 'insurgents.' All it takes is one small bone to be thrown to them by the British, and they'll be persecuting us again!"

And so we walked along, putting up our flyers, talking in clipped sentences, giving our opinions on this and that, expressing our feelings. The walls of Zichron Moshe were done and we went up to Yellin St., then down through the Edison Cinema to Ge'ula, Kerem Avraham and Tzefania St., "decorating" the houses of the northern quarters of Jerusalem. Come daylight, these walls will be proclaiming the message of the *Lehi.*

Here and there we could already see a few early risers, their numbers growing as time went on. Most of them were genuinely going to morning services at their synagogue before beginning their day's labor, while a few went about delivering newspapers – something that had to be done at an early hour. When any one of them passed us we turned our backs to them, hiding our faces. There was one who asked for a copy and, upon reading it, began to bless us fervently: "Be of good courage, God is with you, heroes of Israel!" It was good to hear him. Dawn was approaching as we went on with our work, feeling much better now. I regretted not having asked the good man if he was ready to aid the underground, become one of its sympathizers. Among the adherents of the underground were many middle-aged citizens who helped us greatly, providing us with cellars, rooms, money and important information. I went on zealously spreading glue. What a change! Never before had I seen underground material on the wall without stopping to read it. This time I had to be satisfied with the headlines alone! "Evil Oppression Will Not Crush The Fight For Freedom!"

We had used up all the glue and the job was done. We buried the tin pot in an empty lot and took one copy of *The Ma'as* for ourselves, to be read in private. The rest of the copies would be distributed in letter boxes that evening.

Fixing the time for another meeting, we turned homewards. En route I went into some synagogue and washed my hands of all the glue that had dried and coagulated on them. Then I took out my prayer shawl and *tefillin,* tucking them under my arm, making myself presentable for my parents and giving me an air of innocence. The walls along the way in Mekor Baruch testified that our friends had been here too and the proclamation was shouting from all sides.

At home I received a loving welcome, for hadn't I gotten up at an early hour in order to pray with the congregation? But when I laid down my prayer shawl and *tefillin* I apologized to them silently. Not only had I failed to wind them round my arm or put them between my eyes, as was my custom every morning, but I had used them to mislead others, pretending to go to prayers.

A new man was now in charge of us – Eliezer, replacing Amos. For the first time I was "officially" grounded in the ideology of *Lehi* to which I had been so instinctively drawn before. Ya'ir, founder *of Lehi,* had drafted the objectives of the underground: Israeli sovereignty in the Land of Israel and the erection of the Third Temple. He formulated 18 paragraphs of his *Principles of the Rebirth,* proposing solutions that went much further than just the termination of foreign rule in our country: foreign inhabitants will leave in accordance with a system of population exchange; there will be social justice in the land, inspired by Jewish ethics and prophetic justice. The borders will be those promised in the Bible: "...to your descendants I give this land from the River of Egypt to the Great River, the Euphrates..." (Genesis 15:18). We must not content ourselves with less. Moreover, we were enjoined to remember that there was nothing sacrosanct about the arbitrary borders laid down by the various conquering powers after Turkey's capitulation at the end of the First World War. Because "the sword and the Book came down intertwined from heaven," we must strive to impose the principles of ethics and justice given us by our prophets. The insurrection against the British, the realization of Zionism, i.e., founding a Jewish National Home in Israel, all these were only the necessary stages leading to the greater dream of Israeli sovereignty and the principles of its rebirth.

Eliezer's responsibility for us passed to other hands. This time it was not a man in charge, but a woman, Hanna, the first woman I encountered in *Lehi.* I had known, of course, that there were girls in our movement; probably some of those I knew at *Brith Hashmona'im* were underground members. But how was I to know who was a member and who wasn't? There was also Khissia Shapira, famed for the statement she made at her trial after being sentenced to four years on the charge of possessing arms. But personally I had never met a girl since joining, and Hanna was the first to bring an element of warmth and gentleness into our lives, so charged with tension. Hanna introduced another girl to the cell, Techia, and a boy called Aryeh.

The British Government had decreed that the terror must be stopped at any price, and large numbers of British troops began streaming into the country, among them the "Poppies" (*Kalaniyot*) of the 6th Airborne Division, so called because of their red berets. It was a famous division, renowned for its victories and its prowess against the Germans during the war. This was also the division that had crushed the communist uprising in Greece during the last months of the war. Not content with the "Poppies," the Government sent out a call for police reinforcements throughout the country, while at the same time an enormous campaign for volunteers was launched in England, calling English lads to: "Join the Palestine police and see the world." Israel and Ha'im my cell comrades, remarked ironically that there was a word missing in the above placard, which should read "... and see the next world!"

By now all British Government offices were fenced in with barbed wire, with armed guards on duty day and night. A new, originial use was found for the old alarm systems – relics of the war in case of an enemy attack – a means of fighting the terrorists. According to a new regulation issued by the British, all civilian vehicles had to stop as soon as the alarm was sounded, or their drivers would be shot on the spot. This was thought to facilitate surprise searches in different locales. Some streets would be blocked by the police and army forces, and every passer by made to identify himself, after which he was thoroughly searched. Simultaneously with this, careful house-to-house searches were carried out, each city quarter and borough being combed from time to time, with the older quarters receiving special attention. Members of the Jewish community who had not, till then, realized the inevitability of having to fight the British, had the lesson brought home to them by the enemy himself.

From time to time curfew was imposed on certain

84

neighbourhoods or upon whole urban areas. People would retire into their homes, not a soul coming or going, and with only soldiers and policemen patrolling the streets. The more the Hebrew underground struck at the British, the more frequent the curfews, till it became an almost daily feature. As for us, the more curfews imposed the more pleased we were: it clarified the situation, stopping the foreign power from hiding behind its liberal facade and unmasking its true character – that of an oppressor.

Like any other active member of the underground, I obeyed orders and carried out all the tasks assigned to me, but I always kept my eyes open, for I wanted to do more. My job gave me the entrée to areas closed to the general public, and I was often in the position to report to those in charge any untoward movements of the enemy, newly erected structures, or military encampments that came to my attention. There was also an additional new address for telegrams that received my devoted "care," that is to say, careful copying. This was the head-quarters of a new, gigantic military camp, named El Alamein, that had just been completed at the time on the road to Bethlehem, north west of the Talpioth quarter. This same camp that, ironically enough, was to turn into a vast transition camp for immigrants from Iraq before four years had passed.

But the passing years brought the time nearer when I could no longer serve as a messenger boy. The custom being that at the age of eighteen we were promoted into regular postmen, with the more gifted ones taking a course in radio transmission. Hopefully, I thought I could go on collecting information in the radio transmission room, but very quickly I found out that I was wrong, and decided not to work as a radio transmitter. So, at the age of eighteen I became a postman, and imagine my joy when I realized that here, too, I could get hold of the mail in which the underground was interested.

It was the daily routine of the postmen to classify all the mail belonging to Jerusalem into pigeonholes, one for each district. I too, stood there classifying my quota, and whenever I found an official envelope I would put it in the pigeonhole of my own district. I would also filch registered government letters out of the others niches and put them into mine. My task was often made much easier by the authorities, when they stamped the envelope "Confidential" – indicating its special importance. Section 6, our intelligence department, was particularly interested in those.

All this created another problem: as a postman I was loaded down with a lot of material, too bulky to fit into my pockets, like the few chosen telegrams I had dealt with before. We therefore fixed on a place for a "drop," where I could leave the material for our "Censorship" to go over. The place chosen for this was the Schwedron Kiosk in what used to be Chancellor St., (today Strauss), near the Maayan Stub Store. After it had been suitably scrutinized, the material was returned to me and I would put it back in the mail bags, putting a tiny pencil mark on each envelope to prevent my taking it again, something which happened from time to time when letters had to be redistributed.

I also made good use of my friendly relations with the clerks in charge of the telegraph department, going down to the basement for a chat almost every day. There were three of them working in shifts, and it pleased them to see I had not forgotten them since my promotion to the grade of postman. Nor were they loth to ask me, who had so recently been under their orders, for a "small favor." There was always some urgent business they had to take care of and would I mind very much "replacing them for just a moment?" I always did, of course, well aware that they would be away for some time, perhaps for as long as an hour, which suited me right down to the ground. Mr. Sherrif, one of the staff there, was always particularly happy to see me. Sherrif, excitable Arab nationalist, was always trying to impress me with the might of the Arab nation. He was convinced that the Jews were *Walad el Mitha* (children of death) who could never fight back and were doomed to humiliation. Whenever the underground pulled off some impressive operation, he would try to convince me that it was actually the work of the British in their attempt to threaten and frighten the Arabs. Sherrif was not alone in these ideas, which often found expression in the Arab press. "If the British leave the country and we have to fight it out between us," he once asked me, "can you deny that it will be all over for you?" "I don't understand politics much," I replied, "but it says in our Torah that the whole country, from the Nile to the Euphrates, will be the kingdom of the Jews."

"Don't believe your Torah," he sneered.

"But its yours too, our Torah."

"No! All that is cancelled by the Koran," came his heated retort. "It says there that the Jews will be persecuted forever and that they will never have a homeland..."

Mr. Sherrif enjoyed my company, either because he thought he had made a deep impression on me, or because he wanted his friends at the office to think so. Anyway, the more he liked me the greater his eagerness to exploit my goodness of heart, and he was always asking me to replace him "for a minute" in the telegram room so that he could go about his business. His "minute" was sometimes so protracted that I often managed to copy out more telegrams than I had done when delivering them as a messenger boy.

After the Six Days' War I took the trouble to find Mr. Sherrif and found him still working in the Post Office, at the Herod's Gate branch. The 'brave' man told me that he was suffering from diabetes, a result of the terrible fear he suffered during the war. He looked miserable and worried...

It took me a long time to realize the great importance of my work in the underground "censorship." Not only did it give us detailed information of government plans but we could also see which way their mood was going. We could study their very thoughts, attitudes and reaction to our operations. The private correspondence showed us how greatly they feared us, how they hated their service in "fuckin' Palestine." Neither were there humorous aspects lacking in my work. I remember some letters sent to Ge'ulah Cohen after her escape from prison in Jerusalem. They were sent to her by an admirer in Italy, praising her effusively to the very skies. His letters, sent by regular mail, bore the following address: "To the illustrious announcer of the clandestine Hebrew organization, Miss Ge'ulah Cohen, Jerusalem, Land of the Hebrews, Palestine." The postman couldn't make out the address and pushed the Italian admirer's letters into the niche for illegible addresses. It was the easiest thing in the world for me to have them delivered to her...

Ha'im is Expelled from School

At one of our cell meetings I noticed that Ha'im and Israel were unusually perturbed, but when I asked them what was wrong they just looked at each other and refused to answer. I pressed them to tell me and finally Ha'im, unable to contain his anger, burst out: "Listen, conspiracy or no conspiracy... This is something you should know. We've got a new Principal at our school who's against us. A few weeks ago he got all the pupils together and gave a poisonous speech against the underground organizations. 'What does it matter,' we thought, 'Let him talk!' But he wasn't satisfied with just a talk and this week he sent for my parents..."

As Ha'im's mother was ill and his father busy at the pharmacy, the task fell to his elder brother who, taking his wife along with him, went to the Principal's office for what they thought was to be a quiet talk about Ha'im. What they heard was: "Ha'im had better change his ways or I shall expel him from the school!" Ha'im's brother and sister-in-law were dumbfounded, for they knew that he was honest and industrious, what crime could he have committed to justify expulsion from school? Furiously the Principal pulled out a written sheet from his drawer and began to read it out. The composition, written in Ha'im's hand was, on the one hand, a paean of praise for the Hashmona'im, and on the other a scornful diatribe directed at the Grecophiles (*Mityavnim*), who helped the enemies of their own people. When he finished reading, the Principal handed them the composition, to see their brother's sins for themselves.

They read and re-read it, but failed to understand what had roused the Principal's ire. The central idea of the composition was clearly expressed and the style was perfectly acceptable. Perhaps it wasn't to the Principal's individual taste, but what was there to make such a scandal about?

"Don't you understand?" he ranted, "Don't you see that while he's talking about the Hashmona'im he's actually referring to the dissidents? I've heard rumors that he has joined them and this I won't stand for in my school! I will not permit him to poison the whole class with his dangerous ideas! What do you have to say to that?"

Ha'im was called to the office and asked if it was true that he had joined the dissidents. Seeing that it was no longer a secret, he decided to confess, hoping to avoid entreaties and pressures to leave the underground. "I have sworn by the Bible to be faithful to the underground. This promise I shall never break nor will I give up fighting for my people's freedom!" he declared. Swearing by the Bible was a lie, there was no such thing, but he hoped that, as this was a religious school, they would honor his oath and not ask him to break it. He was wrong! Out of Ha'im's hearing the Principal suggested that the family do everything to get Ha'im away from such evil company. He asked them if they had any relatives in a kibbutz even not a religious one. "Never mind," the Principal replied. "Better that he should give up his faith, so long as he has nothing more to do with those dissidents."

Hurrying home, Ha'im's brother and sister-in-law told his father about their talk with the Principal, but kept the story from his sickly mother. His father decided that they had no choice but to tell her too. Ha'im was a decent honest lad who loved his mother very much and knew how serious her illness was. Surely he wouldn't dream of continuing in the underground if he knew that the anxiety would influence her for the worse and may even shorten her life.

The mother was told, but the result was far from what the surprised family had expected. There was no crying, no breaking down... "Each Jew must try to serve his people in his own way. If Ha'im thinks his is the right one – we have no right to stand in his way!"

So Ha'im was expelled from the Ma'aleh High School because he refused to break faith with the underground.

Ha'im was not the only victim, and on that same day there were other boys expelled from Ma'aleh on the charge of belonging to the underground. Israel's parents, too, were called to the Principal's office, where they were warned that their son had joined the dissidents. Israel was called and asked if he had sworn fidelity to them, which he denied. The Principal warned him to cease having any contact with the dissidents, which the lad promised to do. Yet here he was, coming to the meetings as usual, in spite of his promise. He believed that by pretending successfully he would be able to go on with his studies...

Shortly afterward Ha'im managed to get a job in the Jerusalem office of the *Ha'aretz* daily paper, supplementing his meagre salary by delivering the paper at dawn. Upon his recommendation Israel was given this job too, providing them both with a wonderful excuse for putting up the wall-placards of the *Lehi*. This job did not last too long, however. Somebody saw to it that the office manager got wind of their affiliation with the underground, and they were both fired for this reason.

★

Hanna arrived with some proclamations which were to be "scattered" in the Edison Cinema while a meeting of the Revisionist Party was being held there. It did me good to see her, small and plump, always smiling...

As at all lectures given by members of the Revisionist Party, the hall was filled to capacity. The crowd was even larger than usual that day, for the speakers were Dr. Aryeh Altman, Dr. Jossef Nedavah and Zvi Kolitz – all famous for their exciting oratory.

Ha'im, Israel and I padded our bodies with proclamations and covered them with our shirts. Then, seated "strategically" in the hall, we listened to the fiery speakers. As soon as they had finished and the crowd was on its feet, singing the *Hatikvah*, hundreds of *Lehi* proclamations began flying above their heads. For a moment it seemed to me that the youth sitting beside me had noticed what I had just done, so, pretending innocence I asked him: "What is it? What are you reading?"

"It's a *Lehi* proclamation," he answered, his face serious as he went on reading. No, he had noticed nothing.

We left without saying a word to each other, each going his own way. The road was already blocked and the *Kalaniyot* (red-bereted paratroopers) had spread out and were searching the passers-by, myself and my friends included. But they were too late, we were "clean" and the material had already reached many hands...

At home Father told us that the *Kalaniyot* had stopped and searched him in the street. The incident reminded him of his stay in Mexico when civil war broke out. One day he had been stopped by a group of armed Mexicans, notorious for shooting down their opponents.

"Quien viva?" he was asked at gun point. Realizing that his reply meant life or death, Father had to think quickly. If he said *"Viva Zappata!"* and these were Zappata's opponents – he was a dead man. If he was for Zapata's enemies and these were his adherents, the result would be the same. *'Quien viva?'* they repeated, about to lose their patience. Father had a brilliant idea and cried: *"Viva Mexico!"* (Long live Mexico!). The patriots who had arrested him were pleased to find a man with his heart in the right place and let him go...

"A Girl's been looking for Me"

It goes without saying that we all wanted the membership of the underground to expand, and whenever one of us met someone who expressed sympathy with our cause he was immediately recommended to those in charge. I, too, was naturally interested in enlisting some of my friends, particularly those working in the Post, and this for two reasons. First – they would be invaluable to our Information Department, and second – I hoped that if there were a few more like me from the Post I too would get to participate in active combat. But, though I was always on the look-out for candidates, there was no one among the postmen I considered worth recommending. None, that is, until Benny appeared, a new postman who was turned over to me to learn the rudiments of his new job. As we walked through the streets of Jerusalem it was he who began discussing the political situation, bitterly criticising the British and praising the Revisionist Movement fervently. He did seem to blab too much, but he hated the British and might make a good fighter. Perhaps I wouldn't have recommended him if I hadn't been so eager to recruit a postman to the underground. I could have waited until I knew him better.

One morning Benny came running to me excitedly. "Listen, I've something great to tell you..." I realized it would have to do with my recommending him to the underground and I was deeply shocked. Had no one warned him not to talk about such things?

"You won't believe this! When I came home yesterday Mother told me that a girl had been looking for me."

"You don't say," I replied, all innocence, "a girl came to your place?" "And I wasn't there!" he mourned, "fool that I am! But how could I know a girl would come looking for me? I mean, how could I, really? I'm never at home in the evenings; I always go out. And then a girl comes looking for me, out of the blue!"

"A pity."

"Never mind, she said she would come again this evenning."

"You lucky devil! Girls coming looking for you at your own home. Who is she? Where did you meet her?"

"I don't know," he admitted.

"Maybe she met you at work? Or you delivered a letter to her place and she liked the look of you so much she found out where you lived? I sure have to admit I envy you... You know, I'm not so bad with the girls myself sometimes, but nothing like this has ever happened to me, never.... What did she look like, this girl; what did your mother tell you about her?"

"Mother said she was quite nice, a brunette, a solid type, not one of your cheap floozies chasing the men. She said she prayed I would be so fortunate..." "I hope so too. The girl really seems to have fallen for you. What do you say I come to your place tonight I'd sure like to meet her?" I knew he would refuse before he answered.

"No, buddy! First let me get to know her on my own." He gave a meaningful wink – "Later on I'll introduce you."

I was curious to hear what he would have to say after the

meeting. Even though I knew that if he joined the underground or not his lips would be sealed about his conversation with the girl, I was still curious. After all, it was I who had recommended him in the first place, he was my co-worker. I wondered what fictitious story he would invent about his "lovers' meeting."

"Well," I interrogated him next morning, obviously impatient. "How was it? Go on, tell me! I'm dying of curiosity..."

"What's to tell." He sounded exasperated. "I sat at home all evening waiting for milady – and she didn't show up at all."

"Impossible!" I exclaimed.

"Who does she think she is? Do you know what it means, sitting home the whole evening, killing time? I kept watching the clock and my mother kept watching me, feeling sorry for me... my friends waited outside wondering what had happened to me and why I had disappeared.... Believe me, that's not my style at all, sticking it out the whole evening waiting for some unknown broad... thank you very much, but never again..."

"Listen to me, buddy," I tried to calm him down, thinking all the while that I had been pretty stupid to recommend him in the first place. The man was too nervous and selfish... not a successful combination. "Patience... she may be sick or perhaps had an accident? Something important may have come up. There must be a reason if she didn't show up. If I were you I'd wait for her this evening too, and tomorrow, for a whole month even. A common girl wouldn't come looking for you at home."

"O.K." he agreed reluctantly, "Just tonight and that's all. We'll see what happened yesterday, why she didn't come."

Next morning he was·as angry as ever. "I'm nervous, that's my trouble!" he began, without any prompting from me. "I waited for her till eight but she didn't show up. So I went out. I felt that if I had to wait another minute I'd go nuts. But you know what? When I got back home my mother told me that the moment I left my 'good fortune' appeared. But she's not so stupid, she left me a note. Look!"

The note said: "I would like to meet you. If you can, please wait for me at seven beside the Tachkimoni School, holding a newspaper in your hand." "Her handwriting," I cried, "If she's as

93

beautiful as her handwriting she must really be something! I've got to meet her and I'm coming with you!" "Ezra!" he screamed, shaking me by the arm, "don't you dare! Promise me you won't come!"

"I want to meet her!"

"I'll introduce you to her as soon as I can. Swear you won't come!"

"O.K.! Just don't forget to ask her if she's got a sister."

At work next morning he was uneasy and embarrassed. I understood that my "match" had failed, but pressed him to give me the details. He seemed a bit scared and begged me to stop all that nonsense. "It's only a girl from the Mekor Baruch quarter, waiting for an important letter from a relative in Europe. She wanted to ask me to help her find out why the letter was being delayed."

I would have left him alone but for a sneaking fear that he might suspect me of being a party to last night's meeting. I had to carry the game a little further. "You're not telling the truth. You're scared I might take your girl away from you so you won't tell me anything about her. Do you think I've never met any girls before and haven't got anyone to go out with?"

"Cut it out, Ezra, cut it out! Enough of the girl. I don't want to hear any more about her!" he cried with angry finality.

Looking into his eyes everything became clear to me. He would never be a *Lehi* member.

Many years later, after the State of Israel had been established and the underground movements long disbanded, I met this same Benny in the street, and we stood there for some time, talking about the old days and our work in the Post. While we were talking, a girl passed by – Yona Yeffet, erstwhile *Lehi* member Chagit. She said "Hello" and walked on. Some time later we met, and this is her story: "That man you were talking to in the street the other day, do you know him well? Someone had recommended him for the movement and I was sent to enlist him. When I told him what our meeting was all about he became hysterical and started screaming: 'Leave me alone, what have I done to you? What do you want from me?'" He refused to be calmed and went on protesting loudly, so that she was forced to leave him, after warning him to never tell anyone about their "meeting."

When the attempt to enlist another man from the Post failed, I almost gave up all hope of active combat. But the problem solved itself, and one of the new postmen, Me'ir Sar-Shalom, was enlisted on someone else's initiative, thus providing an additional worker in our "censorship."

A Boy sleeps on the Stairs

Hanna announces: "Tomorrow we're putting up proclamations! We meet at four in the morning."

Ever since that first "pasting" operation I had been nursing a plan of getting my family used to my leaving home very early in order to join morning prayers at the synagogue. I would do this every morning, daily, so that no one would pay attention when I had to get up for morning "pasting" service. Regrettably I had not yet put this plan into operation. Either I never woke on time or, if I did, immediately sank back into my sweet dreams, with a firm decision to begin morning prayers on the following day... And now another "pasting" operation was upon me and this time no excuse would do! Again a whole night on the alert, sleeping and waking in turn, leaving home too early...

We met at the appointed place – Ha'im, Hanna, Techiya and myself. Israel failed to show up. Apparently he just didn't wake up in time. We start pasting and this time we work much faster. I spread the paste and Ha'im smoothes out the sheet of *The Ma'as* over the fresh glue. Hanna is keeping watch in front and Techiya is on the lookout behind us. Nevertheless we are sensitive to every sound. The motor of an approaching vehicle causes us to disappear into the nearest entrance, there to wait until it is gone. Our work goes quickly and we complete it with a quiet feeling of confidence. After all, we are "veterans," to a certain extent. Hadn't we done it once before?

95

A new comrade joined our cell, Issakhar, and now there were six of us, six young people, our ages ranging from fifteen to eighteen. Each one precious and loved by his family, excelling in their devotion, willingly accepting all the duties and dangers inherent in the membership of an organization shouldering the brunt of a war of liberation.

Inspired by their love of their people, these six gave up any ideas of a life of ease and tranquility, surrounded as they were by constant danger. The cell was now their family and each meeting served to strengthen the inner ties. There was a certain compensation in this close friendship for the estrangement and oppression suffered by members of the underground. Should one of us be late for a meeting all the rest were united in our fear for him.

Hanna's proposal was that if you couldn't wake up in time or found it difficult to hide your action from the family, you'd better not sleep at home at all. As to parents – "tell them you're staying the night at a friend's home, to do your homework together." ·

Israel took her advice. One night, before a morning's "pasting," he left home and started wandering around the streets. Finally he became so tired that he went into one of the houses to take a nap on the stairs. It was the entrance to the Hevron Yeshiva and, in spite of the late hour, all the students were still studying Torah. Hoping that no one would pay any attention to him, Israel fell asleep, oblivious to the noise of the students. When the lesson came to an end the students, going up to their rooms, saw the sleeping boy. In reply to their questions Israel told them he was tired and would they please leave him alone. The students didn't understand and refused to let him stay, screaming at him to get out. Israel tried to cajole them, asking to be allowed to go downstairs and join the more diligent students. So they argued until one of the boys sensed the true reason for the stranger's insistence on staying in the Yeshiva during the night. Silencing his friends he said: "My name is Refaeli. Come and stay in my room, there's an empty bed." Refaeli asked Israel when he wanted to get up and promised to wake him in time, which he did.

A few days later we had another "pasting." Aryeh and Techiya decided not to sleep at home and wandered around in the streets for hours. Then, too tired to go on, they remembered Israel's story and decided to go to the Yeshiva. Techiya went to look for the ladies' gallery and when she did, called Aryeh up to join her. There they sat quietly, watching the students below at their studies, arguing with each other with great heat and excitement – a sight neither of them had ever seen before. Both were wary of meeting the students, but there was no need, for when the students found them they treated them kindly and were most welcoming. Once more it was Refaeli who introduced himself and offered his room as a permanent base in which our people could hide. From that time on, when we told our parents we were going to sleep at a friend's house we were no longer lying, for Refaeli was indeed a good friend.

It was years before I saw him again. There was the War of Independence and those that came in its wake, and during all that time I never met him or heard word of him. From time to time I would think of him and wonder where he was, and then, while engaged in the writing of this book, I learnt that Refaeli, our "friend indeed," was living in Bat Yam and acting as Principal of a State-Religious High School in Rishon le Zion. I went to see him, and when we met he told me that when the Yeshiva Principal had found out that he was giving us shelter in his room he threatened him with expulsion.

In those days we used to meet in obscure alleys or on street corners, but there was nothing romantic about our meetings, whose purpose was to carry out assignments fraught with danger. Not a day passed but I expected to be arrested, interrogated, tortured and possibly shot. The only means of safeguarding our freedom, and continuing, even intensifying our intransigence was by maintaining absolute secrecy, by assuming a kind of blurred anonymity. It wasn't easy. Day and night we would be devising stratagems for camouflaging our underground activities in order to mislead our friends at work and at school, and hardest task of all – our family. Conspiratorial meetings for their own sake, of the kind without which no espionage novel is complete, were the last thing we wanted. When we met, it was either for a planned assignment, or in order to maintain communication. Sometimes there would be ideological discussions with someone presenting an assessment of the situation, and then we would talk about current affairs.

One day we went with Hanna to meet a member of the higher echelon "in charge" of the underground. The meeting was unique and unforgettable. Late one night we went to the Valley of the Cross, and when Hanna whistled, an answering whistle came from the dark depths of the valley. Not knowing where we were going we climbed up the rocks, thrusting aside the thorny bushes, until we saw the man who had answered our signal. He persisted in turning his face away so that we wouldn't recognize him and then told us to sit around him in a circle. "My name is Yechezkel," he said, and it soon became clear to us that "Yechezkel" was one of the more experienced freedom fighters in the underground.

He opened with a summary of the birth of our movement, dwelling on the history of some of its original protagonists who had been [youths of] our age at the time. There was Yehoshua Cohen of Kfar Saba, whose true identity had been revealed by the British, (among ourselves we didn't know the real names of our heroes, only their brave deeds). Yehoshua was eighteen years old when Ya'ir was assassinated and other members of the underground were hunted down like animals, arrested, tortured and executed one after the other. The group grew gradually smaller until there were no more active members left. The dead rested in the cemeteries, the wounded suffered in the hospitals and the prisoners underwent torture in the interrogation cellars. The few who had managed to avoid being murdered or arrested did not dare to go on hiding, for they knew the enemy was aware of their true identity and they might be shot at any moment, either in the street or at home. Overcome by fear and despair they decided to give themselves up. It seemed as if the underground was doomed, with no one left to raise its flag of insurrection. The solitary few who had managed to stay free despaired of fighting.

The One Who refused to submit

But in one of the villages of the Sharon there was one man who wouldn't give himself up and wouldn't give up the fight. A man? No more than a boy, about eighteen years old who, alone and unaided, decided to continue the struggle of his people against the British empire.

As the enemy knew his real name, they sent some policemen to his parents' home to arrest him and thus celebrate another victory over the menacing underground. But they didn't find him for, taking his gun with him, he had managed to escape to the orchards surrounding the village. For days they hunted him, placing ambushes around his parents' home and in the orchard paths where he was thought to be hiding. They waited obstinately, refusing to let their prey go, for well they knew that as long as there was one freedom fighter at large refusing to lay down his arms and surrender – their victory was not complete.

Yehoshua's picture was published in the papers every day, above an enormous sum of money promised as a prize for anyone who would get him "Dead or alive", for those out for his blood. Not content with that, the CID men got to work on his friends in prison, tempting them with all sorts of queer promises, if only they would help them lay their hands on him. One of these promises was to release them and give them a free hand so they could "close the account" with the Jewish Agency whose people had turned them over to the police. All this on condition that they gave their word of honor to refrain from attacking the British till after the world war.

In the meantime the one-man rebellion was still going on. For many months Yehoshua hid among the dusty fruit trees, unwashed, his clothes filthy. He had let his beard grow wild and his only food was the oranges he picked in the groves. He saw nobody and nobody saw him – nobody, that is, except for his devoted girl friend Nechama, who managed somehow to meet him under cover of darkness in order to encourage him and be encouraged by him. So they would sit together whispering, making all sorts of plans, never realising for a moment what was the actual power of one boy and one devoted girl.

It was only a few months later that "Michael" Itzhak Izernitzky (today Shamir) succeeded in making his getaway from the Mizra detention camp and reassembled those members of the *Lehi* who had disappeared and were in deep hiding. From this nucleus he recreated a fighting movement, a new branch of dynamic power.

It took the British more than two years to catch Yehoshua and arrest him. But by then there were many others to take up the flag of *Lehi*. Michael was already outside, as well as the twenty who had escaped from Latrun, joined by many others ready to devote their lives to the war. The rebellion declared by *Lehi,* which for long had been like an ember glowing in the dark, endangered by every passing breeze, now turned to a raging flame constantly eating away at the enemy.

Yechezkel's enthusiasm grows as he tells us how Dr. Scheib (today Dr. Israel Eldad) was smuggled out of hospital, his whole body covered with wounds. His friends in charge of the rescue operation had made a mockery of the many guards in whose charge he had been. "The struggle will now accelerate," Yechezkel promised us. "The British say Dr. Scheib is heading the 'brainstrust' of the 'Stern Gang', and they know whereof they speak."

Then Yechezekel began singing, "We are soldiers unknown" while the rest of us listened in charmed silence. We were already familiar with Ya'ir's song, having read it in the underground's publication, and knew every word by heart. But never before had we heard the melody so quiet yet charged with feeling, sung under the open sky and its myriad stars. It seemed to us then that the words and the melody had been formed out of our hearts and emotions and had we known how to write poetry – this is what we would have written! Close as we had been to each other before, we felt that in some miraculous fashion our love for each other had deepened, our ties to each other become stronger than ever. It was a good, warm feeling.

Then Yechezkel taught us another song, one never heard by us before, and once more we felt identified with it, as if it expressed our innermost thoughts – a song of our own:

FROM THE PIT OF THE UNDERGROUND

From the pit of the underground, chained, behind bars,
Our song rises up of rebellion,
It sings of our longing for freedom, release,
For the day we emerge all unfettered.

On this day we have sworn to our brothers now gone
Not to slacken the hand, cease the fire;
The sword we have brandished we never will sheathe
Till this land for ourselves we have conquered.

Though homeless we are and hunger for bread,
We'll overcome all the evil around us:
A brother's betrayal by money repaid,
The whip of the jailer, the bullet that kills –
None of these will ever quench the fire.

On this day we have sworn to our brothers now gone:
In this battle now fought for our freedom
We will strike at the enemy, show no remorse,
Till the light over Zion will have risen!

Years passed before we learnt that this song was written by the legendary Yehoshua Cohen, and the Yechezkel who sang it to us was no other than Naphtali Cohen, his brother.

With a quite murmur my friends slowly joined in – all but myself who could never carry a tune and wouldn't have spoilt this for the world.

"Singing is good," remarked Yechezkel. "The songs of the underground are an expression of its soul." Not wishing to distress him I joined in, conscious of his disappointment even though I couldn't see his face in the dark.

There was some release from the highly charged atmosphere when Yechezkel turned to each of us, asking us how old we were. This gave me the opportunity to let him and my friends know that I was no longer a child, though I knew I looked like one. "I'm over eighteen years old," I declared proudly. High time they were aware of this and let me participate in some real action, with actual fire-arms.

But Yechezkel was convinced I was making fun of him... Pulling at his left eyebrow he drawled out in Arabic "*Aleina...*" meaning, "Look me straight in the eye! Do I seem to be someone you can make a fool of?"

We all burst out laughing. With that one word he had erased the halo of mystery and enchantment with which we had surrounded him, and had become one of us.

We carried the impression of this meeting with us for years, so profound was it. Ha'im, Israel and I used the word *Aleina* whenever we could, and it became a sort of password for us. And when we encountered some British policemen on the way – difficult if not utterly impossible to avoid in those days, we would quietly hum the final couplet of "From the Pit of the Underground":

We will strike at the enemy, show no remorse,
Till the light over Zion will have risen!

One A Communist, One in the Hagana, One in the Etzel and One in the Lehi

I have already told you how eager I was to recruit new members for the *Lehi* and how I "failed" with one of my co-workers at the Post Office who, so I had hoped, would release me for combat assignments. Aside from my friends in the underground I met none of my former acquaintances, with one exception – a lad two years my junior with whom I had lived under one roof ever since we were infants. Always playing together, we never quarrelled, and being older I always protected him from bigger boys who had it in for him. Ours was a true friendship, such as prevails sometimes between brothers. And indeed, that boy was my beloved brother Yehoshua. I had known for some time that he sympathized with us and would have liked to join one of the underground movements fighting the enemy. He often spoke about it, but somehow I didn't have the heart to embroil my little brother in such danger and suffering. After all, I had always been his protector – how could I send him on a way from which so many failed to return? I knew that I would have no rest from the moment he entered the underground, that I would always fear for him. And yet... didn't I believe whole-heartedly that every (Jewish) boy should be happy to give his life for his people? Was my brother in any way better than others? Finally I made up my mind to recommend him. My conscience was clear but my heart strangely heavy...

One day there was a knock on our door and Aliza Attia (today Barmatz) came in, asking for Yehoshua. My parents were used to friends coming to my brother and paid no attention to the caller, but I understood at once, for I had met Aliza at the *Brith Hashmona'im* club and so could guess why she was there. That evening Yehoshua was out, but Aliza found him on the following day and they left together to take a long walk.

During the first meeting, Aliza described the general state of our nation, after which she fixed another meeting for the next day. This time she spoke about the need to act against the British and, as it was getting quite late, suggested that they get together again on the morrow. Losing his patience, Yehoshua said, coming straight to the point: "Enough of this! Do you really want to recruit me to the underground or just to talk and talk?"

Aliza gave him a searching look and asked: "Do you have any idea what being an underground member means? Do you understand what being a *Lehi* man means?" To her astonishment he burst out laughing and Aliza racked her brains trying to remember what it was that she had said that was so funny.

"Can you imagine the salad we're going to have at home now? There are six kids there. The two youngest don't understand anything yet, but the four older ones are each going off in a different direction: Avraham, the oldest is a member of the Communist party. David is in the *Hagana**. Ezra, my third brother, is in the *Etzel* (that's what he thought, for some unknown

---

* He didn't know, and neither did I that David was an Etzel man and had been for many years. How could we know? Each of the brothers kept his secrets and those of his underground movement. We never discussed politics at home.

reason), and now I, the fourth brother, am going to be in the *Lehi...*"

But Aliza would not be sidetracked. Over and over again she explained the difficulties of an underground existence: the constant dangers, the hard work, often boring and lacking in any glamor. Fighting wasn't always done with guns – the work was much more pedestrian, even though no less dangerous. Proclamations had to be put up, information collected and people followed at all seasons and in all weather. Sometimes you had to leave your warm bed at night, summer and winter, in hail or snow, in the heat or the khamsin wind. You might be called to spend a whole night in the doorway of someone wanted by the underground, shivering with the cold, just in order to find out when he came home or left it. You followed him for what seemed an interminable time, hoping that finally some worthwhile assignment would fall your way. No one, of course, would ever know about it but it would be a source of satisfaction for you. And again, after many sleepless nights of waiting – the operation you had worked so hard for might be delayed or even cancelled.

Listening to her gloomy descriptions of the life of a freedom fighter, Yehoshua broke in: "What are you trying to do, make me decide not to join *Lehi?*"

"You must know everything before you decide. You have to realize that you will have to give everything you've got for the liberation of Israel, which you yourself might never see in your lifetime, though, hopefully, our sons will. You must realize that this is not something you are doing for yourself but for the sake of your people. Only if you love the People of Israel, the Land of Israel and the God of Israel can you make the necessary sacrifice."

Yehoshua accepted and was recruited to the underground.

From then on I left the house in the dark of night in the company of Yehoshua to join in the "morning service at the synagogue", i.e., putting up proclamations. We would fix on a meeting place after the pasting operation so that we could return home together from the "service." Nothing made me happier than for Yehoshua to finish before me and to find him waiting for me, safe and sound. Whenever it happened that I was the first to arrive, I would wait there, worried and apprehensive, each minute seeming like an hour.

Yehoshua, who was tremendously popular with his friends in the Ohel Moshe quarter, enlisted them all into the underground. Some of the girls were members already, having followed the example of Sima Assoulin and Nitzhia Levi, who had been enlisted earlier on through the *Brith Hashmona'im* movement. Yehoshua also succeeded in locating a place to cache arms. He was apprenticed to the Potash Works and decided that their supply depots were just what we needed. The "boss" presented a bit of a problem, but Yehoshua got around that too. He managed to leave a window in one of the depots slightly open before he left work, returning through it at night with his friend, Uzi "the red," to tear out some of the tiles in the floor and dig a pit, which they filled with milk containers stuffed with ammunition. In this way the *Lehi* had proprietary rights over a depot where no one would ever think of searching – a most timely arrangement. This was a period of frequent searches conducted in the Bukharim and Sanhedria quarters, where we had a number of caches of hidden arms, but it goes without saying that the British never thought of searching the Palestine Potash Co., a company that could never be suspected of aiding and abetting the Stern Gang.

Brith Hashmona'im secedes from the Lehi

In spite of my many commitments in the underground I never stopped visiting the *Brith Hashmona'im* club, long considered the "incubator" for raising freedom fighters. One day I joined the members on a night trek to Mt., Scopus. We stopped for a moment in the pine woods near the German hospital, "Augusta Victoria," and gazed at Jerusalem below us, glittering with lights. The guides recounted the tales of the Romans who had camped on that spot when they lay siege to Jerusalem. Not far from us there was now a British encampment whose purpose was to combat terrorism... Two thousand years after the Roman occupation the

Hebrews were again engaged in a war for freedom. And where was the victorious Roman empire now, and the proud Roman people, where were they today?

A few days after this outing I was asked to call at Moshe Segal's place in Zichron Moshe. He was head of the *Brith Hashmona'im* movement and had invited me along with the other group members. To my amazement he suggested that we should all join the *Hagana*. At first I thought that this was some kind of ploy. They had decided, perhaps, to send all those who had been found unfit for the fighting underground to the *Hagana,* and had invited all the members for the sake of camouflage...

Some of the members did indeed accept the offer. It was interesting to note that I had always considered them unsuitable material for us, and here was the leader himself confirming my opinion! When it was my turn to be asked if I was prepared to join the *Hagana* I replied that my parents had fobidden me to join any clandestine organization, as it was too dangerous. I was very apologetic about it but insisted that I couldn't disobey them.

It was not until we returned to the club that I realized the offer had been no farce but perfectly genuine. Moshe Weiss, one of Segal's assistants, called me aside and told me frankly: "Now that the Rebellion Movement has been formed, *Brith Hashmona'im* decided to join the *Hagana*. You, who joined the *Lehi* as a member of our movement, should leave them now and join the *Hagana* together with the other members."

I was stunned, unable to grasp that anyone aware of what was going on could reach such a decision. I left Weiss and walked out of the club.

What was there to say? What else could we talk about but the need to get rid of the foreign rulers?

Brith Hashmona'im was no longer a source for fresh underground members, but many of our finest fighters had come to us from their club and there will always be a warm corner in my heart for the place where I had first found friendship, faith and a way of life.

The withdrawal of *Brith Hashmona'im* was a heavy blow to me and I deeply regretted the loss of the club which had been almost like a home to me. My only comfort at that difficult time was the friendship of my cell members. Now that *Brith Hashmona'im* had deserted us, our devotion to one another knew no bounds. We literally felt like a band of brothers tied together by a love stronger than death itself. We met as often as possible, even when there was no meeting scheduled, talking and finding comfort in each other.

Ha'im, Israel and I met almost every day. We talked much about the new "Rebellion Movement" and its chances. One subject of speculation was whether all the youth movements in the country would really unite at last and join forces to fight the enemy. Another recurring theme was our desire to be trained in the use of arms, now that we were finally adults and could fight like adults, gun in hand. We derived much satisfaction from the barbed wire fences the British troops had stretched around their buildings and which they made higher every day, even though they were by now twice the height of any man. Where was their famed self-control and coolness in the face of emergency now?

A constant source of bitterness was the indifference of our own people, who watched our struggle from a distance with a complete lack of comprehension. We, on our part, did our best to explain... Night after night our members endangered themselves, broke cover and revealed themselves to the enemy by going out to paste our proclamations in the hope of making the people understand our activity and of rousing their fighting spirit.

"Two thousand years this nation has been dreaming of salvation, and now, when the opportunity is at hand – it sleeps, forcing us to endanger our lives every night in order to speak to it, awaken it from its complaisance. Look at me," argues Ha'im. "They expelled me from school, fired me from my job, and if I ever get another one, they'll fire me from that too. There's always someone coming out of nowhere who knows you, who saw you putting up proclamations in the street in the middle of the night, and he starts making waves. The Principal of the school hears about it, then your employer, and you're out! But what hurts the most is that hundreds of pupils or workers get to know me in the process, pointing at me and taunting me: 'Terrorist!' Not that I really care, but if the enemy gets wind of the story I might have to pay with my life! I'm ready to lay my life down for these people and they don't give a damn for me or my sacrifice!"

"Yesterday," I tell them, "I brought some mail to the Boys' School in Rav Kook St., when one of the kids winked at me and said: 'You've got cheek coming here! Everybody knows you paste the *Lehi* proclamations on the walls at night, so let me tell you: Get away from here! Go on, get out! There's nothing here for the likes of you! One day you'll get a bullet in the belly!'" What a quirk of fate! Years later I encountered that same person in the Disabled Servicemen's Office of the I.D.F. I reminded him of what he had said that day, in his school yard, and told him that although I had been wounded many times over the years, in almost every part of my body, my belly had somehow been untouched. In reply he told me that he had been shot in his stomach by an Arab in 1948...

I'm A Petit Bourgeois?

The underground acquired a new instrument for propaganda – a broadcasting station named "The Voice of the Hebrew Underground," eagerly listened to by masses of people, particularly in the Tel-Aviv area. On the given hour many of the passers–by in the street would crowd around radio sets in shops selling electrical appliances or in small cafés in the poorer districts, where the radio was tuned in to the right wavelength, listening openly to the transmission. When Ge'ulah Cohen, whose inspiring voice electrified everybody, was arrested, we were all deeply grieved.

Much of our time was spent on activities pertaining to "Section 6." We used to tail British or Jewish detective informers in British pay and so on. Spending hours near their homes – which were mostly in the Talbieh quarter or in the German Colony, we would pretend to be kids, innocently engaged in playing "five stones" or some other childish pastime, though sedulously noting down their times of entry and exit.

In between our "pasting" operations and tailing assignments we managed to meet, with or without Hanna, in some wood or field for ideological discussions. We learnt about Garibaldi, the Italian freedom fighter who succeeded in uniting his country; about the courageous struggle of the Irish underground and most of all about *NILI,* the Hebrew Underground that had far preceded the *Lehi,* combatting the then Turkish Government. We were particularly interested in Aharon Aaronson, who lost his life when a small British plane in which he was flying crashed into the English channel. His body was never recovered. This inevitably brought us to the subject of the Polish leader Schikorsy, who had supplied the British army with a number of brigades in return for the promise that Poland would not be handed over to Stalin. He, too, crashed in a British plane. The theme held many interesting aspects for us.

Nili preceded the *Lehi* in that it, too, was hounded by the "Establishment" of the Hebrew community at the time – the *Hashomer* movement. We dwelt long on Sarah Aaronson who was cruelly tortured and decided to put an end to her life in order to prevent herself from giving away the secrets of *Nili.* Her heroism thrilled us deeply, for at that time, during those talks among the trees or in hidden corners of the field, none of us realised that one of us would be fated to suffer similarly in the near future.

Ha'im and Israel had read *Panpilov's Men*, a tale of the defence of Moscow against Hitler, and told us about it, recommending it warmly. I got hold of the book and read it avidly. What impressed me most was the story about the boys from distant Kazakhstan, in central Asia, who lay down before the enemy tanks, stopping them with their bodies until the troops arrived from the far East.

Those were hard days for Russia. Its life's blood was being shed and it exerted pressure on its allies in the West to open a second front in Europe, thus engaging German forces and easing some of the terrible pressure from itself. In our country members of the Communist Party were covering the walls with slogans calling for an immediate opening of a second front, signing themselves P.C.P. (Palestine Communist Party). Ironically enough, one could still make out their older slogans, written two years ago, in the golden period of the Russo-German "friendship" pact, a period when "the workers of all the nations" were united against a war with Hitler, and those nations who nevertheless dared oppose him were referred to as "speculators," "petit bourgeois," and "war-mongers." "Down with the imperialistic war-mongers!" shouted the slogans on the walls, and there they still were, a constant reminder of their crime, preserved in good quality paint. Even though the U.S.S.R. and ourselves had a common enemy, I never felt sympathy for these "communist heroes." Yet my heart went out to those Kazakhstan fighters, heroes of *Panpilov's Men* who gave their lives to stop the Germans from reaching Moscow, before they could go on to their homeland, Kazakhstan. We all identified ourselves wholeheartedly with the conclusions, so wise and simple, of the protagonist: "The law of the soldier is mastery or death;" "If you wish to live – never speak of your readiness to die, only of the need to kill those who desire your death." Like these men of Panpilov we, too, a cell of six boys aged 15 to 18, discussed the need to fight for our people and our future. Like them, we were prepared to lay down our lives in order to achieve the things we believed in; like them, we knew that if you wanted to live you had no choice but to kill the enemy who tried to kill you. It pained us to see our "leaders" unaware of these simple basic concepts and listen to the empty slogans which they fed the people.

Having finished reading the book, I was impatient for our next meeting with my cell friends, particularly Ha'im and Israel, who had also read it. We met in our "number 2" store, in the Zichron Moshe quarter, which served both as an arms' store and a "work room." First we had to pass our guards posted in David Yellin St., and when they signalled that the area was "clean," with no strangers coming and going, we finally entered, going into the cellar two by two. The floor was covered with copies of *The Ma'as* which we were supposed to fold, ready for distribution. This meant two hours of work, plenty of time for discussing all the subjects under the sun including some jokes about His Majesty King George VI, whose portrait hung on the wall, put there for reasons of conspiracy. When we talked of *Panpilov's Men* we

110

decided that it hadn't been those men who had filled the Russians with patriotic slogans and the need to die for the homeland who had actually done any of the fighting against the Nazis. They and their slogans were crushed under the Nazi boot while the common people – those who knew nothing about ruling by means of slogans but simply loved Russia and its people as a man loves his home and family – it was they who, aided by the guns given them by their "capitalist" allies managed to block the enemy and save Moscow.

We wondered about the modern idol worshippers, those millions who blindly believed the slogans issuing from Moscow, who bowed down before the "Red Foursome": Lenin, Stalin, Russia, the 1st of May. There were five pejorative words in their dictionary: capitalist, imperialist, trotskyite, fascist and reactionary, all tagged onto anyone daring to question the sanctity of the Holy Four. And how was it with us, in our camp? At that very moment, when the British socialists had come into power and been unmasked as zealous followers of the keepers of the Empire who went before them, the *Shomer Hatza'ir* was raising heaven and earth in its campaign against the "Rebellion Movement" – the coalition of the Hebrew Freedom Fighters – calling for a complete break with the dissidents. "Go to one of their meetings," cried Ha'im resentfully, "and what will you see there? The zealous politicians from their Kibbuz Merhavia holding forth to the gilded youth of Rehavia. And what do they talk about? Nothing but the dissidents, messengers of the petits bourgeois, minions of imperialism, no less..."

If that was so, then I was a full-fledged bourgeois! I, who had worked for my living from the age of fourteen; who had not known the meaning of "bathroom" until I had peeked into one by chance while delivering a telegram to one of the "labor leaders" in Rehavia! Or was it Israel, my friend, who was the bourgeois – crowded with his family of six into one narrow room with a ramshackle outhouse open to every wind, somewhere far away in a back yard, with no other option available despite rain, the cold or the heat of summer? Or was it Aryeh and Issachar, forced, like me, to leave school at the age of fourteen to help support their

111

families? Were we the "enemy of the proletariat?" We who were endangering our very lives for our people and our homeland – was it us they were castigating as the "agents of imperialism who were stabbing Zionism in the back?"

We were well-aquainted with these anti-imperialistic heroes, having watched them as they sniffed around us, pointing us out to the police, who were out for our blood.

"Pasting" operations became more frequent and *The Deed* at first a monthly, was now a weekly, so that together with other printed matter that had to be put up we would sometimes have to work as often as twice a week. This became particularly difficult with the onset of winter. Walking the streets of Jerusalem in pre-dawn darkness, which could be very pleasant indeed in the summertime, when the air was cool and clear, was a real hardship on the cold winter mornings. Putting your hand in the tin of cold, coagulated glue hurt as if you had scalded it. But morale was high and the proclamations went up... We had done it!

When the weather forecast was "cold in the mountain region" we knew well what it meant. The hand in the tin of glue would contact a frozen jelly, turning red and swollen and later a frightening blue. Unpleasant, but we couldn't stop. Another wall, another proclamation, and so it went. My hand turned blue and felt as if it was on fire, moving with difficulty. I tried changing hands, holding the pot in my right hand and smearing with the left, but the hand holding the tin seemed to have lost all sensation. Yet another wall, another sheet... While we still had proclamations and walls available we had to go on. I tried to turn the whole thing into a joke: "Let me forget my right frozen hand if I forget your walls, O Jerusalem!" Ha'im offered to change places with me, but I refused. After all I'm not such a sadist.

My work in the "Youth Section" – which included the distribution and pasting departments – was a source of deep satisfaction, even though I never ceased demanding to be transferred to the "Brigade" (three or four cells of the Action Department). I was well aware, of course, of the importance and the danger of the work done by the "Youth," and that many of those who were now directing the activities of the underground had themselves begun by pasting proclamations, so important was it to bring our message to the public. The "twenty" who had escaped from Latrun, whose pictures were in the possession of every British policeman, had done their share of this chore. "Moishe David," a member of *Brith Hashmona'im,* who was famous for his part in many daring operations – no details of which were known – he, too, was arrested while pasting up proclamations. Only much later did we learn of his part in the attempt to kill MacMichael, the High Commissioner. Asher Tratner, an *Etzel* man, was shot and wounded in the thigh while engaged in "pasting" in Haifa. He was caught and tortured by the British till he died.

Every Corner in the City is an Ambush

We were not the only ones to appreciate the importance of our work – the enemy did too. After a while they found out that the "Stern Gang" proclamations were usually put up in the hours before dawn, so they prepared ambushes for the distributors – soldiers and policemen at every corner. *Gestapo* cars (small pick-up trucks so called by the citizens as the police who used them were armed with Bren machine guns and wireless equipment) lurked in the alleys, in the shadows of the houses and trees, the machine guns at the ready.

At one of our meetings Hanna announced another "pasting" operation. As she wasn't certain she could join us, I was put in charge of the cell.

The following morning Hanna didn't show up. The other six all appeared and we set out to the appointed area. Two couples were pasting and two keeping watch. Israel and I were together, with me doing the smearing and Israel the pasting. The other couple were Issachar and Ha'im, the former laying on the glue, the latter putting up the sheets. Aryeh walked ahead, keeping watch in front and Techiya was doing the same behind us. Quickly we "did" the Geulah quarter and went to Ahva, thence to the Zichron Moshe quarter. At the Edison Cinema, our next port of call, we covered part of the display window full of pictures from the movie of the week. Anyone interested in the current movie now had the opportunity of reading the details of one of the most thrilling spectacles ever given by the members of the underground in this country – nine British planes were destroyed in the Kfar Sirkin airport, twenty in Kastina, and one in Lod.

As we were hastening through Yeshayahu Peres St., towards Chancellor, a whistle was heard – Aryeh was whistling the Marseillaise. We froze in our tracks and caught a glimpse of a *Gestapo* car in the shadow of one of the houses. Carefully and quietly we turned into a lane leading to the Berman bakery. There were footsteps following behind us. By the sound of them you could tell they were wearing police boots. We hugged the wall and they bypassed us. Then we heard them going down towards the bakery.

We waited. A long time went by but they didn't return. Where had they disappeared to? Were they lying in wait for us or had they given up and gone away? Thirty minutes of silence passed – no sound and not a footstep. And the patrol, was it still on our tail? We hadn't heard it move. What should we do, wait or leave the alley?

I sent Haim and Issachar to reconnoitre the area and see if the Police had left without our hearing them. If that was the case our friends would give the "all clear" by whistling *Elijah the Prophet*. If they didn't whistle we would understand that we should go on hiding. They left and we stood waiting. Time passed and we became increasingly tense. No sign, no whistle. It would soon be daylight, people would come out into the street and notice us. We could certainly not go on pasting... "Enough!" I told my companions. "We're going!"

The moment we were out of the alley we saw two policemen, one British and one Arab, walking towards us. We decided to walk casually to the corner and then to start running in the direction of Kovach's Photography at the intersection of Even-Yehoshua, Chancellor, Ge'ulah, and Mea Shearim Streets. The policemen were approaching us rapidly, only a few meters separated us from them by the time we reached the corner. We heard them crying "Halt!" and we began running like mad. They fired on us and the Bren gun in the pick-up joined in the shooting. To make running easier we threw the glue pots and the remaining proclamations behind us. Bullets were whistling over our heads and we separated, each running in a different direction. I found myself hiding in one of the court yards of the Geulah quarter.

Now that I had stopped running I began to think over what had occurred. How did it happen that I had endangered my friends and myself by telling them to go out when I hadn't heard the *Gestapo* leaving? Why did we leave our hiding place with the glue pots and proclamations in our hands even though Ha'im hadn't given us the "all clear?" How could I have been so impatient as to find myself in a situation where, instead of Hai'm's whistle, we were treated to the whistling of bullets? I tried to think of excuses for myself – hadn't I always wanted to prove that danger meant nothing to me and wasn't it of the utmost importance that the public should read the proclamations? True, but... such sincere aspirations were not enough, nor should I have been led, because of them, into such carelessness, ignoring the precautions obligatory for any underground man. Courage doesn't justify carelessness, which in its turn must not be mistaken for cowardice. Just as there is a need for courage and self-sacrifice in war so is there a need for carefulness in order to ensure success. I had managed to escape but what about the others, where were they now, had they saved themselves? The British had shot to kill – had they succeeded? The thought of Asher Tratner, who had been killed in Haifa while pasting proclamations, came to my mind, reminding me of what the British had done to him before he died. And what of Israel, who had run with me, did he get away? Where had Ha'im and Issachar, who had gone before us, disappeared? And the "guards," Aryeh and Techiya, what of them? Had they all managed to escape unhurt? And there was my brother Yehoshua, probably waiting for me for a long time now. Did he hear the shooting and was worried about me?

I had often regretted that Yehoshua and I didn't belong to the same cell so that we wouldn't always have to be waiting for each other under unspeakable tension. But now, I thought, it was perhaps for the better that we hadn't been together. He might have been hit in the shooting... And now, was he all right? How was it with all the other boys who had gone "pasting" in the different quarters of the town? Who knows, the shooting incident I had been involved in might have alerted the British and caused other cells to be caught?

I decided to get out of there and left the yard as carefully as I could. There was no sign of police or detectives, so I began walking towards the place we had arranged to meet.

Yehoshua was there, waiting, and, as I hurriedly went up to him I saw the joy and relief in his face. "You've no idea how worried I've been. We heard some shooting while we were pasting, and you were so late. It's been hell... I'm so glad to see you free and unhurt!" On our way home I told him everything. That evening we were supposed to have a cell meeting, and till then I would have no idea what had happened to my friends...

It was getting late, and I left to go to work at the Post Office. On my way there I went into the Nachlat Shiva quarter, where Israel lived, in the Yoel Salomon alley. I prayed I would see him there, outside his house, but there was no sign of him. It was all I could do, not to go in and find out if he had come out unscathed from the incident. But this was one thing I was not to do. We'd had enough trouble due to carelessness. He might have been arrested and the police could be waiting inside, searching and keeping an eye open for more fools to fall into their net. Could he have been hurt? In that case there was the danger that they had discovered his identity and were waiting inside. No, no going in. I must wait till evening. It was a cursed day, damnably long. If only I could have gone to bed and slept through the twelve hours separating me from the time of meeting... But that, too, was forbidden and I had to go to work as usual, pretending that nothing had happened.

I could sense every passing second, time seemed to crawl along interminably and the strain was almost too great to bear. Yet somehow, the morning passed, then noon, and finally it was evening. I left for the meeting, my heart beating faster and faster.

116

Who would be there tonight besides myself? What if only Hanna arrived? It was too painful to picture her anguish for failing to be there with us. At Zefania St., I glanced nervously at my watch. Ten to seven! Ten minutes to go. I was physically unable to wander around aimlessly, the compulsion to know was stronger than myself. Approaching the spot I couldn't contain my emotions: all, all were there, not a single one missing!

No words can describe the joy of that meeting. We looked at each other, caressed each other with our eyes, which shone with our warm, deep love and affection. Then came the stories: how they ran, who ran where, how they had found cover. Aryeh told us that some people, seeing him running, had opened their door and let him in, hiding him till the police had gone away. Ha'im had a similar story. He was even treated to a cup of coffee and breakfast with his saviours. Issachar, less fortunate, was stopped by the police "Where are you going?" they asked. "To work," he replied. "To work? So early? At four thirty in the morning?" It was highly suspicious and he was taken to police headquarters at the Russian Compound, where he was questioned by a trained interrogator. "Where do you work?"

"At *The Palestine Post*." (*The Jerusalem Post* was so named during the British Mandate.) This was no lie, as Issachar was really apprenticed there, and this was verified immediately by a phone call. The interrogator's mistake was in failing to ask at what hour he was supposed to arrive on the job... The boy was sent home forthwith, and they even neglected to take his name and address. Issachar couldn't believe his good fortune. They had even failed to see his hands, all covered as they were with glue. The next to arrive was Hanna who had been lucky enough to have heard nothing of the night's events and only now, at the meeting, did we tell her the whole story.

The story of the shooting and the incredible events experienced by our cell spread like wildfire through the other cells, and, in the way of rumors, was embellished with all sorts of interesting details. Ya'acov, for example, one of our boys in the Ohel Moshe quarter, heard that I had thrown the pot of glue behind me in my flight. But the story as he told it later was that I had thrown it in the face of the policeman who was chasing me. Picturing the policeman with his face all plastered with glue, he roared with laughter. In fact, he liked the idea so much that he decided he would do exactly the same if he ever had the opportunity. Strangely enough, he did. During a pasting operation a British policeman confronted him suddenly. He threw the tin straight into his face and made off. "I pasted him with some white darkness between the eyes," he recounted, smiling.

Gradually I had come to know my cell members very well indeed. In our common work together more and more details would emerge, and this in spite of the conspiratorial nature of our work. Working as I did in the Post Office, I learnt the addresses of Israel and Issachar, and those of the others were revealed one by one, whether by means of an urgent message or other circumstances. I remember one time, when we were sitting in No. 2 Depot, we needed a certain tool and Ha'im ran out and brought it, all in the space of a few minutes. We concluded, therefore, that he lived nearby. Another time, while on my way to that same Depot, I saw him coming out of a nearby house in David Yellin St. Aryeh, for instance, who also lived near this Depot, had a problem – his younger brother was always following him around, perhaps because they were orphans and the child regarded him as a sort of father figure. It was quite an effort for Aryeh to make the lad leave him alone and go back home. The boy would regard him with worshipful eyes, one of them half-closed with some disorder, and in them would be reflected his comprehension of his brother's rejection and of the mysterious affairs which led him to it. The boy, just like Aryeh, his elder brother, had a charming personality. He was very handsome, no less so for his eye defect. No, this lovely child must not be endangered in our company. He had to return home.

Some generations ago the Bardans, Aryeh's family, had lived in Italy. Some of them had made their way to the Caucasian Mountains where their name was changed to Burdanov. The family did well and made a lot of money, and when Aryeh's grandfather began longing for Zion he took his family there, coming to Jerusalem with an enormous fortune. This was at the end of the last century. His love of the land then took him to Petah-Tikva where he purchased a large farm, for which he bought seventy cows, tending them for their milk and selling it. Unluckily the cows all proved to be diseased and died one after the other, so he bought an orchard and also planted tobacco. But this venture, too, was unlucky. The price of tobacco fell steeply and there were no buyers for the citrus fruit either. Aryeh's rich grandfather lost almost everything he had, and took his family to Jerusalem, renting an apartment in the Musrara quarter and living off the remnants of his fortune. Then, when the 1936 "disturbances" broke out, Aryeh's father was killed by Arab marauders. The six-year-old boy and his baby brother, Yermi, were orphaned. Once more the family had to leave their home and settled down with their mother in the Zichron Moshe quarter. Aryeh, having completed his primary school education, became an apprentice clerk in the State Department of the Jewish Agency. Fortunately he could both help his mother and continue his studies at the same time at evening school. His joy knew no bounds when he brought home his first salary, laid it all on the table and cried out: "Mother, look what I've brought you!"

When he read about the trial in Cairo of the two Eliyahu's, Khakim and Beit-Tzuri, he was terribly upset. His admiration for the men in the *Lehi* grew from day to day, and when he heard the speeches of Mattityahu Shmulevitz and others who were condemned by British courts, he felt a surge of pride at their courage and became an indefatigable reader of the *Lehi's* proclamations and leaflets. He was reminded of Shlomo ben Yoseph, who had been executed when Aryeh was still a child. Shlomo ben Yoseph's last request before mounting the gallows was for some shaving equipment. The papers said that he fasted all during his last day on earth, as he had heard of the shameful incontinence of the body when a man was killed by hanging and towards the end his sole concern was the need to appear dignified and in full control – a true Hebrew Freedom Fighter, not an object of pity. Aryeh's heroes were Trumpeldor and Jabotinsky, Protector of Jerusalem. These figures excited his imagination and filled him with pride. For him they were as great as our historical

119

heroes. His one desire was to be a link in the chain of heroism forged by our people throughout their history.

From an enthusiastic spectator of the dramatic events taking place at the time, Aryeh was projected into active participation by means of nothing less than a kick administered to him by a British police officer, and this is how it happened. One day, as he was standing before the display window of the Edison cinema, a group of drunken English police went by and in their hilarity, hit out at anyone they came across. Aryeh was awarded a painful kick in his backside and though the pain passed quickly, the sense of insult did not.

He now felt that being a mere sympathizer of the underground was not enough – he must assist it actively and become a part of it. *Etzel* or *Lehi* were all the same to him, the thing was to become a member of either, whichever one he managed to get into contact with first. So began his quest for a contact. He remembered seeing someone he knew once, putting up proclamations in the street, and got in touch with him, but this person denied having any connection with the underground or its proclamations. Disappointed and depressed, Aryeh couldn't understand why he was being rejected. Weren't the underground movements forever calling for volunteers? What was wrong with him? He didn't know that the man he had approached who had rejected him summarily had given his "man in charge" a recommendation to send someone to Aryeh to assess his suitability. It was not long before Aryeh became one of our cell members.

After the establishment of the State of Israel I met Yermi*, Aryeh's younger brother, uniformed and wearing the red beret of the paratroopers, standing in front of the Edison cinema and looking at the pictures on display. It was the exact spot from which a judicious kick had projected Aryeh into the *Lehi* and where he had been bodily searched. The girls passing by eyed Yermi's beret with affection, and I couldn't help comparing the difference in the attitude displayed then and today... The uniform and the cap were

---

*   Yermi Burdanov, born 1933, outstanding officer in the paratroopers' saboteurs.

identical in color, but what a difference! Gone were the hatred and aversion with which the *Kalaniyot* had always been regarded, to be replaced by the affection and love of all who saw the handsome parachutist.

Shortly after this chance meeting with Aryeh's younger brother, the whole country resounded with tales of his heroism in the IDF's 101st Unit - Yermi Burdanov, whose exploits were whispered around during his lifetime and became part of our national legacy after he fell in the retalliatory action in Kalkiliya.

A Tale of a Passport

One day I was so absorbed in my reading that I was late for our cell meeting – an unheard of occurrence. My friends all feared for me and when I arrived they pressed me on all sides. Hanna asked if I had been followed or if there had been searches along the way. With their eyes turned entreatingly upon me I said: "No one tailed me and no one searched me. I simply forgot myself in the company of other fighters."

"Where were you?" demanded Hanna. "Don't talk in riddles!"

Avraham, my brother, had brought home a new book, a thrilling story about the ancient Maccabee rebellion. I was so absorbed in reading it that, for the first time since I joined the *Lehi,* not only was I not looking forward to my cell meeting, I forgot about it completely. Even now, with my friends, I was waiting impatiently for the meeting to end so that I could return to my reading as soon as possible. But Hanna did not let me go. "Stay here, Datan," she said. And, when the others were gone, went on to explain: "The underground is in urgent need of a passport, so try to get one."

"Get a passport? How?"

At first the assignment seemed impossible. True, the Immigration Department sent its passports to the applicants by post, but it was by registered post, every postman receiving a written list with the number of the articles for special delivery, which had to be signed for by the recipient. The supervisor of these special deliveries would personally hand the postman a package with the list attached. If, for some reason, the recipient could not be found, the package would be returned to the supervisor who would again sign for it.

"Just find a way. I'm depending on you." said Hanna. "We need the passport badly."

I had no idea how it could be done, but I promised Hanna to try. Finally I thought of a loophole in the delivery procedure which I might put to use. The list which had to be signed by the receiver of the envelope contained nothing but the number of the package. It was the postman who had to fill in the name during the delivery itself. My idea was that when the opportunity arose to deliver a passport I would put down the name of some other person instead of the proper recipient and, if I could find someone who was always getting registered mail, I could forge his signature. In this way the supervisor would never find out that one letter was missing, and when the complaint arrived, as was inevitable, there would be no way of discovering how it had gone astray.

The following day I was given some registered mail, including a few passports. Unthinkingly, from force of habit, I put down all the letters given in the list – the passports as well. Only after I had obtained the supervisor's signature did I think of my plan, by which time it was too late. Hanna was so sorry to hear of this opportunity I had lost that I realized just how important and urgent the matter was. In spite of this, I made the same mistake the next day too, and only after I had copied all the addresses into the form did I remember that I should have omitted that of the passport owner. Angry at my own absent-mindedness I did something quite irresponsible, crossing out the address of the recipient and replacing it with a different one. Nothing could go wrong, I thought. How often had I been given a package of mail belonging to another district which I would transfer to another postman and cross off my list?

The supervisor counted the registered envelopes, which came to eighteen. I confirmed the number and signed for the lot. Within an hour the passport was in the hands of the underground.

122

Hanna was glad and I also had reason to be. I knew that a *Lehi* branch had just been opened in England and hoped that the new passport owner would make good use of it inside Britain.

Several weeks passed and I began to believe that I had succeeded in stealing the passport without raising any suspicion, when I was called to the Supervisor. "Several weeks ago a passport was sent to a Mr. X by post, but has never arrived, for some reason. Do you know anything about it?"

"If I don't remember what I had for dinner that day how can I be expected to remember whether I did or didn't deliver a letter to someone who gets letters from me every day?" I answered, pretending innocence. "But why should I remember when we can inspect the lists?"

He agreed, but it appeared that the lists had already undergone inspection – with no results. The disappearance of the passport was still a riddle. No one seemed to suspect that the passport could have been stolen when the thief could just as well have purloined packages containing valuables.

That evening a certain supervisor, one Elkhativ, had another look at the lists concerned. He noticed that a name had been erased and replaced with another. The erasure had been thorough so he couldn't make out the name, but, his curiosity aroused, he applied a magnifying glass to the spot and found that the registered number of the lost package had originally been there, to be replaced by a different one. Again I was called in to his office where he asked me to make an effort to remember who had taken the missing item from me. This was of the utmost importance as the poor passport owner had been forced to put off his trip, and who knew when he could get a new one. "Couldn't I remember what had happened, whom I had given it to? A passport couldn't just disappear like that, as if the earth had swallowed it."

From his tone of voice I inferred that it hadn't occurred to him that the passport had been stolen. But this did not relieve me of the neccessity to explain how it had happened that a registered package entrusted to me – as was proved by the registration list – had completely disappeared.

I had an inspiration! The passport owner had a shop in Jaffa

Road, a street outside the limits of my area. From time to time I would pass his mail to other postmen who worked in Jaffa Road for delivery at his place of work. "This is what I probably did at the time, so that he would be able to sign for it." I told Elkhativ, who began to look embarrassed.

Next day, after working hours, Elkhativ sat down to examine all the lists pertaining to Jaffa Rd., at that time, without finding a thing. He called the postman, Sarour, who delivered the mail there, and asked him if he had not received a registered letter to deliver at X's shop. "I think I did," answered Sarour.

This reply confused the mail supervisors even more. The Post Office Director had no choice but to write to X, explaining that the passport had gone inexplicably astray and suggesting that he apply once more to the emigration authorities. When the passport owner did as suggested, the emigration authorities informed the C.I.D., (Criminal Investigation Department), sending a copy of their letter to the Postal Authority.

Hearing of this development I began to feel like a trapped animal. True, no one at the Post Office had the slightest suspicion of me or why I should be interested in passports. But the C.I.D., was another story altogether. They would know perfectly well how useful a passport could be to the terrorists. As soon as I could, I hurried to tell Hanna about these disquietening developments, asking her to arrange for me to disappear in the underground before the detectives came to arrest me at home.

"It will take a few days until the C.I.D., realizes that the passport is in some way connected with the underground." said Hanna. "In the meantime go on working and I'll try and arrange a hiding place for you."

I spent the next few days expecting a knock on the door, accompanied by the cry "Police!" But a whole fortnight went by and everybody seemed to have forgotten about the passport. Tense and nervous, I decided to ask my supervisors if they had found the passport at last. When they said they hadn't I asked innocently: "And the C.I.D., – couldn't they solve the mystery?"

The Emigration Department had actually asked the C.I.D., to investigate the loss but the latter advised them to issue another passport instead of bothering them, while they were so busy catching and interrogating terrorists... I now began to understand how and why I had gotten away with it.

★

One Saturday morning, as I was on my way home from synagogue there was a tremendous explosion, followed immediately, as usual, by the moan of the sirens and the sound of loud speakers declaring curfew. According to the radio the explosion had occurred in an empty ruin in the Bukhara quarter. Some British policemen were killed and others wounded.

Some time before the explosion, the police had received an anonymous letter, whose writer explained that he dared not identify himself for fear of the Stern Gang. The letter, written in bad English, reported that the ruin "close to the Spitzer school" actually housed the High Command of the *Lehi.* The whole thing was nothing but a scheme of the *Lehi* to draw some British detectives to the spot. A constant watch was kept over the ruin in case it was visited by children playing there who might find the "toys" hidden inside. As the British failed to nibble at the bait and did not show up for several days, it was decided to dismantle the booby-trap and forget the whole thing, when suddenly they arrived – the most infamous investigators of the C.I.D.'s "Jewish Department," hunting for prey treading warily with guns in hand, straight into the trap. One of them trod on the activating mechanism triggering the bomb. The ensuing explosion killed two of the best and most experienced officers in charge of the campaign against terrorism.

★

Early one Saturday morning, as I lay in bed, I heard some water dripping from the container on the roof. Water was expensive in Jerusalem, every drop was precious, not to be wasted, so I got up, left the house, walked around to the back, climbed up to the roof and closed the main tap. Then, just as I was jumping down again: "Halt!" A group of British soldiers appeared out of nowhere, their Sten guns aimed at me, safety catch off. A quick glance at my watch told me that I had broken curfew. It was only ten to six, whereas the curfew was officially lifted at six.

I was pushed into an army truck and driven to one of the military installations in Talbiyeh, where I found myself with about thirty others who had committed similar crimes. Some had gone out to call a friend or relative to the morning service, one had been out looking for a doctor for a sick person in the family, and there were those who had gone to the outhouse in their back yard, only to be arrested and taken away.

I was kept in "detention" for three hours. One by one we were called and questioned as to why we had broken the curfew. Our names were taken and we were warned never to repeat our misdemeanor, after which we were sent home.

Hurrying home to calm down the family I heard familiar voices congratulating me with "Blessed be He who frees the imprisoned." My cell members had come looking for me, only to be told that I had been arrested for breaking curfew "Come on," they urged me impatiently, "There's work to do, some booklets of the movement have to be distributed immediately."

On the way, they told me that one of our caches was thought to be under Hagana surveillance so we had to clear out all the printed booklets stored there and see that they were distributed that very day.

As we stood waiting for the material near the Orion cinema I saw Israel, our neighbour Esther's son.

"What are you doing here, Zuri?" he asked. "I heard you were arrested for breaking curfew?"

"True," I answered. "I was, but they let me go."

"Aren't you going home?"

"I've already been there." I lied, hoping to get rid of him.

The distribution of this particular booklet took a few hours, after which I went home, the work concluded. Mother didn't know whether to be happy to see me or angry. "Is it true that Israel saw you near the Orion cinema?" she asked.

"What?" I pretended surprise. "Would I go walking around in the streets, letting you worry for nothing?"

Mother, who had always disliked Israel, for reasons of her own, now made him the object of her anger instead of me.

A Punch in the Belly and a Kick in the Arse

Aryeh's in trouble. His boss in the Jewish Agency, Ze'ev Sherf (later to be a Minister in the Israeli cabinet) called him in and asked if it was true that he was a member of the *Etzel*. Aryeh denied this vigorously, and he wasn't lying. He really had no contact with the *Etzel*. A few days later he was called in again and informed that they had proof of his connections with the dissidents. He was fired. So, no job. But he could go on with his studies at the night school.

One evening, soon after his dismissal, the school was surrounded by police. They asked for the list of pupils' names, but were interested in only two – Aryeh and another lad. The two were taken to the C.I.D. building and interrogated for many hours, after which they were released.

Week after week Aryeh hung around, unable to find a job, until finally he was given one in the Postal workshop. It was there that he had a painful experience. Just after an explosion at the railway station, all the Jewish workers were given a thorough going over, first being made to stand with their hands raised high. "What've you got in your satchel?" Aryeh was asked, and, wanting to show them the sandwich prepared by his mother, lowered his hands. The frightened policeman jumped backwards, but, realizing that Aryeh wasn't about to hurt him, thrust the butt of his gun into the boy's belly.

"I've been hurt twice by the British," Aryeh told us. "The first time was a kick in the arse. It didn't hurt but I felt so humiliated that I joined the underground. The second time, the butt in the belly was very painful, but it made me feel good to see how scared the man who hit me was..."

Aryeh didn't keep his job for long. He worked under the most difficult conditions and was badly treated to boot. The boy who was so eager to help his mother was once more unemployed.

127

An added affliction was the continual harassment by the police, who had probably been told why the boy had been fired from the Jewish Agency. Twice or three times a week, very late at night, the police would be knocking on his door to take him in for questioning. While they were standing there, pounding with their fists on the door, Aryeh would sneak out the back door to hide with some friendly neighbours until they had gone away. Finally it was decided to send him out of town, to the *Shomer Hatza'ir* Kibbutz in the Emek – Sha'ar Ha'amakim. Although Aryeh did not break his contact with the underground, we were now only five in the cell.

What will I tell my Parents when They ask: "Where is Your Brother?"

Very late one night Yehoshua surprised me with the announcement that there was a pasting operation scheduled for early next morning. I was certain he was mistaken, for Hanna would never neglect to tell us beforehand. Yehoshua insisted that he had to get up early and I began to look for reasons why I had not been called. Had someone decided that our cell was due for a holiday? Did they perhaps wish to surprise us with a fresh copy on the walls, put there by hands other than ours? This seemed most unlikely. It was impossible to believe that others would be sent to do the pasting and we would be allowed to go on sleeping...

As it was too late to contact one of my cell members, I decided to go out the next morning with Yehoshua. If I had been left out by mistake I would be there, and even if I had not been forgotten, it was better that I leave with Yehoshua, who was supposed to be going to morning service...

So we left together, as usual. Yehoshua went to his meeting place and we made an appointment to meet within half an hour at our usual rendevouz.

What a wonderful feeling it was, strolling carefree through the streets, the walls of which were resplendant with our latest poster of *The Deed.* I began speculating why we had not been called to take part in its pasting. Was our cell about to be transferred to a new department? If so, I would have liked it to be the "Division" and not Section 6, the "Intelligence" of the *Lehi.*

Arriving at our place of rendevouz I stood and waited for Yehoshua, my thoughts full of our possible transfer to the "Division." I could already see myself running, grenade in hand, in the direction of *Bevingrad* (the name we gave to the enclosed security area fortified by the British in and around the Russian Compound), shooting whole volleys of bullets at the heads of the C.I.D. But where was Yehoshua? It was getting late and I began to worry. My fear increased with every passing moment and I could feel the irregular beating of my heart. A whole hour had gone by since we were supposed to meet and there was no sign of him. It was an open secret that there had been arrests at almost every pasting operation lately. The number of "journalists" (the name given by the veteran prisoners to the boys arrested for pasting) was steadily increasing at the Latrun Detention Camp.

Like one bereaved and overcome with guilt I decided to return home. How would I go in without my brother? How to face my parents? What will I tell them when they ask me: "Where is your brother?"

*

When Yehoshua returned, he recounted what had happened. Only two members of his cell showed up at the meeting, Ya'el and he. Ya'el was worried as they were supposed to paste in the "Triangle" – a block made up of three streets. Jaffa Rd., from Zion Square to "Ma'ayan Stub" Stores, a part of King George St., and a part of Ben-Yehuda. These three streets comprise the business center of the new city.

Proclamation pasting had become an extremely dangerous assignment, the whole country being full of ambushes cunningly placed by soldiers and policemen to catch the boys and girls. Jerusalem, the heart of British rule, was the most dangerous place in the whole country and the Triangle forming its center was the most critical area. But it was also the most important, for every

Jerusalemite would go there almost daily – either to work, for shopping, or for recreation in the evenings. Ya'el asked Yehoshua if they could do it by themselves, just the two of them. "What's the problem? I'll smear the glue and you paste the sheets!"

So they set about pasting *The Ma'as.* When they reached Ben-Yehuda St., they saw a delivery boy distributing *The Palestine Post.* Between one cry and another he managed to get across a warning to the two: *"Palestine Post! Palestine Post!* Gentiles higher up! *Palestine Post!"* Yehoshua, who was vigorously working, did not catch the hint, but Ya'el understood: "Gentiles, let's get out of here!" and started to run. Jushua made for one of the alleys but found himself in front of a *Gestapo,* so he turned around and entered another alley only to be confronted by a policeman holding a gun. He was caught and taken to a police patrol for questioning. Pointing to his velvet prayer bag he told them innocently that he had been on the way to synagogue for morning prayers when he met a girl who offered him five shillings if he helped her put up some cinema bill boards. Luckily he had five shillings on him which he could show to the interrogator. "She told me to smear the walls and go on before her, while she stuck the sheets on behind me. Suddenly she began to run. I didn't know why she was running but I got scared and began to run too. Then I met a policeman who told me to stop, so I did."

His pockets were searched and various bits of paper taken out, among them a note from the underground. It was a reply to his request to be transferred to the "Division" in order to become a combat fighter. It said that every activity in the underground was important and in time he, too, would be admitted to the "Division." but he must be patient. The note ended with the words: "Read and destroy!" Yehoshua had been in no hurry to destroy it, for he wanted to read it again at his leisure, when he might find some hint that the time was not too far off before his request was granted.

"What does it say here?" asked the interrogator, pointing to a salary sheet lying among the papers. Yehoshua explained that he was employed at the Potassium Co., and that these were the details of his salary. The man called up the company and they

130

confirmed that they did indeed employ a boy of that name. He was now holding the incriminating note in his hand but strangely enough the interrogator evinced no interest in it. Returning all the papers to Yehoshua he told him that he could go. Yehoshua went to the door, not believing that he would actually be able to go through it to freedom. The spirits of his ancestors must have been protecting him, and the prayer shawl and *tefillin* made a favorable impression...

But less than two weeks later the police broke into the house, made a thorough search and took Yehoshua to the police station where they informed him that he was under arrest for distributing illegal material.

By some strange coincidence two of my brothers were brought to trial on the same day, both on a similar charge: Avraham Yakhin was tried for distributing proclamations of the communist party. This party was legal, but they had no license for putting up proclamations. He and his friend, Wolfgang Ehrlich, a well-known communist, were let off with a token fine. An hour later Yehoshua Yakhin appeared on the charge of pasting *Lehi* proclamations. The Judge asked if the two were related and when he heard that they were brothers he quipped: "The one goes with the Stern gang and the other with the Wolf gang..."

The sentence was one month in prison. He was sent to the central jail in the Russian Compound. At the end of this period his whole family stood waiting for him outside, ready to greet him with the blessing: "Blessed is He who frees prisoners." He asked why they didn't let him join his family and go home, but was told to wait. It was not long before an armoured car drove into the prison yard and took him to the Latrun Detention Camp.

THE ISRAEL FREEDOM FIGHTERS (LEHI)
AN ANNOUNCEMENT

Since the arrival of the immigrant ship "Exodus, 1947" and the banishment of its immigrants, the Israel Freedom Fighters have begun a systematic campaign against the enemy forces, its vehicles and installations. From Friday, July 18, 1947, the following attacks have been carried out:

1. On Friday, July 18, at 8.00 hrs., two vehicles of the British army were attacked in Jaffa Rd., in Jerusalem. Automatic weapons and grenades were used. The British were conducting searches and identification parades at the time. Finding themselves under fire, the British threw down their arms, ran into the nearby alleys and lay flat on the ground. A few minutes later reinforcements of soldiers arrived and opened fire indiscriminately. The enemy suffered casualities.

2. On the same day, at 20.30 hrs., an enemy sentry post at the Jerusalem "Security Area" in Aza St., was attacked by grenades. Three enemy guards were wounded.

3. On that same day, at 19.45 hrs., a police armoured car was attacked by incendiary bombs in Ben-Yehuda St., Jerusalem. The men inside the car jumped out and escaped. The car was completely demolished.

4. On Saturday night, the 19th of July, at 8.00 hrs., a military vehicle was attacked in the Jerusalem Sanhedria quarter. The vehicle was destroyed and three British soldiers badly wounded.

5. At the time of the above operation a group of Freedom Fighters was confronted by a police patrol and ordered to stop and be searched. An incendiary bomb was thrown at them and the group retreated.

6. Simultaneously with the above, incendiary bombs were thrown at a police car in Agrippas St., Jerusalem. The fire was extinguished.

7. At the same time in Haifa, in Hehalutz St., some plainclothes policemen were attacked. Two were fatally wounded.

8. On Sunday morning, July 20, all the main railways of the country were mined. At 8.45 hrs., a goods train on the Jaffa-Lod line was mined – the engine and the lines damaged. At 8.00 hrs., a mine blew up under a goods train in the vicinity of Haifa and, at 12 hrs., the same thing happened on the Haifa-Lod line. Three other mines on the Lod–Jerusalem, Lod-Kantara and the Haifa-Zemach line were found and dismantled by the enemy.

9. On Sunday afternoon, a military vehicle was mined in the Ra'anana

area and was completely demolished. One soldier was killed, three were wounded.

10. On Monday, at 9.30 hrs., a military vehicle was attacked on the Tel-Aviv –Haifa Rd. The vehicle was damaged.

11. On the same day a police sentry post in Mahane Yehuda in Jerusalem was attacked.

12. On the same day, at 17.30 hrs., a mine was activated under a police car in Hehalutz St., in Haifa. Two British policemen were badly wounded.

13. On Tuesday, July 22, at 8.00 hrs., incendiary bombs were thrown at an armoured car in the Bukharim quarter of Jerusalem. The damage was slight.

14. On the same day, at 15.00 hrs., grenades were thrown into a military car and at a sentry post near the Syrian Orphanage in Jerusalem. The grenades exploded inside the vehicle and there were casualties.

15. On the same day, at 17.00 hrs., automatic fire was opened on an R.A.F. vehicle in Keren Kayemet St., in Jerusalem. The enemy suffered casualties.

16. That evening incendiary bombs were thrown at vehicles in three places in Jerusalem: in Zion Square and Agrippas St., an armoured car was destroyed by fire.

17. Simultaneously with the above, the Mahane Yehuda Police station was attacked. The enemy responded with indiscriminate fire for about two hours.

18. On Wednesday, July 23, at about 9.00 hrs., two military vehicles were attacked in the vicinity of Rishon-le-Zion and completely destroyed. One officer and one private were seriously wounded; five privates slightly wounded.

19. The same day, at 14.00 hrs., a commanding officer's patrol car was attacked on the Haifa–Tel-Aviv road in the Shomron region. A jeep was destroyed and one soldier wounded.

20. Later that day, mines were activated in various places of military concentrations, sent there to enforce the curfew in Haifa.

21. On Thursday morning, July 24, a railway bridge on the main route of Haifa-Kantara was mined and blown up in the area of Benyamina. All trains between Haifa and Jaffa were stopped as a result.

22. On Thursday, noon, enemy check posts in the Goldsmidt Building in Jerusalem were fired at.

ISRAEL FREEDOM FIGHTERS
(LEHI)

From the Underground – July, 1947

PART II

MY COMRADES, SONS OF GLORY

In the "Division"

Good news! It was decided that our cell members be promoted and the cell itself disbanded. Issachar and I were transferred to the operations department; Ha'im was made responsible for a new "youth cell" and Israel went to Section 6.

I was now under the charge of Tanchum and introduced for the first time to the framework of an established cell. From time to time I met members of other cells and was allowed to take part in various operations. I also learnt that I would shortly be called to take a course in the use of firearms. Till then all I had done was go on "tailing assignments." Now more attention was being paid to theoretical training, involving extensive reading and many lectures.

There was one theoretical discussion I shall never forget: a certain person, not introduced by name (not even by his underground alias) met us in a shack in the Kiryat Shmuel quarter, not far from Aza St. I have forgotten exactly what he said at the time, but the impression of his frail and gentle personality, so different from the standard "fighter" image we had expected, is still with me. His real identity was revealed to us only after his death: Zion Abugov, victim of a malignant disease. What a bizarre way for an underground man to go. Mr. Schwedron, the shack owner who was taking a great risk in putting it at our disposal, was an old acquaintance of mine, for his kiosk in Chancellor St. had become the collection center of our mail for the "censorship."

The printed material which we studied so intensively at the time was mimeographed. It covered a variety of subjects, all of them intended for internal distribution only among acting and future

134

group leaders. Among those I remember, was a certain booklet: *Basic Guidelines for Hebrew Foreign Policy,* which showed how a militant underground movement was assisted by various foreign factors. Another booklet, *The Accused as Accusers,* described in detail the appearances of our comrades before the British courts of law; another dealt with the ideal image of a freedom fighter – one we all strived to emulate. I kept these publications at home, hidden in a tin behind the wardrobe.

When my annual leave was due I asked Tanchum to get me some assignment. I told him I could use my leave by taking a course in firearms.

"You're scheduled for a course quite soon," he told me. "Right now conditions are unsuitable, but we'll find something else for you to do on your leave."

The upshot of it all was that I spent two boring weeks doing observations – something which at least gave me plenty of time to think. For hours I hung around in the vicinity of the Roumanian Church in Hanevi'im St., waiting for a car bearing a certain number in order to ascertain the times it passed that spot. The car belonged to a high British official, and between its appearances I stood staring at the church, ruminating upon the "church epidemic" in our city. So many churches, Christian hospitals, schools and missionary charities abounded in Jerusalem! There was not a country in Europe which had not been waiting expectantly for the Ottoman empire to fall so it could establish its holdings in Jerusalem. The priests were the forerunners of the armies, the diplomats and the governors. France built monasteries and orphanages without end; Germany – orphanages, vocational schools, hospitals and agricultural villages. The Russians built their Orthodox churches and the British-Protestant missions infiltrated the local population.

How to get a "Sick Report"

My leave was up and I returned to work. A week later Tanchum let me know that I was being sent on a course in firearms which would take two weeks. At 11.00 hours I was to be in Tel-Aviv, at Fein St., and stand there, scratching my thigh. There were three other Jerusalem boys joining the course with me. "The evening before we leave," said Tanchum," we'll get together and make all the arrangements."

"Of course," I answered in a confident tone, but actually I was at a complete loss as to what I would say at the office.

After Tanchum and I separated, I began racking my brains. What was I to say at home, and how could I explain my absence from the office? I had only just returned from a two weeks' holiday. I thought of ways to wangle a "sick report," but it wasn't that simple. What doctor would take the risk of giving me one? Then I thought of Dr. Heffner, a patriot who was always ready to help both the *Etzel* and the *Lehi.* His sons had been arrested some time ago and deported to Kenya, while he himself had spent some time in Latrun. If I asked him for a fictitious report and was caught – he would be the victim. No, Dr. Heffner was out of the question. But if not he, who would give me such a report, without which there was no way I could participate in the course.

It never occurred to me to give up the course. I had joined the *Lehi* in the first place in order to fight, and without the proper training what good was I? Come what may, I would go to a doctor and complain of some aches and pains. Then I remembered that in order to give a legitimate sick report the doctor must visit the patient at home, to certify that he was too ill to get up and go to a government doctor... What was I to do? It wouldn't have been so difficult if the course had been for two or three days, but fourteen days? I was at my wits end.

A friend at the post office once told me how he had obtained a "sick report" from a certain Dr. S. for a sum of money. I knew this Dr. S., who lived in Mekor Baruch in my area, Zone 5, where I delivered the mail. He seemed desperately poor, a man who would welcome any sum that came his way, and I wondered if I should risk approaching him. There was also the problem of what my friends at work would say when they heard that I was so ill I had to stay in bed for a fortnight...

Dr. S. was no stranger to the supervisors at work and many of them availed themselves of his good services. When a postman brought a "sick report" for a few days they would shut one eye, understand and forgive; but two weeks! – and that immediately following a leave of the same length?

Mr. Hayut, with his thundering voice, wouldn't tolerate it, not under any circumstances. Possibly the only thing to do was to confront him with the fact that I was a *Lehi* man and warn him not to tell a soul. I believed that if I put it that way Mr. Hayut would cover for me and keep silent, but I couldn't do it without telling Tanchum first. What if he didn't agree? Why should he put himself in jeopardy, as well as myself, when there were so many other candidates for the course? Weighing up all the possibilities I finally decided that it would be best to present him with a *fait accomplit* – come to him after making a deal with Hayut and tell him about it with a big smile... I felt certain he would approve of my initiative and enterprise.

But there were other problems. Bizhe, for example, who delivered the mail in our quarter and would often come in during working hours to rest a while, to lay down his heavy mail bag and have a cool drink. If he heard I was so ill he would surely make it his first duty to visit me. How to avoid it? I could never tell my secret, to him, a man who could never keep his mouth shut.

"Listen, I'm going to give myself a treat!" I told Bizhe as he was coming out of the post office in the direction of Storrs St. He eyed me, his curiosity aroused. "My uncle is coming on a visit from France and there's no one but me to take him touring round the country. He's rich, you know, and it's my plain duty. Sometimes he remembers us and sends us money and packages... I'm clearing out for two whole weeks."

Eyes wide with surprise he cried: "How will you manage? You've just returned from a two weeks' leave?"

"I'll get a two weeks' 'sick,'" I retorted.

"Two weeks' sick?" he exclaimed, unbelieving: "Do you realize what you're saying? What doctor in his right mind will give a healthy rascal like you a sick report for two days, let alone two weeks? And the office, do you think they'll take it lying down?"

"If you keep mum about it, so will the others. They'll believe I'm ill, why shouldn't they? And as for the doctor, I'll let you in on a secret. There's one who's ready to give 'sick reports' for money – at fixed price for every kind of illness."

I revealed the name of the doctor to Bizhe and he was duly grateful. He, too, had heard about such a doctor but no one had ever told him his name for fear he would blab about it. Now he, too, could take a "rest" sometimes, when the work became too much for him. In return for the favor he undertook to tell the people at the office that he had visited me at home and found me in bed, running a high fever and suffering from some contagious disease.

This ensured that none of my friends from work would pay me any visits in my absence, and I now had to find a suitable excuse for my parents. I told my mother that a school friend of mine now living on a *kibbutz* had sent me an invitation.

"You must be crazy," cried my mother, thinking I was making fun of her. "You've just had your yearly vacation!"

All innocence, I told her that all my colleagues were in the habit of getting "sick reports" for all kinds of queer reasons, and why should I always be working like a donkey? My parents, guessing that I was perhaps lying to them, regarded me with mixed feelings. They suspected that I was off on some underground assignment and would have done anything to prevent my leaving for the *kibbutz*.

But they realized it was not that simple and they hadn't succeeded in stopping me in the past.

They were in a quandary, but both were convinced that I had to be stopped and diverted from such dangerous ways. And what if I wasn't lying, was really going to a *kibbutz?* This might even be a good thing, a real rest from the hard work at the post office, where they did work me too hard, as if I were a slave!

Another point in my favor was that they were well aware how opposed the *kibbutzim* were to the underground movements. This

138

was not exactly to their credit but they might influence their Zuri and clear his head of all those dangerous ideas. After all, hadn't the family suffered enough with Salvo (Yehoshua) imprisoned in Latrun?

"What *kibbutz* are you going to?" asked Father.

I must confess that I was at a loss for an answer. I hardly knew any *kibbutzim* but for two, the names of which I remembered because of the freqent searches for arms to which they were subjected. They were Doroth and Ruhama. "Doroth," I replied, fully aware that as soon as I went out they would set about ascertaining if there was such a *kibbutz* in the country, and its exact location. Some time later they asked me where it was, and I told them in the Negev, even supplying some information about its agricultural products. This seemed to calm them a little.

It was early evening when I went past the market, crossed Agrippas St., and entered the Mishkanot quarter, where I found the place where Mr. Hayut the Post Supervisor lived. He was sitting with his wife on the veranda and I called out: "Hayut, there's something important I have to tell you. Could you come down for a minute?"

"What is it?" he asked, his voice like thunder, as usual. Mr. Hayut was no common character and not everyone was privileged to reach such a high rung in the post office hierarchy. That was the reason, perhaps, why he spoke so loudly making sure no one was left in doubt of his importance. A further incentive was his wife, sitting nearby and listening. "Have you lost a registered letter? Have you got into some kind of trouble?"

"No, no. it's nothing like that. Could you come down for a minute?"

When I had said what I had to say he was struck dumb with astonishment. "I'm a member of the *Lehi* and I've been ordered to leave town for two weeks." "You!!!" He couldn't seem to grasp that Yakhin, the shy and silent character who always ran to obey his supervisors when others protested and complained, that this Yakhin would come and talk to him like that.

"Yes, Hayut, I. Nobody must know what I've just told you, not even your wife. You can concoct any story you like but not a word of what I've said!" Then, just as I was about to mention it myself, he suggested: "Get a sick report!" "I'm going to, but you'll have to smooth things over, see to it that the directors don't begin to smell a rat."

Calming down a little he asked in a friendly tone: "So they're planning a serious operation, what?" Never had I heard him speak so softly. "Sorry, but I'm not allowed to talk about it!" I answered in a firm voice looking him meaningfully in the eye. "I hope you have really understood what I've just said, that there is no mistake about my meaning..."

"I understand perfectly, and I'll do everything I can to help you." he promised. "As for the job, leave it to me and don't worry!"

I could now go to see Dr. S., in the Mekor Baruch quarter. I knocked once and no one answered; again, and still no reply. As I stood there, uncertain what to do, an elderly Arab came up to the door and also knocked. He told me that he had come from far-away Ein Karem because the village was full of the wonders and miracles performed by the good "Doctor," who was also famed for his goodness of heart and his extremely low fees. When this new "friend" heard that I worked in the post he immediately offered me his good services.

"Listen," he told me eagerly. "I want you to get promotion and it is within my power to help you. All the high officials, Arabs, Jews and Englishmen are my good friends and I can do anything I like with them. Do you know X? A big shot, isn't he? Well, he's a regular visitor at my home. He eats at my place and I eat at his. I'll see to it that you are promoted over the heads of all your friends... I began to wonder what he was nattering about and why he was so flattering. Why should he go out of his way to "help" someone, a stranger he had first met three minutes ago?

In the meantime, the "Doctor" appeared. Pleased at being able to get rid of this tedious acquaintance I offered to let him go in before me, even though I was a bit pressed for time, out of politeness and as a reward for his avowed generosity. He wouldn't hear of it and added that he had something to tell me after I had finished.

140

Dr. S.'s home was shockingly filthy and neglected. When delivering mail to a doctor I always found clean rooms, polite manners and decently clothed tenants, an air of wealth and respectability. Yet the man sitting here was unkempt and dirty, disorder and dirt all around him.

"Well, what do you want?" he asked, his eye blinking.

"I need a 'sick'."

"It will cost you five piasters a day. How many days shall I put down?" "Five piasters is too much. I want a wholesale price – for two weeks." "Two weeks!" His eyes opened wide. "It's a fixed price, for a day or for a week – the price is the same."

I delved into my pocket and shelled out a handful of coins which I counted shilling by shilling, fourteen shillings in all. "A few more clients like me, Doctor, and you can buy yourself a new suit."

I asked for two separate "sick reports," one made out for each week. Reporting sick for two weeks ahead seemed even to me a bit too daring and might easily arouse suspicion.

"In that case, why don't you come again next week for another report?" "I don't mind coming every day, but why should I bother you? By next week I might get well and spend all this money, so why should you be the loser?"

"And your employers, won't they ask questions?"

"Why should they? On the contrary I'll tell everybody about you and they'll come to you. You'll end up a rich man because of me."

"Okay, Okay! What disease shall I put down?"

"How should I know, am I a doctor? You should know the diseases that go on for a fortnight."

The important man of medicine got up and drew a book out of a packing case on the floor. It looked like a medical encyclopaedia. He leafed through it and finally pronounced: "Influenza! Okay?"

"Fine."

"In case anyone asks you, tell them that I visited you at home and found you in bed with a high temperature, 40^0, to be exact... I ordered you to stay in bed."

"Should I complain of a sore throat?"

"Good idea... Remember: 40^0 and a sore throat." He reopened his desk drawer and again counted the coins I had given him. Yes, they added up to fourteen shillings. Tearing two pages out of a notebook he wrote down something and began looking for his seal which he found, after much opening and shutting of drawers, lying in front of him on the desk. It had been so long unused that only by breathing heavily on it could he dampen it enough for it to work, then stamped it heavily on the two notes.

"That's it! Try and lie down with a high temperature."

"And a sore throat," I added.

As I left the doctor's room, there was my friend from Ein Karem, seemingly overjoyed to see me again.

"Right then! What is it you want? And tell me quickly because I'm busy and haven't much time."

He certainly had something to tell me, but I saw he didn't know how to begin. If he were a Jew I'd have suspected him of wanting to enlist me in the underground... Finally, when he realized that I was about to go, he managed to blurt out a few words that clearly implied an offer of a homosexual nature... Filling my mouth with saliva I spat straight into his face and left for a meeting in the underground. On my way I stopped at home for moment to give my father the second "sick report," and asked him to bring it to my supervisor in a week's time. If he was interested in my state of health, father should say that I was still suffering from a high temperature.

Father didn't seem over eager to fulfill my requests, but after all, what wouldn't the family do for their Zuri?

Off to the Course... and the Sea

Meeting the three who were to join me in the course I saw that one of them had gone to school with me. "Ginger" Greenberg was now introduced to me as "Aviram." "Good," I quipped: "I am Datan and you are Aviram. Let's hope the earth doesn't open its

142

mouth to swallow us up because of our evil deeds."* Then there was Shlomo, who was new to me, and the third – none other than Ha'im! We shook hands happily, unable to hide our joy. "At least we'll be together during the course," I told him. We began reminiscensing nostalgically about our former cell, famed for being the best "Pasters" in Jerusalem. It seemed so far away now, as if many years had gone by. Not that we regretted the disbanding of the cell – our chances for some "real" action were so much better now. Still, we had all been saddened when the time came for the "Brethren of the *The Deed*" to separate, for we had grown very close to one another. It was good to be together again, exchanging confidences for days and nights on end as we loved to do, discussing every conceivable subject under the sun; to argue about politics, the future of the underground and the possibility that the whole nation would join us in our insurrection. Who knows, after the course we might even meet in joint operations!

Ha'im was now in charge of a new youth cell whose task was the distribution and pasting of proclamations, but a promise had been given him that from time to time that he, too, would participate in actual combat, and the very thought that we might act together excited us greatly.

We decided to leave two hours earlier than the time set for the underground meeting. This would give us time to go down to the sea.

The sea! How commonplace it is today. There was hardly a child in Jerusalem who had not seen it, swum in it from early childhood. However, it was far different when I was a child and even when I became a teenager things had not changed. There was an exciting magic about a trip to the seaside, unlike anything I have ever experienced. It was a prize one could win, if ever, once in many years, to be prepared for as if it were a trip abroad. Those fortunate to have spent some time there never tired of talking about it to their friends, dwelling repeatedly on each fascinating

---

*   Reference to the incident of Datan and Aviram recounted in Numbers 16:30. The two men conspired with Korach to challenge the authority of Moses. The latter called them to a judgment before the Lord and "... the earth opened its mouth and swallowed them up and their homes."

detail. Six years before the time of my story I had been there as a guest of a Yemenite family, the Madars, friends of my parents living in Bat Yam. They sent one of their children to us for a week and, in turn, I was sent to spend a week with them.

Jerusalem seems Further and Further Away...

There was no sleep for us on the night before the trip. At seven that morning the four of us met at the Central Bus Station. Again we calculated how much time we had at our disposal: two hours for the journey, two for the seashore and then off to the course!

Each pair of us boarded the bus separately and we sat in different parts, this for reasons of security. Ha'im sat next to me, of course. We hardly spoke but were both exhilarated, and showed this in our eyes. As the wheels rolled on the black asphalt, we viewed the enchanting scenes of Jerusalem through the windows. I had a strange feeling that Jerusalem was going further and further away, and we ourselves were not sure of our destination. Everything was suddenly unreal. I couldn't imagine a Jerusalem without Ha'im and myself. How good it was that he, at least, was with me.

We were now passing through the orange groves, a sign that we were nearing Tel-Aviv. If Jerusalem was surrounded by mountains, one could say that Tel-Aviv (at that time, at least) was encircled by citrus groves. Finally we arrived. The bus stopped and we got off. It was still early, before nine, so that we had two hours before us. Where was the sea and how to get to it?

"What's the problem?" said one. "Let's ask. Everyone in Tel-Aviv knows where the sea is."

We asked a bearded old man passing by and he, thinking we were making fun of him answered irately: "In Honolulu!"

I remembered hearing once that the sea which appeared at the end of Allenby Rd., actually continued to the shores of Spain.

"Why don't you ask how to go to Spain then?" one of them joked. We all had a good laugh and asked for the way to Allenby

Rd. and thence – straight to the beach!

Ah, the sea, the sea! The promenade with its small cafés, the smell of the salty water (pollution was an unknown word then) and the pretty girls in their bathing costumes! What a sight for Jerusalem boys: girls with their nakedness barely covered, all arms and thighs, slender nymphs and plump ones all tanned and warm.

The time flew by, there was so much to see. But when it came to the hour of our meeting we departed from this Eden without any regrets and hurried to Fein St., the gathering point from which we would go towards the fulfilment of our innermost desire, the end for which we had planned and plotted so deviously and dangerously. We were setting out to learn "the use of our hands in fighting and of our fingers in the art of war."

So I stood there, scratching my right thigh, my friends regarding me from a distance.

A young man stood before me. We exchanged passwords and he told us to follow him. We boarded a bus and left for Ra'anana, where we got off and walked a bit till we got to a lonely shack, where we were introduced to six other youths who had come from all over the country. Each one introduced himself, myself being the first of the Jerusalemites. Trying to be impressive I said: "Freedom Fighter Datan." My Jerusalem friends followed suit: Freedom Fighter Aviram; Freedom Fighter Ha'im etc.

The other members of the course thought that this was the custom in Jerusalem and were a bit embarrassed that they were simply "Yoram," "Avner" or "Amos." They began feeling better when the instructor appeared and introduced himself simply as "Yehoshua," not "Freedom Fighter Yehoshua."

Yehoshua was very tall, slim, blonde and very straight, with a glint of fun in his eyes, radiating authority and complete trust. Later I was to learn that "Yehoshua" was "Eli," a Haifa man, one of the first in *Lehi*. There were also two lovely girls with us, one a red-haired beauty called Tamar, and the other a Yemenite – Dvorah.

We were given our orders. First – arrangements for standing guard. During the day, guards would relieve each other every thirty minutes. Each of us would in turn be on the look-out stationed on the roof and, in case of approaching British, would call out: 'Gentiles!' at which we had to get away as fast as we could, shooting as we retreated – that is, if we had managed to learn how to by that time... At night the guard would be relieved every hour. Throughout the course we were to sleep in our clothes, including shoes, which would make it easier to escape if we were caught.

The first day was devoted to the program of the course and the various arrangements. There was also a lecture on the firearms we would be using. When darkness came we began to stand guard, taking our turn as it came. Some of the lads fell asleep at once and their snores disturbed the others who were trying to sleep. Some had never slept away from home before and couldn't relax. Wearing all your clothes and shoes didn't help much either. In my case all these were at work together, keeping me awake. But most of all it was the excitement of knowing that I was about to "teach my hands to fight and my fingers to make war" and this quotation from the Psalms kept ringing in my mind.

I watched the guards changing one after another, every hour exactly. It was a wonder to me that some of the lads slept so soundly they had to be shaken repeatedly to awaken them from sleep and make them understand it was their turn to keep watch. When they finally stood up they tottered as if they were drunk, stumbling after those who had roused them to take them to their post. The day's exertions must have tired them out.

The next day we had a lecture on the use of a pistol in combat, and the difference between an automatic pistol and a revolver. We were told that revolvers were best as an attack weapon, for in case of a dud bullet we could turn the drum by pressing the trigger, thus activating the hammer and releasing the next bullet. It was also faster, for there was no need to open the safety catch and press before shooting. Conversely, in retreat, the automatic was the better choice as its magazine held more bullets and could be loaded at one go.

I remarked that the word "Automatic" seemed more suitable for the revolver, whose action was more automatic than that of the pistol with its magazine. But I found it difficult to remember all the other names of the pistol components or their specific functions. Perhaps it was because I had never before dealt with machinery or mechanical instruments, or because I was suffering from lack of sleep. Yehoshua's personality, too, was so compelling that I was fascinated, and this distracted me from the subject under discussion.

At the end of the second day I finally fell into a deep, refreshing sleep, waking up by myself half an hour before I was due on guard duty. Everybody was surprised at this except myself, for I had developed a kind of sixth sense that worked like an alarm clock, rousing me at the required time. The many nights of "pasting" had done their work and it didn't fail me now. If it was motivation, I had no lack of it. As the bridegroom says in the Song of Songs: "...Do not rouse her, do not disturb my love until she is ready." My love for my people was deep indeed and I was ready to act for its redemption.

The third day began according to plan: getting up, morning exercises, breakfast. There was a knock on the door. Dvorah, our liaison officer went out, followed by Yehoshua. Within five minutes he returned and asked us to excuse him but he had to go out for a while.

An hour went by, then another and another, each longer than the last. Yehoshua failed to return.

To alleviate the tension we tried thinking of something to kill the time, otherwise it might kill us... Pistols and revolvers are, of course, useless as weapons against ennui so we began "shooting" jokes, some very old and some new to us. Dvorah, who was sitting next to me, murmured something or other in my ear and realizing that the others had not heard, I decided to play a joke on them. "Listen kids," I said conspiratorially, "It's a pity I can't let you in on why Yehoshua had to leave... truly a pity, but never mind! It's going to be O.K.!"

Everybody suddenly came alive, asking me, no begging me to tell them the truth: "He's out on an operation, isn't he?"

"Are you crazy? Now that we know the difference between a pistol and a revolver they'd send him and not us?"

"Come on, Datan, be a sport!"

I kept diplomatically silent.

"I know," came the remark. "He's gone to bring more weapons for the course." "Right," I confirmed, "Cannons!" Everybody burst out laughing but, calming down they renewed their supplications, so that I was forced to tell the truth. I had no idea where Yehoshua had gone nor what was delaying him! They all agreed it was a good try so I decided to go on pretending to them. With a meaningful smile I turned to Ha'im and asked him to tell the joke about Stalin's moustache. Poor Ha'im blushed. True, he had told the story to Israel and myself with great gusto but here, in front of girls?

"There's a Sternist for you. They don't mind undressing the British Empire and displaying it in all its nakedness... but tell an off colour story before girls... that can't be done!"

The Return Home

It was noon by the time Yehoshua returned. Surrounded by our expectant faces he gave us the news, which wasn't so good. The course had to be stopped at once as the British might be conducting searches in the area. Precautionary measures had to be taken.

"But what about us, what are we going to do?"

"You're all going back home!"

Home? How could we, dear God, how could we? After all our enormous efforts and deceptions – go back now? After the "talk" on Hayut's staircase, after the "rich uncle" invented for Bizhe, the "sick" given me by the doctor and the "kibbutz in the Negev" – after all this to return without having achieved a thing? I felt sick with frustration, my throat choked with tears.

Ha'im tried to comfort me: "At least we managed to see something on the beach," he winked, but it was no good.

Everybody began speculating about the new development. An important operation against the British was probably in the offing which would result in widespread searches. Stopping the course was a logical preventative measure, but what a pity! It could have taken place earlier, while I was on vacation, and by now I would have mastered the art of firearms, might even have participated in the present operation. Damn the British! With all my heart I hoped they would pay dearly for everything – even the bitter disappointment of having the course annulled.

Looking back I realized I had done well to divide the "sick" into two separate reports, and I could go back to work at the end of the first week. Hayut, when he read the papers, would be sure I was one of the terrorists causing all the trouble, and treat me with due respect.... Poor comfort! I had no desire for the glory due to others and, had it been permitted, I would have told Hayut the real reason. Oh well, let him think what he liked. It wouldn't hurt anybody and it might come in useful in the future if he stood in awe of me.

"You're back already?"

My family was surprised, and I had to tell them a tale about the breaking out of a typhoid epidemic in the kibbutz. "All the guests and those who refused immunity shots were sent home."

My parents had a good laugh for they were aware of my incurable fear of injections which had for long been a source of family jokes. Yehoshua, my brother, used to say I was lucky that the underground had to fight British soldiers armed with guns, not doctors armed with syringes... It all sounded so natural that I added the daring information that the visit to the *kibbutz* was only postponed for the time being and I had a raincheck for a fortnight in the future. In this way I prepared the ground for the time when I would leave on another course.

Returning home one night we learnt that the "Rebellion Movement" had attacked some military camps and railways. When I showed up at work Mr. Hayut treated me with profound respect, so much so that I had to warn him to behave towards me as he had always done in order to avert suspicion. Indeed there was room for warning. Here and there I heard murmurings about "Yakhin the bastard" who had bribed Hayut to keep his mouth shut. What other explanation could there be for this sudden affection for a postman who had dared take off for a whole week, having a good time, his only excuse a bit of paper, the "sick" signed by Dr. S. – which, as everyone knew was easily available to anyone with a bit of money. As for me, I wasn't worried. So long as they thought I had been living it up in my absence, with no suspicion of my membership in the underground – there was no reason to be. Fortunately no one suspected anything, believing me to be a "mother's boy," both because I looked younger than my real age and because of my shyness and unobtrusive behavior. I always made for home after working hours and whenever anybody invited me to go out on the town I would say I belonged to the H.T.T.H., Club (Happy are Those who dwell in Thy House).

Many weeks went by as we waited for the renewal of the course – a period of stormy turbulence for the country.

The course was to be renewed and this time everything was much simpler. At home I said that the epidemic had passed and I was going back to Kibbutz Doroth; at work Bizhe was informed that my uncle, who had put off his visit for business reasons, was coming at last. Hayut just had to be informed as our former conversation had prepared the ground. Again I called on Doctor S., but this time gave him only 7 shillings. I didn't fail to mention that the following week I might be too ill to come personally for a further "sick" and would send someone from my family (thus saving 7 shillings in case the course broke up again). The ceremony of moistening the seal by breathing on it repeated itself, and I told Doctor S. that with the money he made from me he could buy a pad and some ink for his stamp.

Again we went to Tel-Aviv, not omitting the visit to the beach. Finally we found ourselves in the shack in Ra'anana but with a different instructor, Ben-Nun.

Everything went according to plan. We learnt how to use pistols, dismantling some then putting them together again. We learnt their names and those of the various parts. We fired some air-guns and had a lot of fun with "Ginger" Tamar's problem – she could never remember the word "parabellum" – name of a German automatic pistol. Nothing we tried seemed to do any good. Finally Ben-Nun said firmly: "Pay attention, Tamar! The parabellum is your pistol. Remember, the name of your gun is 'parabellum!' "A few minutes later he asked her: 'What is the name of your pistol, Tamar?'

"It's... It's my pistol..."

From that momment we all called the parabellum "Tamar's pistol." As for me, I didn't do too well either at learning to recognize its various components. I was always forgetting their names and functions, and getting confused when it came to dismantling them and putting them together again. But to compensate for this I was quick on the draw and a good shot with the air-gun we used for practice.

We learnt about explosives – both the repellant and the pulverizing kinds, as well as the use of grenades. We were taught how to put a grenade together and how to produce several types of "homemade bombs." We also learnt how to produce and throw Molotov cocktails.

On the seventh day we began studying "heavy artillery" – sub-machine guns. At midday, as we sat down for lunch and Ben-Nun wished us a good appetite, to which we replied "strong and bright!" there was a knock on the door, and before we had taken a bite into our mouths Ben-Nun was called outside. He returned quite soon only to declare that he was sorry but the course had to be called off for fear of searches in the area..."

Rising, I pulled at his sleeve: "Listen! we've finished the course. We've learnt everything we had to learn!"

"You know everything, I suppose. Sub-machine guns too?"

"Yes" – we chorused, hoping we would now be accepted as regular combat men and not have to wait for a further course before participating in operations.

We returned to our homes. Well, I went back to work and Dr. S. lost 7 shillings. It was a pity the course had to be stopped, but we found comfort in the heavy toll the British had to pay. Dorn, an officer in the C.I.D., was killed in the *Lehi* attack on the Jaffa office. Martin, renowned for his sharp eyes and redoubtable memory and the one who had identified the member of our Central Committee, Michael (today Yitzhak Shamir, who had been hiding under the cover of a rabbi in Tel-Aviv) – was killed in Haifa.

The "love affair" between the underground organizations and the *Hagana* came to an end. After the "Black Saturday" the *Hagana* gave in to the British and the "Rebellion Movement" was officially dead.

This was the time for the underground organizations to launch an intensive attack. *Etzel* and *Lehi* fought the enemy in different ways. In one of its operations the *Etzel* literally reduced the British Army to nakedness: some British officers were caught, relieved of their pants and flogged in their tenderer parts. This was an "educational" reply to an "educational punishment" favored by the British – flogging. A youngster caught pasting Etzel proclamations had been cruelly whipped by the lash and the British were now given a taste of their own medicine.

The sight of the British officers reduced to such pitiful straits did much to undermine the prestige of the British Empire which was now made an object of ridicule, and laughed at by the whole world. The ugly practice of flogging was discontinued...

Mr. Khalil's Stick

I have personally known corporal punishment and few things can anger me more than seeing it in use. As a pupil at the Ratisbonne School I learnt to regard the stick as an integral part of the teaching process, more frequently used by the teachers than any text book. The English teacher – an Arab by the name of Mr. Khalil – outshone all the others in its use, and would accompany the beating with a stream of abuse that more than indicated his anti-semitism. Yehoshua and I learnt English in Mr. Khalil's class. One day, before the lesson had started, my brother asked me to lend him a book we shared in common. As soon as the teacher entered the room, the monitor in charge of keeping the class quiet, one Shweiki, hurried to inform him of Yehoshua's "crime"... He was called up and told to put his hand out. My brother tried to explain that he hadn't been chattering but had asked for a book – Mr. Khalil was deaf to the explanation. My blood boiling, I watched him strike my brother's hand again and again.

Next day before the lesson I turned intentionally to my bench partner in order to provoke Shweiki to tell on me as well, but he refrained. So when the teacher entered, I began pulling Victor's (my neighbour) school bag. The two of us were called up to take our medicine. Poor Victor didn't dare protest at being punished for something he had not done, but when my turn came to hold out my hand I refused. In a voice that seemed strange even to myself I declared: "No, I won't hold it out!"

It's hard to say who was more surprised, Mr. Khalil or the class. The cheek of it, daring to disobey Mr. Khalil – it was something completely unheard of in the history of the school. Grabbing hold of my hand he raised the stick powerfully to strike, but I managed to catch it with my other hand and pulled it away from him. After a short struggle he managed to retrieve it but when he tried to strike again I caught it again. This went on until the stick broke.

Mr. Khalil refused to let me go. Shweiki was sent to Mr. Kammalle to borrow his stick, a solid, thick one no child could break with his bare hands. The struggle was renewed. For a second the stick was in my hand and I threw it outside through the open window. It made a beautiful arc as it flew from the third floor down into the school yard. The good Shweiki was sent down to fetch it and the struggle was renewed. In the course of it Mr. Khalil bent down and his glasses, as well as an expensive fountain pen, fell out of his pocket. I was so mad that, not stopping to think, I stamped on both objects and crushed them with my shoe. Then I straightened myself, held out my hand and cried scornfully: "Go on, hit it as much as you like... You've got a reason now!" And hit me he did, again and yet again, until the pain became unbearable. But I kept on laughing in his face and, the more it hurt, the more I provoked him to go on hitting me. I was determined he would not have the satisfaction of seeing me cry or groan and as he struck I would laugh. The hand was already quite swollen and there I was, telling him to go on, to hit again. Finally he stopped. Not that he was feeling sorry for me or worried about my hand – he had simply tired of the whole thing and stopped.

At home I declared that I would never again attend Mr. Khalil's classes unless I was promised he would not touch my brother or myself with the stick again. It took some time to convince my parents but finally they realized I meant it and reluctantly went to talk to "Pére Laniado," the Principal of the school who was a convert. It wasn't easy but they extracted a promise that the Yakhin brothers would be exempt from Mr. Khalil's beating in the future. The latter now changed my name from "Ezra" to *Ozre'in,* or "devil" in Arabic.

The British seemed to be losing their self control. For decades the principle of "divide and rule" helped them to rule the many nations and tribes of their colonies and despite their vaunted liberalism, they never hesitated to restrain or even physically destroy any independent group that might threaten their sovereignty. Here in our country, too, they did not hesitate to use unscrupulous methods. They had managed to create an image of indestructable force which could never be overcome, bolstered by an aura of moral superiority, justice, honor and liberalism. They incited the Arabs against the Jews, at the same time as they ruthlessly suppressed anybody who might present a potential danger to them – as had been the case with Ya'ir.

But this time it didn't work. On the contrary, the underground expanded, and its operations were multiplied. The people sympathized with the fighters, even though there was no lack of leaders willing to collaborate with the enemy, who were now unable to isolate us from the rest of the nation.

The British found themselves in a cleft stick: true, they succeeded in finding and arresting many "terrorists," but there were always others, many more, to take their place. Nor did the terrorists lack bases from which to carry out operations and return to after combat.

All this was beginning to get the British down and every Jew, however innocent, was suspected of being a terrorist. A good example of this was the Jerusalem Rabbi they arrested in Paris, on his way to New York on family business. He was taken for a thorough interrogation at the Intelligence Center in Cairo where they hoped to reveal his true identity and the evil plots hidden underneath his long beard...

Every day there were reports of soldiers shooting at people indiscriminately, often at their own comrades whom they suspected of being terrorists masquerading as British soldiers...

All this was a strain on the nerves... *Ha'aretz* (The most popular Hebrew daily) of January 15, 1947, reported a strike in the British Army. Protesting against their prolonged service in Palestine, 150 soldiers declared their refusal to accept orders. Four were arrested for incitement to rebellion and that same week eight "Poppies" (nick-name of the 6th Airborne Division) were similarly indicted.

Mothers and relations of British soldiers serving here flooded the British government with letters demanding that their sons be returned to them – an unheard of phenomenon in England.

Sans Home, Sans Family

British offices and barracks had by now been turned into fortresses, impregnable and isolated. They were surrounded by high fences of barbed wire, behind which were firing positions backed by searchlights. The guards were actually imprisoned by their own fences, from which they dared not venture outside. Peering through their windows at the houses of the Jewish community, apprehensive of the danger lurking there, they would expropriate a whole row of houses, evacuate the Jewish inhabitants living there, and fortify the area with barbed wire. Even then, looking out of their windows, they still felt the danger and threats on every side.

This process continued until – in order to protect their offices in the King David Hotel – all the buildings in the vicinity extending to Arlosoroff St. in Rehavia were expropriated. Similarly, to ensure the safety of the Russian Compound and the Post Office Building, a large part of the city center was sequestered and surrounded by barbed wire and firing positions. About a thousand families lost their homes, but the British were still dissatisfied. All the families of the civil service men and those of the British police were sent out of the country (in spite of the fact that the

155

underground had never harmed women or children) and the represetatives of foreign rule found themselves isolated and alone, without home or family, a prey to constant fear. Their roads were mined, shots were fired at them from every corner, cars exploded in the heart of their "Security Zones..." Many policemen wished to resign from the service, giving as a reason their unwillingness to be separated from their wives and families who, in their turn, added their voices to the clamor raised in the press and demanded: "Bring back our sons from Palestine!"

Brilliant generals like Cunningham and Barker were sent to cope with the freedom fighters, but to no avail! Many advisers, among them General Dempsey and Field Marshall Montgomery himself – the man who had directed the campaign against the hordes of Hitler – were invited here for consultations. Montgomery came to Jerusalem to study the situation at first hand and was indeed given a lesson... His first night at the hotel was spent to the accompaniment of ceaseless fire. The guards of the illustrious general had been thrown into a panic by the shadows of some dogs prowling in the area, resulting in a shooting match which continued for hours...

Another weapon tried by the British Government was that of exerting political pressure. Hardly a day passed without the Jewish Agency leaders being brought in and their full cooperation demanded in the suppression of the terror, on pain of "drastic measures" against them, such as martial law. The leaders of the Jewish community were at their wits end. Inciting the public, they demanded that "extreme measures be taken against the dissident terrorists" – but the people heeded them no longer. Thus ignored, they tried to create an image of themselves as leaders of the "struggle" against Britain, but the community treated this ploy with the contempt it deserved...

Actually the official leaders of the community could have acted effectively against the British by simply declaring a state of civil disobedience without resorting to armed rebellion. It would have sufficed for them to break all contact with the foreign administration and stop all payment of taxes. Another effective measure would have been to call on the Jewish community to

156

destroy all its identification cards, etc. Such universal opposition would have deprived the British of any ability to exert authority, being a bitter propaganda blow, and a clear moral indictment. After all, how can one deal with a whole nation which has declared civil disobedience? One can only prolong the arrest of its leaders, and that at a time when ordinary *Etzel* and *Lehi* soldiers were being marched to the gallows with a song on their lips...

The ferment in the *Hagana* was getting out of hand and there were cases of men deserting from the *Palmach* to join *the Lehi.* The *Hagana* counter-acted by organizing refugees in Europe in a network of illegal immigration to circumvent the White Paper edicts. This organization opened a new chapter in the struggle between the illegal immigrants (*Ma'apillim*) and the British. At first the refugee ships were stopped at sea and the immigrants imprisoned in Atlit, thence to be released at the rate of 1,500 a month – the quota permitted by the White Paper. When the Atlit Camp was filled to overflowing, the new arrivals were concentrated in a camp in Cyprus. In some cases the refugees actively resisted arrest, and many were killed on the beaches...

But the ships persisted in coming, seeking to unload their human cargo in obscure beaches, under cover of night. To combat this the British created a whole navy whose sole task was to fight the refugees. Little by little it became obvious to the most obtuse, that any hope of an eventual peace between the Jews and the British was now out of the question.

Nevertheless, the British persisted in their policy: once more they demanded full cooperation from the community leaders "within a few days," threatening them with "extreme sanctions" if it was witheld. The latter did not reject the ultimatum, offering the excuse that they were doing their best in their efforts to prevent bloodshed. Ben Gurion, who was then in Paris, talked to the press, belittling the underground movements and their operations and presenting their whole campaign as "terrorist acts of a few Yemenites..."

Here is an incident typical of the time: two lads of the *Hagana* were putting up proclamations of *The Wall,* the *Hagana* mouthpiece – on the houses of Tel-Aviv, when they were surprised

157

by two policemen who tried to arrest them. The boys resisted and managed to relieve one of them of his machine gun, at which both policemen ran away in a panic. We were all delighted when we heard about it, believing that the *Hagana* leaders would learn the moral of the story as demonstrated by the men in the rank. But next day we learnt from the press that the *Hagana* had decided to return the machine gun to its "rightful owners." It was abandoned in one of the back yards and the British Intelligence was informed, together with appropriate apologies...

Yehoshua, my brother, was released from Latrun and came home, but it was conditional release. Twice a day he had to report at the Mahane Yehuda Police station and sign a register. He was also placed under house arrest from six in the evening to six in the morning – a treatment which many of those released were subjected to by the British. From time to time they would burst into the house for "surprise" inspection, in the hope of catching him breaking the rules. It often happened that when Yehoshua was absent from home at night, Mother would lead them to my bedroom where they would beam a torch onto my face and then go away.

The comrades released from prison were not usually allowed to enjoy such house arrest for long. Regarded as hostages, after every successful underground operation they would be re-arrested by the furious British and packed off to prison again. Neither was Yehoshua permitted to enjoy the mountain air of Jerusalem too long. Three weeks after his release, the British were dealt a heavy blow by the underground, and my brother was returned to the detention camp in the valley of Ayalon.

"You're on Observation Duty this Evening"

Tanchum's orders were that, together with M., I was to be on observation duty near the railway lines at the Mekor Ha'im quarter that evening, and we were to set out for the assignment at ten o'clock. When we got there we had to note every train passing through and the exact moment of its arrival; count the number of freight cars and fuel tanks, and let no detail of the traffic arrangements or other procedures escape our notice.

I was glad it was M. I was going with, he was such a pleasant fellow. Like me, he had been through "Youth" training and, even though we had never worked together, I hoped we would get on well, an important element in alleviating the tension of observation duty.

The night was cold and the humidity high. Putting on my winter coat I informed my parents that I would spend the night at a friend's place. Having by now gotten the idea of what I meant by sleeping with "friends," they pretended to believe me, begging me not to go out on such a cold night. As usual, I had to turn a deaf ear to their pleas.

M. and I looked at the heavy clouds, through which not a single star could be seen, and exchanged worried glances. We were about to spend the night beside the railway lines, under the open sky, and there were all the signs of a heavy rain in the biting wind and the black clouds.

As we were walking along M. surprised me by asking me if I could carry out the assignment by myself. He was very sensitive to cold and should really be at home in such weather. I was stunned. Freedom fighters of this kind were a new experience for me. I knew that there were members who had dropped out for ideological reasons, as, for example, the *Brith Hashmona'im* movement; some had left because they were unfit for a militant framework such as ours, and there were even those who could not withstand their parents' pressure. But to be afraid of a little rain? This was a rare bird indeed!

Not that I found the idea of spending hours in the rain particularly attractive. But to try and get out of observation duty, leaving the dirty work to your friend while you cuddled down under the warm comforter at home? No! It was out of the question. "You're a *Lehi* man and you're coming with me," I snapped.

We took the bus to the Mekor Ha'im quarter, getting off at the last station and walking the rest of the way to the railway lines. It was so dark that we could barely make out the path, feeling our way along the rocky terrain step after step, until, after some 200 meters, we felt that we were walking on the lines.

As we sat down beside a rock it began to rain heavily, slowly at first then faster and faster. M. was shivering. "I can't take this any more," he muttered, "I've got to go home."

I tried to talk him out of it, telling him of the terrible sufferings of his comrades in the interrogation cellars, and literally working on his patriotic feelings. This seemed to work for a while but the heavy rainfall quickly melted his wavering will-power. Again and again he begged me to let him go until I tired of the whole business. "Get out!" I told him, and he did so with alacrity. I felt easier without him and there and then decided I would see to it that he was expelled from the movement. Types like him would certainly add nothing to our glory.

Someone had once told me that long-term prisoners were in the habit of counting the days to their release from their first day of imprisonment, ignoring the days that had already passed. I tried to emulate them, sitting there by the rock under the merciless rain and counting the minutes to the end of my assignment. After a quarter of an hour I made out a dark object moving towards me. "*Min inta?*" (who are you? in Arabic) asked an apprehensive voice: "I've quarrelled with my parents," I replied. "They wanted me to give them all my earnings. It's not that I'm a bad son," I hastened to add, "I'm willing to share with them, but I wanted to keep two Lira for myself. After all I'm *shab* (young man in Arabic) and I want to live a little while I'm still young. If not now, when will I ever be able to? But they refused to understand and pestered me so that I left home. I swear I'll never go back there, even if I die out here in the rain. I'm going to sleep outside, that'll show them!"

The dark mass was full of understanding, as I knew it would be. All too often had I heard the Arab youths at the Post Office discussing a similar situation with their parents, which would result in their running away from home. The man evinced some concern for me. "Are you crazy, sleeping in the open?" he asked. "Do you think that the rain is the only danger here? You may not know it but there are terrorists in the vicinity. What will you do if they attack you? And then there are the British who might suspect you of being one of them and shoot you down! No, son, I won't let you stay the night here, it's too dangerous. Come with me. I'll take you to Mekor Ha'im where I know some kindly people who'll put you up for the night, and tomorrow morning you'll go and apologise to your parents, like a good boy..."

"O.K., I'll take the bus home."

"It's too late, son; the buses aren't going at this hour. Come with me."

I couldn't refuse him as that would have aroused his suspicion, so I had to do as he asked. He told me that he was going home to Beit Tzafafa and he thanked Allah for putting a good deed in his way. I began to realize what a fool I had been to sit beside the track in order to observe His Majesty's trains and be seen by any chance passer-by.

At Mekor Ha'im my "good friend" told me to knock loudly on one of the doors. I gave it a light tap, but there was no answer.

"Not so softly, no one can hear you. Give it a good bang!"

"I'm ashamed to; it's late and they're probably all asleep."

Suddenly there were footsteps approaching. Some Supernumerary Police were patrolling the quarter. My protector told them the whole story: how he was walking home in the rain and found me wandering around. So, taking pity on the foolish boy, he decided to try and find him shelter for the night. The two Supernumeraries berated me for my foolishness. "Don't you know that this is where the terrorists lie in ambush for the trains. Those murderers would shoot you down like a dog if they met you. Come along, child. You can sleep in the synagogue till the morning."

They opened the door of the synagogue and when I entered I had a pleasant surprise: one of the windows in the wall overlooked the railway lines.

Finally they left and I felt wonderful, having got rid of them and of the soaking rain. This was a look-out post deluxe, absolutely secure from any passing British soldiers. Not five minutes later I heard the wheels of an approaching bus. "Dear God," I prayed. "Don't let the Supernumeraries see the bus, or they'll come and call me to go to town on it." But my prayer wasn't heard and there were the Supernumeraries calling me: "Hey! Come quickly! there's a bus going to town... the driver's waiting for you, you lucky rascal!" There was no alternative but to go to town, and then go back by foot to my observation post. But then I heard the noise of the train engine, the one I had been waiting for. The whole night had been a complete waste and the observation would have to be repeated next day. Leaving the rain-drenched city outside I tip-toed into the house, fearing to disturb my parents.

★

On the 2nd of March, 1947, Tanchum finally informed me I was to join an operation that very night!

Yochanan and I met for our briefing: each one of us was to get a Molotov cocktail to be thrown at an armoured car which was out on patrol every Saturday night, at about ten p.m. in Metudella St.

We left immediately to go there, to the southern part of the Rehavia quarter, and reconnoiter the area.

It was a Saturday morning. Worshippers were returning home from morning service. We stood in the street and Tanchum pointed towards a stone fence built upon a rise beside the road. "You'll stand behind this fence and when the armoured car reaches you, throw the bottles at it and run away! Don't look back, just run..."

He was still speaking when boom!!! – a terrible explosion rent asunder the Sabbath quiet.

"Oh, no!" cried Tanchum. "They've gone and done it just the same! Sorry, kids, but I'm afraid the operation we planned for tonight is off for the present!"

"Why, what's happened?" we were curious to know.

"It's a big *Etzel* operation and we have to make ourselves scarce. Go home and if there's a night curfew we'll meet half an hour before it, at the usual place."

The wail of the sirens reached us before we got home. Its shrieks were longer than usual seeming to go on forever. This time it looked as if "martial law," which had so long been threatened, was about to be imposed. No one knew what it meant exactly but it was certainly something the leaders of the community had long been afraid of. As a matter of fact, every act of the insurgents was always followed by the High Commissioner's sending an invitation to Mrs. Golda Me'irson and threatening her with it. Again and again she would assure him that the "organized community" had nothing to do with the latest terrorist acts, and beg him not to impose martial law on the innocent, peace-loving population.

But now it would appear that we were to learn the secret of this mysterious weapon: "martial law."

But what, actually, could they do? We were already familar with several kinds of curfew: night curfew; inter-urban roads curfew; day curfew and one lasting several days. Tel-Aviv had tasted the "Great Curfew," accompanied by house-to-house searches and mass arrests, over a period of several days. What more could they do? After all, they couldn't send all the Jews of Palestine to Africa, could they? They would now be forced to invent something new, a kind of "special" curfew such as had never been seen before, or the threat would be regarded as empty bombast.

I was dying to hear the news, and more than irritated by the *Etzel* for stealing my thunder on my very first operation. But, needless to say, the British were still with us and the day would come for us to meet...

The news: the Goldschmidt Building located in King George VI St., a noted club house of His Majesty's officers, was attacked by terrorists and demolished. Many tens of officers were killed, some of them still buried under the rubble.

Hats off to the *Etzel!* Any child could see how well-fortified the Goldschmidt Building was and, after the King David Hotel explosion, it and other centers of power were even more intensely guarded. But the Goldschmidt Building was considered to be impregnable. It transpired that the desire of the British for security at any price caused its downfall. The inhabitants of the adjacent Helbreich building had all been avacuated in order to ensure the safety of the Goldschmidt Building. Had there been Jewish families there, the *Etzel* would not have risked a frontal attack with such an enormous amount of explosives, for fear of endangering the Jewish neighbours...

And now we had "martial law." It covered the whole of Tel-Aviv and the northern parts of Jerusalem. These last were separated from the rest of the country by masses of barbed wire, with no one coming or going under threat of being arrested or shot. The people inside the enclosed areas were to stay inside their homes, with permission to go out granted only for a few hours a day – to buy the necessary food. In addition to this, all of Jerusalem was under curfew from six in the evening to six in the morning.

★

"No sleep for you tonight," says Tanchum. "You're to go to the Abu-el Bassal quarter and mark the movements of the army there. What we need is information about the movements of military vehicles in the path joining the Beit Ya'akov and the Zichron Yoseph quarters."

We went to look for the place best suited for a look-out base, finally choosing the brick factory in Saydoff's yard, where I could hide all night behind a pile of bricks and observe the movements of the vehicles on the path. I didn't go home this time to tell my parents that I was "sleeping at a friend's place." I simply couldn't face the fearful look in their eyes, knowing full well how anxious they would be. Obviously they would not be slow in making a connection between my absence and the acts against the British, and their feelings, when I failed to return that night, were not hard to imagine. On the other hand, if I didn't let them know in advance, they might comfort themselves with the thought that I had been caught breaking curfew and arrested. This wasn't pleasant, but implied a fine at the most.

So – no going home. As curfew time approached I was ensconced behind my pile of bricks. Each of the neighbours nearby took a last look at the yard before lowering their shutters and locking their doors, and they all saw me there. To avoid their worried glances I slipped around to the other side of the pile, making myself fully visible to the patrols enforcing the curfew. Only after everybody was shut inside the houses did I slip back – only to be cordially invited by someone peeping through the shutters to go in and stay till the morning. Ignoring the invitation I waited tensely for darkness to fall.

The noise of army vehicles touring the area filled the night. Sometimes they would stop to permit a foot patrol to get out. At times some men, talking English, approached my brick pile, and I couldn't tell whether they were just loitering or going straight for me. Hearing a vehicle approaching I would raise my head to see it, risking being seen by a passing patrol. I could hear them but it was too dark to see them. Conversely, I realized that my dark figure could be easily made out on the background of white bricks, and that I was just what the enemy was looking for. There... they were coming, now! They had seen me and where could I hide? They were getting nearer. Their English fell painfully on my ear. No place to run...

They stopped close to my pile. What were they plotting? I hadn't heard them moving away, so they must still be there! My heart beat so loudly I was sure they could hear it.

I held my breath. Footsteps again, this time from another direction. Probably reinforcements. When did they call for them? The footsteps came straight towards me and... passed me by. Only then did I see it was just a pack of dogs. But the British were still there, with only a pile of bricks between us. The minutes crept along, an eternity – but they were still there.

My limbs were cold and cramped, but I dared not move them. Finally a British truck arrived, stopping some distance from me. My "neighbours," the patrol, finally left my pile, went to the truck and left. I waited a while before I dared stretch out my limbs and straighten up for a minute, when I suddenly tensed up. It was the pack of dogs "visiting" me once again.

It seemed that my brick pile was the royal court of all the strays in the area. The darkness made it difficult to discern a dog from an Englishman. At long last the dawn appeared but the light was a new hindrance! The early risers in the Saydoff House eyed me with wondering looks. I told them that my watch had stopped and I had been caught by the curfew far from home. I had been too scared to knock on one of the doors and ask them to let me stay the night for fear they would think I was a terrorist...

I hurried home, walking as quickly as I could, worrying about what the night had done to my parents. As I reached Tachkimoni lane and our house, I saw my mother leaning on the balcony rail, her eyes searching the street.... Who could tell how long she had been standing there? As soon as she saw me she disappeared inside the house, so that I wouldn't notice how worried she had been. Father, too, behaved as if nothing untoward had happened and I told them about my night's adventures: "A quarter of an hour before curfew, as I was on my way home, the British stopped and arrested me, along with many others. We spent the night in jail and were questioned by some officers in the morning. They believed me and the others when we claimed that we had not broken the curfew intentionally. We were all released..."

Father and mother looked at me, their faces frozen. It was impossible to tell if they believed me or not.

Suddenly mother began hugging me with all her strength and I could hear her murmuring: "May God keep you wherever you go, protect you from evil... May your enemies be struck by blindness and not see what you are doing..." Poor woman she had no idea of the surprise in store for her that day.

In addition to the dramatic steps taken by the British as a result of the martial law declared after the explosion at the officers' club, they also took the usual measures after every such incident. The commonest of these was the immediate internment of those who had been released from past arrests. Our house was visited by three policemen, two British and one Arab, looking for Yehoshua. They took the opportunity to make a thorough search of the house. One of the Englishmen spoke Hebrew and was immediately attracted to my brother Avraham's room, which was full of communist literature. The detective was drawn to the printed word and eagerly grabbed the works of Marx, examining each book minutely. Not a booklet or leaflet escaped his examination and he seemed to be looking for some clever piece of camouflage. While he was reading, sunk in the mysteries of communist theory, his companions, the Englishman and the Arab, went into the living room, which also served as a bedroom. Shimeon, who worked for Abarbanel the upholsterer, was sitting there quietly, like a good, obedient child. The British always insisted on a witness being present during their searches who would later sign a document testifying that the search had been orderly and nothing had been stolen. Though from time to time the searchers would take some valuable "souvenir," the witness would nevertheless be forced to sign that all had been done according to regulations.

They searched the cupboards, opened drawers, fingered the clothing, overturned mattresses and comforters – not a spot was left unattended. The Englishman looked the whole room over, trying to guess where an underground man could hide incriminating material. There was a small cupboard in the corner which aroused his suspicion. He had guessed right – when it was moved, a suspicious tin box was revealed. Confidently he picked it up, the box containing my collection of publications printed for *Lehi* activists and, on opening it, found it to be full of booklets. His curiosity aroused, he brought the box to his friend, the speaker of Hebrew, but the latter was still engrossed in the communist propaganda that seemed so suspicious, so much so that he refused to be diverted. He therefore turned to Shimeon, the upholsterer's apprentice. "Yes Sir!", replied Shimeon politely, rising obediently to his feet. The Englishman pointed to the heading on the top leaflet: "Read it!"

It would never have occurred to Shimeon to refuse to obey a British officer in those difficult times. He willingly opened his mouth to read, but remained thunderstruck and silent when he realized what lay before him. The heading read: *Being a Freedom Fighter*. The word *Herut* (freedom) was one with which every Britisher in Palestine was more than familiar, particularly as it was one of the three words making up the name of *Lehi: Lohamei Herut Israel* (Freedom Fighters of Israel) – none other than the notorious Stern Gang.

The Britisher began to grow impatient with poor Shimeon, standing there openmouthed. What was it that had made the youth so nervous, shuddering, blushing and paling in turn?

"Go on, read it!" he repeated peremptorily. Shimeon knew that you couldn't cheat the British, a dangerous thing to attempt at the time, and he couldn't just stand there dithering forever either, or they would begin suspecting him too. Obviously making an effort he tried to read, but at that moment the Britisher came to the end of his patience: "Nothing?" he asked sharply. "Nothing," repeated Shimeon, mumbling.

The Englishman passed the booklets that had passed inspection to Mother who, in her turn, looked questioningly at Yehoshua. "Burn them!" he whispered to her in French.

The search was over. Shimeon signed a statement to the effect that the searchers had behaved properly and taken nothing (except for Yehoshua, of course). Mother burnt the booklets.

It was only after I returned from work that evening that I learnt the whole story, and I didn't believe my luck. If the British had known what was written in those booklets they would not only have arrested me but my three older brothers and perhaps even my father as well, for there was nothing in the material to indicate whom it belonged to. But, whoever owned that material was obviously a dangerous terrorist trained by the Stern Gang.

Realizing that she couldn't prevent me from keeping forbidden material, Mother called me outside quietly and, taking me by the hand, led me to the kitchen in the yard, at some distance from the house. There, in a hidden corner, stood an old wooden crate. Pointing at it she said: "From now on, if you have something to hide, put it there. If they search the house again I'll leave them inside saying I have to go to the toilet, sneak to the kitchen (which was near the W.C.) and hide it in my clothes. Then I can flush it down the toilet!"

Friday night. Tanchum came to tell me that Yochanan and I had orders to join an important operation next day, on the Sabbath, after morning service. We met in the Mekor Baruch quarter for a briefing.

It had been ascertained that at eleven o'clock Brigadier Davies – Commander of His Majesty's Ninth Division, and just recently nominated commander of the "Pill Operation" (name given to the martial law operation in Tel-Aviv and some Jerusalem quarters) – was in the habit of leaving his home on his way to the Schneller Camp via Hatturim St. He was to be ambushed there by our people and shot to death. Yochanan and I were assigned to a diversionary group, drawing the enemy's attention and covering the retreat of the fighter force.

We were given some empty wooden crates with the word "Mine" written on them in English and Hebrew. Right after the shooting we were to place them on the roads leading to Hatturim St., thus delaying the reinforcements rushing to the scene after the shooting, and ensuring our men of a safe retreat.

We were at our appointed place, sitting and waiting for a sign. As we talked, Yochanan told me the story of his induction to the underground. He was born in Vilno, son of a very large family abounding with uncles, aunts, cousins and their children, all of whom had been exterminated by the Nazis. He and his mother were all that was left. Even those who had made it to the forests and joined the partisans were dead. His sister, whose beauty was a byword in the ghetto, spied for the partisans and was betrayed by them to the Germans, who made her undergo unspeakable tortures before she died. Her death was a great loss to the fighting underground of the Vilno ghetto where she had been admired for her devotion and courage. Her name is mentioned in books describing the Vilno ghetto – Mira Goniondska. He went on to tell me that in 1942, after most of the ghetto had been destroyed, there came a period of relative quiet and there was a lull in the mass executions, Jews being killed only "here and there" in shooting "incidents." The partisans were at that time in a terrible plight, especially the Jewish ones. The Judenrat of the ghetto and his helpers held public meetings at which they denounced the partisans for their "irresponsibility," calling them "insurgents against the public authority who stick a knife into its back"... The public was called to hunt down and denounce these men who "lacked all responsibility."

Somehow Yohanan was among the privileged few who managed to reach Palestine, only to hear those same curses against our freedom fighters from the mouths of our leaders. Over there, in the Vilno ghetto he had been a small, weak child incapable of joining the partisans like the rest of his family. But now, after arriving here, he knew well where his place was.

The minutes passed and Brigadier Davies should be making his appearance at any moment now. At the corner of the street I made out Ben-Zion, accompanied by Achino'am (today Sima Assoulin). I had met Ben-Zion before, a dark, quiet chap, whose very silence seemed to be somehow eloquent. I felt they were there on duty and pretended not to have seen them. Yochanan, who had never met either of them, pointed the couple out to me.

"Look at them," he said. "Somehow they don't look like a natural couple to me... Funny, they don't look like lovers."

Near the Mekor Baruch playground, some distance from us, stood "Old" Danny and "Ginger" Uzi and I saw that they were hiding something under their coats. At that moment a command-car loaded with soldiers appeared, crawling along very slowly, looking in all directions, particularly down the sides of the street. We turned our backs to them and sauntered along in the direction of Alfandari St., returning to our posts as soon as the command-car had disappeared, and expecting at any moment to hear the sound of shots. Time passed slowly. More than an hour had gone by and our Brigadier had failed to show up. Then Tanchum appeared and told us it was all off: "He won't come today. We'll have to do it some other time."

Three days later Ben-Zion was caught in that very area, in Rashi St. This was the beginning of an epoch of heroism which shook the whole country and made a deep impression on the outside world. It was then that I told Yochanan that Moshe Barazani, who had been caught with a grenade in his hand in Rashi St., was none other than the dark-complexioned youth we had seen that Saturday in the company of a blond girl at the corner of Alfandari St. Yochanan was deeply moved when he heard this and changed his code-name to Ben-Zion.

"Datan, I envy You!"

Careful as I was to observe the rules of conspiracy, there was one pleasure I refused to give up, even though it was a distinct infringement of a strict underground rule – I had to meet my friend Ha'im from time to time, despite the fact that we worked in different departments.

It was a turbulent time, not a day going by without something happening. Some of it was of our own doing, and we had a profound need to talk it over with each other. Not that we ever divulged any underground secrets when we met. I never mentioned my affairs at the "Division," to Ha'im or to anybody else. Our discussions were mostly centered on the political situation and possible future developments. Ha'im would lead me to a secret place where he had hidden a freshly printed proclamation of *The Deed* especially for me, so I could read it in quiet, unseen by prying eyes.

I was well aware, of course, that I was breaking the rules of conspiracy, but those meetings were vital to me and I could not have continued without them. Our friendship, nurtured by long dialogues about dangerous situations we had faced together, went on far into the night. Our joint faith was so deep that we believed it would protect us from evil. It was a bond of love, affection, friendship and mutual trust; separation would have been unbearable.

It was the time of Ben-Zion's trial. We knew he was facing the death penalty, and our apprehension was great as we awaited the news.

The expected had occurred! One day, on my way to a meeting with Ha'im, I bought the paper and there it was, the heading on the front page, in screaming black letters: "Moshe Barazani condemned to death by hanging." I was galvanized by shock and my hair literally stood on end.

Ha'im was as stunned as myself, ceaselessly repeating: "They won't hang him; they wouldn't dare. They know how dearly they'll pay for it." But obviously he couldn't convince himself and we were both saddened, and burned with the injustice of it all. "If they hang him we'll pay them back... There'll be a bloody massacre," he said.

"Yes indeed, but the pity of it, a man like Ben-Zion... What a terrible waste!" "You know, Datan, sometimes I envy you. I really do."

I pretended that I didn't understand him, but I did. It hit me suddenly, when I had read the news confirming the fate awaiting Ben-Zion – it could have been me! Like him, I had stood in Hatturim St. that same Saturday when we were planning to ambush Brigadier Davies.

"Do you know why I envy you? I'll tell you – it's because your sacrifice would be so much greater than mine. I'm not seventeen yet and in their eyes I'm not worthy of the death penalty..."

"Better so," I comforted him. "That way your chances are better to go on fighting. There have always been escapes from prison and there always will be. Those that get away get to fight again."

"You're wrong, Datan. To go to the gallows is a very great privilege, for every hanging brings us that much closer to salvation. Every hanging widens the chasm between them and our people. They have always hated us and always will, but if it will make our nation rise up against them, then we must suffer, sacrifice our lives, go to the gallows... You and the other comrades are in constant danger while I, I'm too young..."

Instead of four men wearing the red robe there were now five in the Jerusalem Central Prison. There was Dov Gruner – an *Etzel* member condemned to death after being taken by the British during the attack on the Ramat Gan police station. The others were Eliezer Kashani, Mordechai Alkachi and Yehiel Drezner, all from the *Etzel,* caught after the Night of the Flogging. They were now to be joined by our Ben–Zion Moshe Barazani.

The fury of the underground expressed itself in more frequent and more intensive operations against the British. The soldiers in charge of imposing "Martial Law" became living targets. The Schneller Camp – Jerusalem headquarters from which the orders were issued – was attacked by the *Etzel*. The *Lehi* Center, which now found it difficult to communicate with its branches because of this law, gave each branch *carte blanche* to act independently, without waiting for confirmation of the Center. The branches went full swing into action and not a day passed without mines exploding on the roads and military barracks attacked.

The British were not so lucky this time. During the whole period of martial law they had failed to catch even one of the wanted underground members, and were forced to fill their cells with all kinds of small fry in order to be able to claim that the "object of the operation has been fully realized and many suspects arrested." This was also a good excuse for terminating Martial Law...

On March 17, 1947, two weeks after the British had loudly proclaimed the abolition of martial law, Tanchum informed us that the ambush plan for Metudella St., was again feasible. He gave us two fruit juice bottles and went over the old instructions with us, not forgetting to stress: "As soon as you have thrown the bottles get out! Don't wait for results or look back!"

On the hilltop behind the stone fence we stood watching the road that ran beneath us, the bottles gently held by their necks in our hands. "I wonder what Tanchum was thinking when he drank the orange juice out of the bottles," I muttered. "Do you think he drank it all, two whole bottles?" wondered Yochanan. "Why not? For such a purpose I would have drunk ten bottles..."

There was the armoured car, right on time! As we tightened our hold on the bottles it moved up directly beneath us. We let fly and they shattered on the steel body. There must be no looking back! Run! Unable to resist it, we snatched a quick look at the car. Damnation! The bottles had shattered but failed to ignite.

The bren gun was pointed in our direction and we fled for our lives.

Another Hebrew fighter condemned to death! Me'ir Feinstein, an *Etzel* man who had been badly wounded after the *Etzel* attack on the Jerusalem railway station. He wasn't armed at the time but the British found some ammunition nearby and claimed it was his. They gave him the death penalty.

★

I knew Me'ir well, the son of the late Eliezer, the long-bearded owner of a grocery store in the Kerem quarter. Before moving there they had lived in our lane, in the apartment beneath our veranda. What a stately figure he was, even when serving customers in his little shop. I was always being sent down for something, and Me'ir and I (we were the same age) often played hooky, playing some game or other together.

General Barker left the country, to be replaced by General Macmillan. Both the *Etzel* and the *Lehi* were disgusted at the way Barker had escaped without a scratch, in spite of the many attempts on his life. He was the most hated man in the country. The whole Jewish community resented his crass brutality In one of his "Orders of the Day" he forbade British soldiers to enter any Jewish place of business, his explanation being that: "If you want to hurt the Jews, hurt them in their pockets." This remark was passed on to the public by the underground and aroused everybody's ire.

Before leaving, Barker was careful to confirm the sentence passed on Eliezer Kashani, Mordechai Alkachi and Yehiel Drezner. Dov Gruner's sentence had been confirmed some time before, but its execution was delayed by the kidnapping of Judge Windham and several British officers. The British, naturally, refused to admit that this was the reason for the delay, saying that they were only waiting for the hearing of an appeal presented by the attorney for the defence, Levitzky, in London. The Etzel couldn't keep the kidnapped men too long and let them go. On the morning of April 18, 1947 the whole country was in turmoil: it was learnt that during the night Dov Gruner and his three comrades were transferred from Jerusalem to Acre and there summarily hanged. They were not even given the chance to take leave of their families. The furtive massacre, committed in such haste, revealed once more the panic that had overtaken the British who no longer considered themselves bound by any form of the law obligatory to a governing power, if only for the sake of appearance. They had been lying shamelessly when they declared that Gruner would not be executed until the appeal was heard – a ploy to release the hostages whom the *Etzel* threatened to kill. Some days after Dov Gruner and his comrades were hanged, Macmillan confirmed the sentences of Me'ir Feinstein and Moshe Barazani.

Moshe – our Ben-Zion, and Me'ir, son of Eliezer the grocer.

A Trap set at Night, during the Curfew

Tanchum and I met at "T" (our nickname for the Knesset quarter where two streets met to form a T. "Wait for me near the Menora Club at 9 o'clock. Sha'ul and Hanokh will be there as well. I may be late."

At nine we were there and had to wait for half an hour. This meant something big, we thought.

Tanchum arrived: "At six in the morning two bren carriers go through here, on their way back from controlling the inter-urban curfew. You'll ambush and attack them. Come back at 10.30 and wait for me. Don't go away even if it takes a few hours – I'll come. There are rumors that they're going to hang Feinstein and Barazani tonight. If they impose curfew tonight the operation is off." He left.

We dispersed in order to meet again in an hour. Everyone was on time but Tanchum didn't show up. We waited. "The curfew is a good thing," said Hanokh. "We can attack them with perfect confidence – no need for precautions or anything . Anyone driving on the road is British, there aren't any civilians about during curfew."

Tension was mounting by the minute. There were very few people in the street so we asked if the radio had announced curfews.

"No. No curfew was announced!" That meant there would be none. The British were in the habit of announcing it by means of loudspeakers from their armoured vehicles, which were ceaselessly driving through every street and alley, in addition to the radio announcements. As nothing had been announced on the radio, we were convinced that there was no truth in the rumor. True, the streets were empty, but that in itself did not presage curfew. These nights people preferred to lock themselves inside their houses, fearful of going outside. The streets were crawling with British soldiers who would shoot at passers-by indiscriminately, as the spirit took them. Many were hurt in those "Nights of Horror" (so named by the press when describing these wild outbursts, which were lately becoming a matter of routine). Twice or three times a week they would shoot their light and heavy machine guns from the *Mustashpha* (police station) in Mahane Yehuda and the Schneller Camp. A prowling dog or a passing cat was enough to set off hours of crazy shooting by the terrified look-outs, usually after they had turned on the sirens.

As the street was quiet we thought there was no curfew and stood there waiting for Tanchum, while he prepared the material – a matter of some three hours. We had no idea, and neither did Tanchum, that all the time we had been standing thus, openly in the street, curfew had been declared. The announcement had been given at a time when most of the people were busy and did not listen to the news. We were not the only ones who did not know. A Jew called Ovadiah Mizrahi, father of ten children, was walking along innocently when he was cut down by a passing patrol. A woman who went into the street, unaware of the curfew, was badly wounded.

The days of imposing fines on curfew breakers were long past, nor was any warning given. The "best" thing that could happen to you these days was to be arrested (if not shot) and brutally beaten with fists and the butts of their guns. And there was I, standing between Hanokh and Sha'ul, eagerly awaiting the "Dawn Operation."

Sha'ul was a youth from the Kurdish quarter, one of many who joined the *Lehi* from that area. About half of our young members were from that quarter, including girls who were noted for their strength and courage and had proved themselves as peerless fighters. Many of them who had not come to us went to the *Etzel* – only a few to the *Hagana*. Hanokh came from the Ungaren Houses in the Mea She'arim quarter. It was years since he had cut off his side-curls and stopped observing the commandments. Yet he felt uneasy among the unorthodox people he now lived with, and his membership in *Lehi* gave meaning to his life.

When his mother began suspecting that he was a member of *Lehi*, she became very nervous – this was a worse sin than that of cutting off his side-curls. Angry with him for thus putting his life in danger, she told him there was nothing for him at home. He left, never to return. He worked "full time" in the underground.

176

In time his mother began to regret her hasty temper. Passover was approaching and she couldn't bear the thought of sitting down to the Seder without her Motti. Blaming herself for her thoughtlessness, she left for Tel-Aviv, there to consult her Rabbi. The Rabbi told her to calm herself and promised that Motti would be there for the Seder.

On Passover eve the father and brothers all went to the synagogue, but there was no sign of the boy. They returned from prayers and sat down at the festive table without him, the mother quietly weeping. Then suddenly the door opened and there stood Motti.

"I've had enough. We shouldn't quarrel on the night of the Seder. Even if you send me away, I won't go!"

*

We were beginning to worry about Tanchum. Something had to be very wrong for him to be so late. But finally he arrived, carrying two satchels, one in each hand. In one there were three dismantled machine guns that we would have to put together again before the operation; in the other – explosives.

Tanchum briefed us in detail: an additional floor was being built on the roof of the Etz Ha'im Building at the entrance to Jerusalem. The scaffolding, which had been put up some time ago, had been abandoned and was now deserted, all building having stopped for lack of funds. It was on this floor that we would lay an ambush for the armoured trucks patrolling the Tel Aviv–Jerusalem Road. The moment the trucks appeared, we were to bombard them with the hand-grenades that were tied to highly charged explosives and – as soon as these had gone off – open fire with our tommy guns. In the meantime, till zero hour, we were to hide in a room in the Zichron Yoseph quarter, where we would also be given further instructions.

Just a few hundred meters separated us from that room, but curfew was already in force that night, and our hands were full of explosives and machine guns, the penalty for carrying them (or even being suspected of having traffic with them) was death. Tanchum and Hanokh carried a bag between them, and so did

Sha'ul and myself. Walking along we could hear English voices coming from different directions – the area was crawling with them... The guns in our sacks were still dismantled, so there was no comfort there if we were caught, and the thought of this was very real just then – if they caught us we would surely be hanged. Now, for the first time, I was upset by the thought that I might be taken before I had time to use my gun.

To be taken prisoner did not mean that a freedom-fighter had finished his job. On the contrary, he was now embarked on a new campaign – appearing at the military courts-of-law. How would I behave if I ended up there, I asked myself. Would I make a declarative statement? There seemed little point, after so many had been delivered there by now and the public had become indifferent. The "Workshop" prisoners had made some impression, sitting and singing all through the trial. But I was too poor a singer, and nothing was more irritating than a grating voice, the last thing to arouse any feelings of respect. Finally I did think of a plan that would make a mockery of the British Court Room: every time the presiding judge opened his mouth I would begin quoting some appropriate passages from the liturgy or the Bible. Knowing these by heart I would be able to declaim them loudly and clearly, in a voice so charged with emotion it would drown the remarks of the judge. I had even decided what quotations to use – we Jews have no lack of appropriate quotations for all contingencies. The one I liked best was from Moses' Song of the Sea, sung after he and the Children of Israel had successfully crossed the Red Sea as they were pursued by the Egyptians: "Terror and dread fell upon them; through the might of Thy arm they stayed stone-still while Thy people passed, O Lord." (Exodus, 15: 15–16).

But what about *Hatikva?* If they sentenced me to death I would have to stand up and sing the national anthem, and I shuddered to think what my rendering would do to our "Song of Hope," and that in the presence of journalists and the British oppressors. With my kind of voice I was liable to turn those sacred moments into a farce, a disgrace to myself and the *Lehi*...

★

We were trapped between the British patrols that were stationed at every corner and moved along every street. They were so near to us we could smell the whiskey on their breath. Could it be that they had really missed us? No sooner had we caught our breath at the narrowness of our escape than there was another patrol in front of us. So we progressed, making our way between the patrols. Not a soul was out in the streets but for ourselves and those who sought to kill us as we crawled along, lugging the incriminating satchels between us and evading the patrols and ambushes on every side.

We did it! It was unbelievable, but we were in the Zichron Yoseph quarter, a door was being opened to admit us. Tanchum pushed us into an empty room and the door was immediately pulled shut. Turning to Hanokh I told him he should grow side curls again and say the Benediction of Deliverance (*Hagomel*). I wasn't jesting and nobody laughed. Tanchum excused himself, saying he would be back later, and we began preparing the "Tommies" for action assembling the various parts and greasing them. Finally all was ready, but Tanchum had not returned. Zero hour, 6 a.m., was fast approaching, but there was no sign of him. Where could he be?

Six o'clock. We looked ouside in the half light and got the shock of our lives: the whole quarter was surrounded by soldiers and we could see them entering the houses, accompanied by detectives in civvies. Relentlessly approaching our hide-away they were conducting room to room searches. The ring was closing around us and soon they would reach our room. Hanokh stood up straight and very quietly began singing *Hatikva*.

"We have to be ready," he explained.

"Not on your life!" I berated him. "Not with Tommy-guns ready at hand. Let's think how many of them we can take with us before we go."

I stationed Hanokh behind the door and I crawled under the bed, weapon triggered for action. Sha'ul lay on top of a wardrobe. As soon as they were all inside we would shoot them down before they had even caught sight of us, and go on shooting till they

179

mowed us down. I thought we might take about twenty of them with us.

The nailed boots of the soldiers were now directly beneath our window and we could hear them talking near the door. Caressing the trigger-guard with my finger I began saying *"Shma Israel"* in a whisper. We were ready now, expecting the worst. Nothing for it but to wait. For a moment I thought they had entered our building but I was wrong – it was the adjacent one. The search was very thorough and we could hear every word they were saying, the noise of the objects pushed around, and the curses. We were next in line and getting impatient. Let them come – we were ready for them.

They entered our building and our impatience began to mount. Their footsteps passed by our door but continued towards the stairs leading to the floor above. "They want to live for another ten minutes!" said Hanokh.

The search went on for about a quarter of an hour. Ordinarily, fifteen minutes equal a fourth of an hour, an infinitesimal unit of time in a man's life. But for us it signified nine hundred seconds, each one of them an eternity.

They came down and we could hear them talking in a heavy English accent, as if their tongues were scalded. Where the hell were they going now? Why didn't they come in? Didn't they realize we had a warm welcome ready for them? But, wanting to drive us crazy, they chose the opposite apartment, the other one on our floor. Through the thin partitions we could hear everything that was going on there: drawers opened, furniture moved around, mattresses thrown – all to the tune of questions and invective. It was almost more than we could do to control our trigger finger, but we forced ourselves to wait, to be patient for another second, another minute...

Time seemed to have become a changed dimension. It had grown heavier, every second assuming immense proportions, pressing down to crush us. Our bodies no longer felt as if they belonged to us, each part of them seeming to have grown a will of its own. I was no longer "I" but a conglomerate of nerves and limbs. My finger was independently aware of its duty to press the trigger properly and at the right time; my eyes were riveted to the door, to catch the enemy as soon as he entered; the arm to which the finger belonged sensed the need to support the hand; the lips knew that they had to murmer a prayer for our delivery. From time to time we would grind our teeth and bite our lower lip, the tongue slipping between the teeth and softening the grinding. Our ears were tensed, absorbing any sound, however slight, even the words murmured by the enemy behind the wall. But tensest of all was the heart, beating loudly and strongly as the heavy minutes pressed upon it; beating out the pain for my friends Sha'ul and Hanokh, Hebrew freedom fighters like myself, now waiting for their death, which might come at any second. My heart-beats accelerated wildly as I thought of Father and Mother, of the parents of Hanokh and Sha'ul, the terror-stricken faces of brothers and sisters when they heard the worst from the messengers... What unbearable pain we would cause our dear ones, what torture were we inflicting on our most beloved...

My eyes were suddenly bathed in tears which began coursing down my cheeks, bringing relief to the over-heated brain. Each part of the body knew its appointed task and all it had to do now was wait.

An unbelieveable message was suddenly heard: "They are leaving!!!"

How can that be? They must be hungry... going for a snack... Their breakfast is waiting for them outside and they'll be back right after. But the signs are unmistakeable – they go further and further away, up to the high rise of the alley, where they take the turn and disappear...

"Hanokh, go to the window," I whisper. He leaves his post behind the door and looks outside. "They're gone!" he announces.

Sha'ul climbs down from the wardrobe and leaves the room, saying he was going to the neighbours to find out what had happened. Sha'ul knows the people who had loaned us the room. We had no idea who they were but he certainly did – they were his brother and sister-in-law.

When he returned, he brought us the ill tidings that Me'ir

Feinstein and Moshe Barazani had killed themselves by detonating a bomb pressed between their two bodies. This tragedy occurred in the Jerusalem prison shortly before the British were to take them to be hanged.

The curfew was over, the British gone. There was not a house in the quarter that had not been thoroughly searched, not a room, not a cupboard left unturned. The one room they had managed to overlook had been ours... a miracle!

A Grenade between Two Hearts

Robed in crimsom garments, Me'ir Feinstein and Moshe Barazani, both condemned to death, languished in their death cell in the Jerusalem prison. When the British decided to carry out the execution, they called Rabbi Aryeh Levin to visit the prisoners and hear their last confession.

Fearing that his weak heart wouldn't stand the strain, the Rabbi declined. He also insisted that people about to be martyred had no need of confession.

Rabbi Aryeh knew the prisoners of the underground very well, particularly the two who had been condemned to death. He had visited them often in their cell and had grown deeply attached to them. The aging Rabbi had never before been put off by the sight of pain or suffering – day and night he would be out on some errand of mercy for the oppressed and the miserable, the suffering and the rejected. Be they prisoners or lepers, it was with them he spent his Sabbaths and Holy Days, giving them support and new-found courage. He regarded the prisoners of the underground as so many devoted sons and was like a father to them. They, in turn named him "Father of the Imprisoned." The wonderful old Rabbi was full of admiration for their peerless courage and whole-hearted sacrifice, and thus there grew a relationship of profound love between him and the prisoners. But now, on being asked to go and hear their last confession, he feared he would break down in their presence, "And why cause these lads any more suffering?"

The prison authorities then asked Rabbi Goldman, representative of the National Council in charge of the religious needs of the prisoners, to come and hear the last confession of Feinstein and Barazani.

At 9.30 p.m., the Rabbi met them in their death cell and they knew the reason for his coming, having been informed three hours before that they would be executed at sunrise. The two lads, clothed in the red robes of the condemned, asked the Rabbi to say goodbye to their families for them and begged for their forgiveness for all the sorrow they had brought upon them. Moshe Barazani apologized for their unorthodox clothing at this meeting with so important a personage, and said: "...We were just going to bed."

Me'ir Feinstein said that they had no regrets. "Better to die with a weapon in your hand than live with your hands raised in surrender."

Rabbi Goldman told them about our national martyrs, Rabbi Akiva and his friends; the countless martyrs who had sanctified the name of the Lord in the days of the Roman conquest, during the many Crusades and under Hitler. He called himself unworthy to hear their confession! He envied them, for it was not given to every Jew to lay down his life for the glory of the Lord.

Most of us lived out the span of our lives with nothing to show for it but bitterness and frustration. Happy were the heroes of Israel who had found a meaning in their lives and therefore in their death.

The two were overcome by his words, repeatedly asking him for chapter and verse of all the ideas he had quoted to them. From time to time they joked and even laughed with him, to the everlasting wonder of the guard sitting there during the Rabbi's visit. "Never," he told the Rabbi as the latter was on his way out, "have I seen anything like this. Who would believe that men can behave like that in the very presence of death!"

Rabbi Goldman suggested that they all read the prayer *Adon Olam* (Lord of the World) – praising their Maker for having granted them this unique opportunity. They agreed and asked that they be allowed to sing it.

And so the three stood up and sang "Lord of the World, who

ruled it before any living thing was created." Their voices rose higher and higher, the English guard standing and listening open-mouthed. When the song reached its end the Rabbi promised to return on the morrow, to be with them in their last hour. They begged him to spare himself the trouble, but he insisted that he felt he had to be with them, to tell their friends, their families, the wide world...

Feinstein and Barazani had a secret but they couldn't let the good Rabbi in on it. They had a basket of oranges which contained two hand grenades, one for each of them and for their hangman as well. That was why they begged the Rabbi not to come. When they realized that no power on earth could stop him they parted from him amicably. After he had left they decided to give up their idea of dying like Samson, taking their torturers with them, for this might now endanger the Rabbi. Clutching their grenades close to their heart, the two embraced, with Feinstein holding Barazani with his one hand, having lost the other in fighting. Barazani also held Feinstein with one hand and with the other released the pin.

A terrible explosion shattered the quiet of the prison and the hangman in it...

The Target: Macmillan

"Ginger" Uzi wanted to have a talk with me, and informed me that I was to join him on an important operation. As I looked at him I realized what a deep affection I felt for him, as well as profound admiration. I had already seen him once, from afar, when, together with "Old" Danny he was waiting to ambush Brigadier Davies. And now we were face to face. "What a Hercules," I said to myself. It was men like him who gave the phrase "the arm and muscle of the *Lehi*" true meaning and content. Like everyone else who came in contact with Uzi, I was immediately enveloped by the strength and confidence he exuded. Much later I was to hear about some of his heroic adventures: how he was the only one who had managed to escape from the bloody night battle at the Workshops; how he had cut his hands, first the one then the other, on the electrified fence at Latrun, on his way to freedom and rejoining the fighting. But by the time these stories reached me I knew Uzi well and nothing could surprise me any more. On the contrary, it seemed the most natural behavior for him.

Uzi began explaining the operation. The target: General Macmillan.

Macmillan – Commander-in-Chief of His Majesty's Forces in Palestine and Trans-Jordan, heir of Barker, the antisemitic general who had signed the death sentence of Me'ir Feinstein and Moshe Barazani – would not get away alive. A powerful mine had been placed by our people in one of the twists of the road leading out of Jerusalem. It was the General's custom to leave the city for several hours, between eight a.m. and 4 p.m., by that route, and our men were waiting for him.

On Sunday he failed to show up, on Monday too. Eli and Drora had waited for him in vain. No matter, we would wait for him on Tuesday and Wednesday, and on Thursday too... But the look-outs had to be relieved. "You and Ahino'am will be waiting for him on his way out of town. You will meet each morning at eight o'clock at the corner of Jaffa and King George Streets and take a leisurely walk to the west. If you see the general leaving, send Ahino'am home at once and come to me," were Uzi's instructions.

He explained that the General's convoy was unmistakable. He always drove a luxurious yellow car, preceded and followed by jeeps with mounted machine guns. I was given a photograph of the General with the impressive moustache. "For the first five minutes of every hour I'll be waiting for you on the steps of the Nachlat Zion quarter," said Uzi. "From the moment he leaves town until he returns there'll be plenty of time for us to get the weapons and reach the place of ambush."

I had a two-day "sick," two shillings' worth from Dr. S. This "sick" might prove much more costly if the British should find out the true diagnosis of my illness, I ruminated. I had Dr. S., working for the underground and he wasn't even aware of it.

At eight o'clock next morning I met Ahino'am near the telephone booth at the Mahane Yehuda quarter. Ahino'am, red-cheeked and blonde haired, was a girl of Mugrabi origins. She had a lovely voice and a pleasant appearance. I had met her long before the underground brought us together, for her father owned a grocery store in the Ohel Moshe quarter, and we had both been members of the *Brith Hashmona'im* movement before joining the *Lehi.*

In order to avoid any chance meeting with a postman passing by, we quickly left the center of town and went in the direction of Rommema, where we sat down on the steps of the "Old People's Home." There we got into conversation with three oldsters, the sum of whose years was surely around two hundred and eighty, and enjoyed their company no less than they did ours. After all, we did make an interesting change in their humdrum lives, and at the same time gained a short interlude of respite from our constant state of tension. There was one old man who took the greatest delight in our company, a granddad whose great-grandchildren were by now themselves parents. His joy knew no bounds when he realized I understood many languages. He started off with Hebrew, went on to Arabic, then to French and from that to Ladino – Jewish Spanish. Not every day could he meet someone conversant in all these languages... It was a wonderful opportunity for him to show off his linguistic versatility – perhaps the last in his life.

He talked and we watched the road. He recounted the adventures of his youth, when the Turks ruled the country, while we followed with our eyes each passing car. The kindly grandmothers and grandfathers made us promise to abide by the Commandments and seek to do good deeds, for it was those things only that one could take with him to Heaven. Listening to their gentle preaching, I couldn't help wondering who would get there first – these kindly old souls or my friend and I... Pleasant as it was, sitting there on the stairway to their Home, we suddenly became impatient, took our leave of them and started walking. Leaving the Rommema quarter we turned gradually westward, toward Lifta, where we looked at an Arab school in Upper Lifta, near the main road.

"Canoodling behind the Rocks..."

A couple of Arab youths came out of the school yard, eyeing us wildly and whispering excitedly. My hearing was excellent and I could hear every word they were saying, as well as note their smallest movements. They were obviously speculating about us... Young couples strolling along a Jewish street were commonplace but not so in an Arab village, where such a sight was inconceivable. If the couple was engaged – they would be surrounded by members of the family, if married – the woman's place was in the home or in the field. Should the two have to go out together, the man would go a few paces before the woman, on foot or astride a donkey, completely free of any burden, while she followed him on foot, a basket loaded with vegetables or goods on her head. One of the boys was now telling the other loudly, and clearly: "Over there, do you see the place? That's where he shoved it into her..."

The two were now joined by a few more, all staring coldly at us. The one who had "guessed" what we had been doing behind the rocks now forgot that it was just a guess and began telling the others exactly what he had seen us doing there, his companion swearing by Allah and the Prophet that it was the truth and he, too, had witnessed the deed...

Ahino'am sensed that all was not going well and asked me to tell her what they were saying, something I was too embarrassed to do. "Let's get out of here!" I said, but this was easier said than done. School was over at that hour and a growing mob of pupils flowed into the street and surrounded us, their impudence growing by the minute. Some of them came near enough to touch Ahino'am and even push her. When she tried to get away they asked angrily: "Aren't you ashamed to lie with him, you whore?" cursing and spitting at us. Realizing the danger, we began hurrying towards the Rommema quarter where there were many Jews, but as soon as we had put some distance between us they began throwing stones, slowly at first and then a veritable hail, ranging from pebbles to rocks. We began running in earnest. A stone grazed my earlobe and another touched Ahino'am's hair. We began to doubt that we would get out of there unharmed, and indeed they pursued us well into Rommema, where they finally gave up and returned to their village. Ahino'am and I looked at each other in wonder – we were both unhurt, not a scratch on either of us. What luck!

The following day I went to Rommema again, accompanied this time by Geulah. We walked along, stopping from time to time. During one of our stops we looked into the entrance of the Sha'arei Zedek Hospital where there were a few ambulances in one of which the driver was sleeping, his head on an open newspaper. "Are you thinking what I'm thinking, Geulah?" I asked her.

"Of course."

"Well, what was I thinking of?"

"The ambulances. How they would all get moving when..." She gave me a meaningful look and I knew that she had read my thoughts.

"I wish he would hurry up, that General, why doesn't he come..."

This was the fourth day we had been waiting for him – four days since he had last left Jerusalem. This was unusual, for Uzi had told us he left for the Plains at least twice a week.

Again we came to the steps of the Old People's Home and sat down, hoping to kill time in conversation with the inmates. But the steps were empty. It seems that the heat had driven the old people inside, and no wonder. Were it not for my "appointment" with my General I too would have preferred to stay inside.

To amuse Geulah and relax the tension a little, I began recounting the tales told by the aged centenarian the day before. But it was too hot to sit there in the burning sun so we got up and continued walking listlessly till we arrived at the Etz Ha'im Yeshiva where we stopped, the events of the day before having stirred my curiosity about Lifta. Sitting on the fence opposite the Women's Aid Hospital, we tried to catch what was being said by the inmates there, all of whom were mental cases. The men in the male branch were shouting something to the women in the other parts of the building. As I raised my head I realized I was looking at the unfinished building where we had been forced to abort our last operation.

"What's so interesting there?" asked Geulah. I couldn't tell her, of course. Not even Ha'im had heard the story of that night. "Hey, MacMillan won't come from there, you know. He'll come by road!" She was right. I turned to look at the road and at that very moment saw the jeep, on which was mounted a Browning machine gun and a Bren. It was followed by a yellow car and then another jeep. "You've no idea how right you are," I told Geulah and took a good look at Macmillan, sitting at ease in the back seat.

A quick glance at my watch told me it was 10.45. Good! I had fifteen minutes till my meeting with Uzi; just the amount of time needed for a leisurely walk.

Geulah agitatedly wished me good luck as we parted. She left me and I went on slowly towards the Nachlat Zion quarter. Uzi arrived just as I reached the steps and when he heard that the General had left, was clearly excited. Hard to believe but true – Uzi was agitated! For all his famed imperturbability this was no ordinary operation...

"We've got plenty of time to prepare everything carefully. Wait for me here. I'm going to bring the weapons."

Within ten minutes Uzi was back with a rucksack on his shoulder. "Come on," he said. As we walked he gave me the details of the plan. "There are five grenades in the rucksack – four for you and one for me; two flash bombs, one for each of us and two pistols, one for you and one for me. There's an electric battery, a switch and a pair of binoculars. When I press the switch the mine will be activated. You, Datan, will throw three grenades on the front and rear jeeps. We'll each keep a grenade in reserve, together with the flash bomb and the pistol, for our retreat. No grenades in a populated area, remember. We don't want to harm civilians. A flash bomb will scare off the pursuers."

"What if the mine doesn't destroy the General's car?"

"In that case the blast will blow him down the steep incline and he won't have much chance of staying alive. It's a very powerful mine and I wouldn't be surprised if the rear jeep was blown up too."

As we passed by the Giv'at Shaul quarter, Uzi pointed out where the mine had been buried and showed me the end of the wire which we had to join to the battery and the switch when the time came. We now climbed up a hill at a distance of some hundred and fifty meters from the mine. Here Uzi looked through the binoculars and handed them to me, pointing to a certain part of the road, about five kilometers long and lying south-west. "This part has to be watched every moment – we mustn't let it out of our sight. When our 'Friend' comes here we'll have plenty of time to go down, join the wire to the battery and wait."

After a while Uzi said: "It'll be easy for you. The grenades will roll down in the right direction of their own volition, because of the incline. The only thing we can do now is pray that no Jewish vehicle will show up here when the General arrives. If one does we have strict orders not to activate the mine."

It is no easy task to watch through binoculars on a hot day at midday. That critical section of the road had to be under observation every second or, we might miss our chance. We took turns at it, with Uzi showing much more stamina at the job than me. After three or four minutes I would lose my power of concentration and pass the binoculars to him. He could hold out for a quarter of an hour...

"The General!"

Time passed and the heat became oppressive. Our sight was becoming blurred. After three hours had gone by we suddenly became wide awake for he could be expected at any moment now. Alert and almost unbearably tense we waited for a whole hour before Uzi cried: "I can see a yellow car!"

"The General?"

"It's hard to say. There were other vehicles there and I couldn't see if they were jeeps, or something else."

"So what are we to do?"

"Go down towards the road and see if it's really his car."

I did as he told me and a strange sight was revealed. Hundreds of vehicles filled the curve in the road which hid the end of the convoy in the distance. When I told Uzi he said: "They may have discovered the mine and stopped the traffic. Wait here, while I go down and see."

Uzi returned very quickly. "What a mess! Let's get out of here. They've found the mine."

We decided to hide the weapons in a nearby cave Uzi knew of, in case we were searched in one of the Jewish quarters at the entrance to town. No sooner did we set out for Giv'at Shaul than we saw hundreds of British soldiers, armed and led by dogs, coming directly towards us. The dogs went along, sniffing their way, and the soldiers followed them, their eyes on the ground. We were in an empty, bare area and our only chance was to try to get lost in one of the alleys of Giv'at Shaul, about fifty meters away. But to do this we had to advance towards the British, who were about a hundred meters away from us, the distance lessening as we moved in the same direction from which they were coming.

"When will they raise their heads above the dogs?"

"When they see us we'll make a run for it to Giv'at Shaul," Uzi whispered. "Till then let's walk quickly but not run."

And so we walked towards them, their eyes riveted to the ground. The distance between us was diminishing. They were watching the dogs sniffing along. We were walking quickly in a field full of stones. For some inexplicable reason the many rocks we trod on in our hurry never slipped or made a noise. Here, at last, was the alley. Another ten meters, another seven, five.... the miracle of it! We were inside! Out of sight. We started running madly. Never would I have believed I could run so fast. In a few seconds we passed the main road dividing the quarter along the center. We "flew" through Kiryat Moshe, crossed the road leading to Beit Hakerem and reached Zichron Yoseph. Only then did we begin to feel safe.

"A pity!" remarked Uzi. "When we were planning the operation I suggested that another mine should be planted to trap the British reinforcements who came after the first explosion. The Center didn't accept my idea."

It was indeed a pity, for it would have been some compensation for our failure when the first mine was discovered. "Yes," I replied. What more was there to say?

We parted with some emotion and I went home, full of frustration at the failure of our operation. At the time I derived no satisfaction from the fact that we had managed to escape nor had I any thought of what our fate would have been if we had hung about there for a few minutes more, to be caught with the grenades and the binoculars.

That evening we heard a tremendous explosion. The Police announced that its sappers had blown up an enormous mine found in the Jerusalem-Jaffa road.

*

Full of frustration, I couldn't reconcile myself to such a run of bad luck. What was happening to us lately that everything was going so badly? The discovery of the mine intended for MacMillan – was that just bad luck? And the Saturday when we lay in ambush for Brigadier Davies and armoured cars appeared in his stead in Hatturim Street at midday was that, too, pure chance? And the way they caught Ben-Zion – chance again? Then there was a whole series of operations planned against certain Englishmen who suddenly disappeared for no good reason. How could they have all gotten away just when we had our plans for them? Could it be that the *Hagana,* which by now did not dare attack us openly, had infiltrated an agent into our lines, an agent or agents who reported to the enemy and gave him ample warning... Hadn't the Jewish Agency promised the British to fight against the "terror" not only verbally but actively?

Tanchum heard me out thoughtfully. He himself had had many "accidents" which he could not then discuss. Still, they might all have been just that – "accidents."

Shortly after our talk, suspicion fell on a certain person and he was expelled from the organization.

*

Bitter experience had taught the British to admit as few citizens as possible into their security zones. It was information supplied to the underground by civilian government workers that facilitated many of our operations. For this reason one day, together with a young Arab postman, I was called to the Post Office aministration where we were told that, for reasons of security, all permits for postmen to enter Security Zone "B" (extending from the King David Hotel to the heart of Rehavia) were cancelled. We two, out of all the postmen, were the only ones considered loyal and worthy of entering this zone. We were therefore sent to have our photographs taken by the Armenian photographer near the Fast Hotel. A few days later we were handed our special permits. My job was to deliver the mail to the Jews who had not been evacuated from the area, and my Arab colleague would be my replacement if I should ever be absent from duty.

It was no surprise to me that I should arouse such trust. The "terrorists" were envisaged as violent, frightening characters while I, even though I was already over eighteen and no longer a child, was thin and innocent-looking. It was inconceivable that a harmless type like me would have anything to do with "that kind of business."

When I went into Zone "B" I would show my permit to the guards who examined my post bag, looked at the packages, and showed an interest in the stamps. None of them bothered to open any of the packages, for a postman with the right papers and the appearance of a well-behaved child aroused no suspicion whatsoever.

In time the guards got to know me and stopped asking for my permit. Nor did they bother to inspect my bag... Sometimes, their eyes filled with longing, they would ask me: "Any mail from my girl?" "Sure," I would reply, opening the bag and pulling out a bar of chocolate. "This is from your girl." I would offer him a piece, and his companion, who also got some, asked: "Why does she send you Lieber chocolate and not Cadbury?"

The soldiers got to know me well and were quite friendly. I felt confident that I could enter the Zone at any time, even if the permit were rescinded. Thus convinced, I began thinking of various possibilities of striking at His Majesty's Forces... From time to time I proposed certain operations to the Center. One of these was to steal a military car, load it with dynamite and drive it into the security zone, where it was to be parked – not just beside any building housing soldiers but – beside General MacMillan's house. It transpired that no vehicle could be parked there. The building, formerly used by General Barker (today the residence of *Lehi* Commander, Prime Minister Yitzhak Shamir!) was so heavily fenced by barbed wire that the General himself was forced to park at some distance away from it.

One morning as I was coming down the steps of the King David Hotel, where I had just made a delivery, I felt myself rudely pushed aside by some soldiers who told me sternly to stand back as a very important personage was on his way. "The G.O.C., is coming!" they said. I had hardly grasped what they meant when I saw my old "friend," General MacMillan there before me, surrounded by a group of colonels, his thick moustache covering most of his red face. They passed me by without a glance quickly followed by their rear guard – four soldiers carrying rifles and machine guns.

If only I had a grenade! I would have thrown it without hesitation at the head of the G.O.C., not giving a damn if I was blown up with him...

The opportunity passed. But who knows, it might return in the future.

Upstairs in this building was his place of work. A quick glance at the watch – eight thirty. Did he come here every day at that hour to go up to his head-quarters in this hotel? I would have to return and find out. It was also important to know what route he used from his home to the hotel. As soon as I had ascertained all these details I would try and appropriate a grenade from the underground stores. This presented difficulties, for the Center would never countenance such an operation, just as it had always turned down suicide operations. I would have to get the grenade secretly... Was there a chance I could possibly convince them? No. It wouldn't work. I had to try and work out a way to retreat after it was done.

From that moment I began to shadow MacMillan. Every morning I followed him from his home. It was an easy task. The man was punctual. At eight twenty-five every morning he would emerge from his house and go on foot to Wauchope St., (today Moshe Hess St.,) walk around the tin fence surrounding the Y.M.C.A football ground to Julian St., where he crossed the road and entered the hotel. At eight-thirty exactly he went up to his head-quarters, accompanied by two or three high ranking officers. Three to five soldiers armed with rifles and machine guns preceded him to clear the way, and the rear guard, some ten meters behind, also comprised some three to five armed men.

If that is the usual procedure within the security zone, I thought – where only a chosen few are permitted to enter – how does he behave outside?

If I were to wait for him there, at the corner of the Y.M.C.A. fence, I calculated, I would be visible only to someone who was no further than a few meters from me. I would let the forward guard go past together with the General and his companions, and then, just before the arrival of the rear guard, throw the bomb at him and immediately fall flat on the ground where I would be protected by the fence. With the danger of shrapnel past I would grab my bike and fly for Rehavia... The rear guard and other soldiers alerted by the explosion would at first be too busy looking for cover and only later remember a postman flying by on his bike, by which time I would be far from the scene of action.

Great! – I thought. Not only the General would be taken care of, but so would a few members of his staff...

The next problem would be: how to get out of the security zone? My special permit enabled me to come and go at will in the area, but after the explosion it was reasonable to suppose that all points of entry would be closed. What, then, was I to do? Then I remembered a certain place in Arlozorov St., which provided me with just what I needed. Between the enclosed zone and the open one in Rehavia there was a barbed wire fence which was so positioned that it was invisible to the soldiers guarding the gate in Ben-Maimon St. Nothing would be easier than laying my bike across the barbed wire to form a bridge to the other side. Even if I was seen there was no problem, because friends would be waiting for me with a car and they would take care of the soldiers.

195

Once I had carried out my project I would have to leave home and my job, disappear in the underground. Ezra Yakhin, postman, would be a thing of the past. Anyone desirous of winning the prize which would surely be offered for his head would have to try very hard to find him. He would have a new name, a different appearance and a new address.

I now decided to prepare a detailed plan and present it to the Center, but before this could be done I had to verify just how practical my idea was. Every morning I began going into the security zone, stop at "my" corner and appear absorbed in arranging piles of postage material on the fence. The first time I did this I was approached by the General's forward guard and asked what I was doing. I told them I was sorting out the material for delivery, and a quick glance at my bag satisfied them. After that I stood there every morning, classifying the mail or cleaning my bike, and they got so used to seeing me there that they paid me no more attention.

At this stage I sent a note to my division commander, telling him that I was in the position to liquidate MacMillan. I gave the note to Tanchum and two days later was called for an interview with Dyll, Commander of the Jerusalem Division.

After presenting my plan in detail, I suggested that the bomb be placed inside a package of books, one of those that I used to deliver daily to the English Mission in Mammilla Rd., – inside the military zone. The bomb could be activated by one of the strings with which the package was tied, and explode immediately, within two seconds. This would give me time to fall down flat but would take the General completely by surprise. He would be dead before he realized what hit him!

Dyll listened and examined the details of the plan, which seemed good and feasible. The chances that MacMillan would get away with his life were minimal, but on the other hand, so were mine... After all, the whole area was crawling with soldiers like vermin, and once they caught sight of me...

"Listen! Don't you think it would be worth your while to throw a smoke bomb?" Dyll suggested. "The smoke would provide you with cover and make your getaway easier..."

When all the contingencies had been covered Dyll said: "Can you do it the day after tomorrow?"

"The day after tomorrow?" I repeated after him, my enthusiasm rapidly mounting. "Yes. I'll ask the Center for their approval and if I get it there's every chance it can be implemented immediately."

We made an appointment for the following day, in the alley adjoining the *Matza* factory, to which I promised to bring some packages of "Holy Writ" designated for the English Mission.

Just before the meeting I hid the books in an empty field, so as not to meet Dyll with the packages in my hands. All I needed was to have him arrested for stealing the stuff..

I was on tenterhooks to learn if the Center had accepted my plan – but Dyll wasn't there as we had agreed. I waited for a quarter of an hour; half an hour; a whole hour. The Center had to accept my plan.. But what if they didn't? We all wanted to do away with the General, but perhaps they thought I couldn't get away with it? Underground members had carried out many dangerous missions, but never where a way of retreat was not assured beforehand. The underground did not countenance suicide missions. Was it possible that the Center considered my idea an offer to commit suicide? In that case I would have to force them to accept it. I would tell them bluntly that I would do it anyway. If they helped me, I would have a good chance of getting away. If not – then it really would be a suicide mission. What were we waiting for? Did we want MacMillan to escape like MacMichael and Barker before him? So I stood there, my mind churning with what I would say to Dyll, but still he didn't come. Finally, despairing of him, I gathered up my parcels and prepared to go in search of Tanchum – when there he was.

"What happened?" I inquired, my eyes full of hope and even supplication.

"Sorry. I couldn't make it in time."

"Well?" I asked, my voice firm, as if I was the one in command.

He gave me a strange look, and I repeated my question, this time letting a hint of apology into my voice, as if I regretted my outburst, yet insisted on an explanation.

"Listen Datan," he replied in a fatherly tone, putting his hand on my shoulder. "The Center is studying your plan, examining it from all possible aspects. There's a good chance it will be confirmed in the near future and till then, Datan, patience! Be patient, Datan. And in the meantime keep yourself in readiness. The confirmation may come any day."

We parted and I felt terribly bewildered. He had said the chances were good, but when? One needed to have nerves of steel to sustain such tension, day in day out, hour by hour, not knowing what to expect. Till that moment everything had seemed so clear-cut; either the plan was confirmed or it was turned down. If the latter – I had intended to move heaven and earth till they reversed their decision; but if that didn't work then I would have gone the way of Samson, who chose to die with the Philistines... I had certainly not expected to be left dangling thus in uncertainty, in a constant state of expectation for I knew not what...

Outwardly my life went on as usual. I got up and went to work every morning, knocking on doors, bringing good news or bad, as the case may be, but in reality obsessed by my daily confrontation with that army commander near the Y.M.C.A. fence at half-past-eight. Never did the villain let me down – always there on the dot and obviously never in need of a "sick" for a single day...

All the soldiers stationed at the gate of zone "B" knew me well by then, considered me their friend. They had long ceased asking about letters from their girls back home and whenever they saw me came straight to the point: "Any chocolate from my girl?" Those on patrol around the Y.M.C.A. fence were accustomed to seeing me there every day, sorting out the mail and arranging the parcels of books for the Mission. Fortunately for them the parcels really contained what they were purported to contain at the time! Even the G.O.C. himself was familiar with me by then, and would return my salute.

As a child I had been enchanted by the movie "The Invisible Man" and dreamt that I, too, would one day become a powerful magician capable of observing everything and everybody while remaining unseen myself. What tricks I would play then! That dream was now a reality. There I was, a veritable invisible man, able to watch the enemy of my people, follow him, lay a trap for him while his guards looked on, ignorant of what they were seeing. To them I was just a young postman, a pleasant youth eager to supply them with mail and chocolate. Datan the freedom fighter, the real me, was invisible to them!

The Center is Silent

It was a turbulent time, not a day going by without some underground operation. The railway lines were often mined by *Lehi,* and traffic by train was almost at a stand-still. Driving on the roads of the country became the Englishmen's nightmare. The oil pipe line was constantly being sabotaged by the *Etzel* and the *Lehi,* and enemy strongholds were attacked by the *Etzel,* who used barrel bombs (barrels filled with explosives which were catapulted by lever from trucks). In their treatment of the enemy there was now virtually no difference between the two organizations, and I realized the Center might be too busy to consider my proposition. Yet I was convinced that killing MacMillan outweighed any number of other operations, and the conviction changed me from a passive follower of orders into a somewhat impatient critic. I would ruminate on the Biblical Ehud Ben Gera, who took it upon himself to stab and kill Eglon, King of Moab, who had long oppressed our people; or David in the Emek Ela, striking down the giant who had cursed the Israeli forces. How I envied Ehud-Ben Gera, it had been so much easier for him; he had no need of permission from a Center that kept such an inscrutable silence...

I was obsessed by that silence day and night, wearing myself out in the effort to understand it, when the astounding events in Acre put an end to this fruitless speculation. *Etzel* prisoners interred in the Acre fortress managed to break through the wall, enabling tens of underground men to escape. The whole thing was unbelievable! The prison was an ancient crusaders' fort, well-buttressed by enormously thick walls and located in a predominantly Arab neighbourhood, unfriendly and violent. The price exacted by this operation was very high indeed: nine men were killed during the break-out and the getaway. But for the British this was the last straw! They had long learnt to distrust their prisons and strongholds, but an escape from Acre Prison, that impregnable bastion, was something totally unheard of. The freedom fighters had achieved the impossible...

I consoled myself that the Center, fearing to endanger the escape, had set aside the plan for assassinating MacMillan until the former was safely over. But now there was nothing to hinder them from accepting my plan. Yet several days went by without a word. I began sending those in charge numberless notes and reminders, begging them to agree. They replied that the time was not right, that there were good reasons for delay and that I should stop worrying, as they had not forgotten me.

Three of the raiders on the Acre Prison were caught and sentenced to death: Avshalom Haviv, Me'ir Nakar and Ya'acov Weiss were awaiting execution, and I realized that the Center could not act for fear of forcing the hands of the British and making them rush the execution. Conversely, if the sentences were carried out, my operation would be a fitting act of reprisal.

Full of apprehension I waited to see what the fate of the three would be. They were duly hanged, but still no confirmation from the Center...

Exasperated beyond reason I sat down and wrote a letter, more in the nature of an ultimatum than a request for explanations. I warned them that I would carry out my intention even if they withheld their permission and assistance, well aware that this was suicidal. If they wanted me to have some chance of success they had better accept my plan and work out the details as soon as possible.

This time the answer was not long in coming. The very next day I met the new Division Commander, Amihai – none other than my former firearms instructor at the course we had in Ra'anana. He agreed that my plan was good but told me that the Center was considering another one, far less dangerous. If that failed they would then try mine.

Shortly afterwards I learnt that a large mine, intended for General MacMillan, had been discovered in the Rommema quarter. At this news my hopes rose again, beginning a new period of tension and suspense.

Every day brought its quota of sadistic reprisals perpetrated by the British: private homes were fired into, "illegal immigrants" deported, civilians arrested and killed. Yet the Center, though it was well aware of the fact that I was in a position to strike at the man who pulled all the strings, kept silent.

Then came the greatest crime of all, horrifying the whole country and causing me much personal grief and anguish.

★

A short notice appeared in the press, reporting the formation of "Special Counter-insurgency Squads". There were two such groups, each consisting of ten men, some of whom, it was rumored, were members of the Nazi Mosley party. There were all kinds of adventurers in this group, as well as military officers, dissatisfied with what the ordinary army had to offer. David Charteris*, in his study of the Jewish-British conflict at that particular period, has this to say about them:

> "Field Marshall Montgomery had been pressing the Government for a
> tougher stand against terrorism and by January 1947 his view was
> gaining ground; the Cabinet approved a directive to the High
> Commissioner that, 'Such actions as you may take to implement the
> policy... will receive the full support of His Majesty's Goverment'.*
> This was surely nothing less than a 'blank cheque' from the cabinet..."

As for us, we couldn't imagine what these squads could do to us that had not been done already. Our instructions were to be doubly careful.

---

* Charteris David A., *Special Operations in Counter-Insurgency: The Farran Case, Palestine 1947. p. 58* Department of History, University of New Brunswick, Canada.
* Ibid, Cabinet Minutes, (47), 6th conclusion, 15 January, 1947, CAB. 128/9.

Where is the Boy?

Whenever I saw a new poster of *The Deed* on the walls of Jerusalem, I used to go and see Ha'im to talk over its contents. This time I met Issachar on the way, and was stunned to hear that Ha'im had been arrested.

Somehow I couldn't take it in, it seemed so unreal. Who would put up *The Deed* now? At first we used to go out pasting together – twice even three times a week. After that Ha'im continued with other lads, but what now? And what would become of me? How could I go on without my best friend? There wasn't another person on earth I could talk to so openly, with such trust... What would I do without Ha'im?

I asked for details: How had he been caught? Where? Where was he being held? Would he be exiled to Africa? What were his chances of escape? Was he armed when they got him or just carrying the sheets?

The first real news we got of him was very disquietening. The British police denied having arrested him at all – they had no such prisoner – and this in spite of witnesses who had seen him being forcefully dragged into a car by them.

Before the arrest Ha'im had been sitting in "Cellar No. 2," boiling the paste. He was notified that Hanna was unable to come and get it as she had been asked by Section 6 to meet someone else. She therefore asked Ha'im to send the paste along with somebody to the public garden opposite the Rehavia Gymnasium where she would be waiting for it. At that time Ha'im's group was busier than any other so he had been released from this particular pasting operation. Hearing that Hanna couldn't come, he said he would bring her the material himself, as he didn't want to bother anyone in his group. He left Cellar no. 2 with the paste, on his way to Rehavia Garden, and had not been seen since. Hanna and her group waited for him in vain.

The family began searching for Ha'im. His picture appeared in the *Yediot Acharonot* above the usual information about missing persons:

Alexander Rubovitch, sixteen and a half years old. Address: 22 David Yellin St., Jerusalem. Left home on Tuesday, May 6, 1947 at 6.30 p.m. and not seen since. Description: Tall, slender, wearing a dark blue beret, a khaki shirt and long khaki pants, black shoes. Wearing glasses. Anyone knowing of his whereabouts please contact the nearest police station, or the family at the above address.

Following the appearance of the notice in the paper, the family found a number of notes left on the doorstep by people who wished to remain anonymous and left them there without identifying themselves. The notes contained details of Ha'im's arrest. They recognized the boy from his picture and said they had seen him fleeing from an Englishman in civvies who chased him, caught him and dragged him along by force. Someone asked the assailant where he was taking the boy and was showed a paper saying he was a police officer. The boy tried to fight back, calling the passers-by to help him, when a car drew up. There were some Englishmen inside, one of them wearing a peaked policeman's cap. The boy was thrust into the car, which then quickly disappeared. On the ground was the kidnapper's cap, lost during the struggle.

Despite all this evidence, the British Police maintained that they did not have the boy, vehemently denying that their men had any connection with his disappearance. Pretending innocence, they told the apprehensive family that it might have been the *Hagana* that had kidnapped him. They had nothing to hide, they said, and offered to open all the prisons for a thorough search. Ha'im's brothers went from jail to jail, from detention camp to detention camp, their despair deepening after each such inspection. They even went into the prisons at Ramleh and Ramallah, inhabited only by Arab criminals. Their secret hope was that the boy was being held under an assumed name.

Ya'akov and Nehemia, Ha'im's brothers, gave up their regular work and business, and spent all their waking hours looking for some clue that would lead them to their brother. Much of their time was spent in the offices of *The Jerusalem Post*, whose many reporters had good connections with government circles, where they listened to the most trivial rumor for the sake of the family. Itzhak Ben Dor, *Davar* reporter in Jerusalem, devoted himself completely to the search. Upon his advice, Ha'im's brothers printed all the details known about the disappearance and distributed the sheet among the reporters, who were holding a meeting in the Eden Cinema. This idea proved highly successful, as the information raised a veritable storm among the newspapermen, who proceeded to fill the papers with the details every day, regardless of their political inclinations. Not a paper came out without the accusing headlines: Who kidnapped Alexander Rubovich? Where is he? What has happened to him? Is he still alive?

The slightest rumor was immediately given prominent coverage. One day the brothers found out that a certain Yeshiva student, one Kaminetsky had the cap lost by the kidnapper, having obtained it by nothing short of a miracle: he had found it lying on top of a pile of wood some children had collected for a *Lag Ba'omer* bonfire (a Jewish festival celebrated by bonfires) and had picked it up a few moments before the flames reached it. He was afraid, however, to hand it over to the brothers, who turned to Rabbi Harlap – the beloved Rabbi of Sha'arei Hessed – asking him to intervene in the matter. Only after he had done so was the cap handed over.

The cap was marked with the name "Farran." The fourth letter was a bit smudged and could be read as "k," that is, Farkan. It was now established that the kidnapper's name was Farran or Farkan. The *Lehi* Center, apprehensive about the fate of the boy, now published a proclamation containing all the known details which the censor had held back from the public, as well as the name Farran or Farkan. The *Lehi* issued a warning that if the British did not immediately reveal the whereabouts of the boy there would be nothing for it but to conclude that he had been tortured to death, in which case "the British criminals would be given their just deserts."

Farran's cap was brought to the Mahane Yehuda Police station by the Rubovitch brothers, where they demanded that its owner be questioned. They were told that the police knew no one of that

204

name and were advised to go to the C.I.D. office in the Anglo-Palestine Bank building. There they found a Jewish officer, named Langer who, as soon as he heard the name "Farran," declared that he knew the man. When asked where he could be found, Langer left the room to find out. He was gone for quite a long time and when he returned they saw that he had decided to change his tune. It was all a mistake, he said. The man he knew wasn't called Farran.

Langer wasn't alone in claiming that he didn't know Farran. All the police and intelligence officers insisted that there was no one of that name within their ranks.

But another clue was discovered at this time, tying the British C.I.D. with the mysterious Rubovitch kidnapping. A Jewish youth, suspected of being an underground member, was arrested and brought to the C.I.D. cellars for interrogation. He noticed the name "Alexander" written on the wall there. The youngster was released and revealed what he had seen. Levitsky, the family's attorney, asked permission to see the inscription. It was photographed and inspected by a civilian graphologist, who identified it as the handwriting of Alexander Rubovitch. The police graphologist, on the other hand, found no connection between the inscription in the interrogation cellars and Alexander's hand-writing.

The *Lehi* attempted to kidnap a high-ranking official in Jerusalem as hostage for the release of Alexander – a Mr. Major, who worked in the Chief Secretariat. It was thanks to his Jewish wife, who was with him at the time, that the man was saved. When our people tried to grab him as he came out of his home in King George St., she began screaming so loudly that her cries were heard by passing military vehicles, and a shooting match ensued. One soldier was wounded and our men had to retreat without taking Major with them.

I was devastated to hear that the attempt had failed, for I knew the foul-mouthed bastard well and had learnt to hate him in my days as a telegram boy. Still, there was a certain compensation in the attempt itself. The *Lehi* always kept its word. British policemen and soldiers were found dead in different parts of the country and the *Lehi* let it be known that they would all be hounded so long as the assassins of Alexander Rubovitch enjoyed their freedom.

The retaliatory acts of the *Lehi* and growing public anger forced the British to send Farran out of the country. He was taken in secret to Syria, but it wasn't long before he got into trouble there as well. The Syrian papers published a story about some drunken British officers who had gone berserk and caused a disturbance in a pub in Damascus. One of them was named Roy Farran. Thus was the prodigal son found, and the Syrian authorities decided to send the whole group back to Palestine. But one of them, Roy Farran, requested that he be kept out of this group, as he had killed a Jewish terrorist. This fact, too, appeared in the Syrian press and increased the agitation in our country. The authorities found themselves in an embarrassing situation, having been caught brazenly lying, when they had declared there was no one by the name of Roy Farran in their service. They were now forced to admit that there was such a man, but claimed he had deserted to Syria. The *Lehi* was not satisfied with this belated explanation and took their revenge for the death of the boy on more and more of the enemy. Neither did the Jewish press take it lying down demanding insistently: "Where is Farran?" "Where is the killer of the boy?"

The British now claimed that the name "Farran" was so common, it was impossible to tell whether the Farran who had deserted to Syria was really the owner of the cap that had been found bearing his name. Their efforts only served to make them more ridiculous. They went so far as to open a sports-goods shop near the O.B.G. Stores in Jaffa St., bearing a sign "Farran and Sons." But no one was taken in, of course. Even *Ha'aretz, Davar,* and *The Jerusalem Post,* papers that were always trying to outdo each other in condemning the operations of the underground, now felt that the British had gone too far. All their editorials dealt with Alexander, demanding the truth about his disappearance.

The Chief Commander of the C.I.D. in Jerusalem now informed Ya'akov and Nechemia Rubovitch that he had received secret information conclusively proving that the boy was dead. If he had hoped that this announcement would calm everybody down he was in for a bitter shock. It only served to intensify the storm and everywhere, in every home and in all the newspapers the question was: "Where is Alexander Rubovitch? Where is the boy?"

The papers were relentless in demanding explanations. If the boy was known to be dead – who had killed him. Where was the body? Why weren't the murderers charged and put on trial? Nathan Alterman, the national poet, wrote the following in his "Seventh Column" of *Davar* newspaper.

Where is the Boy?

On the agenda today is the subject
From which we must not be diverted.
For none of us but stands at the mouth of the pit
Where the truth of the bloody riddle lies buried.

Reply, Government of Palestine, say, where is the boy?
And the Police, keepers of the peace, where is the boy?
Or the C.I.D., investigators of crime, where is the boy?
Civilians, forever demanding law and order, where is the boy?

That is the question, it will not be evaded
Until it is solved. Of burning importance, it will not be ignored.
There is none more important in this country, none!
No, no other. Let me put it this way:

Even if he were not just a Jew, 'tis his voice alone
Is heard screaming behind the curtain,
Moving no one, ignored in silence...

Yes, deep as the sea are the woes that engulf us.
In their light this would seem but a detail.

But his hand on each door is endlessly knocking –
He is important!
As the great universal questions are important,
Raised by the anguished cry of a woman, a man or a boy!

Where are the police of the land? We demand explanation!
Why aren't they out in ceaseless search? Is there, at least,
Some officer in charge? Did they hold identification parades?
Time was that governments fell for failing to answer such questions.

Is he living or dead? We demand a reply!
This way by his cries for help we are haunted.
There is one single question in the land today:
Where is the boy?

★

The authorities were in an awkward position indeed. What could they say in reply to the accusation of murdering Alexander Rubovitch? Even a child could realize that Farran and his gang had been acting, if not under government orders, at least with its unspoken sanction. How could they continue to protect Farran without implicating themselves? They announced that Farran had been extradited and duly interrogated, and would be put on an identification parade.

Three people declared themselves witnesses to the kidnapping of Alexander Rubovitch: two boys - Moshe Heshin, thirteen years old, and Meir Cohen, fifteen years old – and Mrs. Ruth Serlin. The three remembered the face of the kidnapper well and had described it so exactly to Rubovitch's brothers that they were sure they could recognize him passing in the street. Farran fitted their description perfectly. The British, well aware of this fact, were worried and tried to intimidate the witnesses by having brought to the identification parade a negro driver, a veritable giant then serving with the police. But Moshe Heshin's father encouraged them, enjoining them to tell the truth without fear. The three of them, each one separately, identified Farran beyond any doubt, a fact that was duly published by all the papers. But the official announcement the following day said that they had failed to identify him, pointing out another man!

Nevertheless the British couldn't avoid putting Farran on trial, so they started looking for ways and means to save him from the unpleasantness of a civilian court. On the advice of his superiors, Farran resigned from the police force and returned to the army. This guaranteed him a military trial, which had its own rules and regulations.

The witnesses were brought to the Allenby Camp and interrogated as to the evidence they had given to the police. Once again Farran was identified as the man who had kidnapped the boy. When the witnesses wanted to point him out they were told to keep silent, to reply only to the questions put to them.

A few days later feelings were raised to the boiling point; Roy Farran, the man accused of kidnapping and murder, had "escaped" from the Allenby military camp, in full uniform and wearing his insignia of "Major." He was also reported to be in possession of all his papers.

Ha'aretz asked: If Farran had not been identified by the witnesses, what need was there for him to run away? The man was no coward, as was well proved by his past. What, then, had been his motive? Why did the authorities assist him in his escape? What did they have to hide?

Davar editorial stated, that in escaping to Syria, Farran had his own good reasons. If he was innocent, there would have been no need for such a step. The Government of Palestine had demanded his extradition with good cause. It is true that the Press Bureau claimed Farran had not been identified by the witnesses but Farran himself seems to have been ignorant of this announcement and decided to run away. How could the Government expect the public to swallow all this in silence?

The storm had by now assumed international proportions, the affair being heavily publicized by the American press. The *New York Times* and the *Herald Tribune* were harsh in their attacks on the Government of Palestine. The British press, too, discussed the subject in detail, the *Daily Mail* announcing that the unmasking of Farran had destroyed any chance of success of the secret police squads especially created for combatting the insurgents. Tempers were high in the British Parliament, many of its members pestering the Government with their demands that Farran be found and tried for the boy's murder.

"Ha'im's" family was adamant in demanding the boy's body for burial in Israel and turned to the heads of the Jewish Agency and the National Committee for help in their search for it. At first they tried to avoid the issue, on various pretexts, but finally agreed to cooperate with the family, suggesting the area around Ma'aleh Edomim as the place to start. The leaders of the Jewish Agency hoped, perhaps, in this way to throw some light on another, different mystery: In the days of the "Rebellion Movement" fourteen members of the *Palmach* left on a mission to blow up the bridge of the Achziv river. Only one body was found there afterwards – that of Yechiam Weitz, the others having disappeared without leaving any trace. Had they been taken prisoners by the British and killed, their bodies then hidden in Ma'aleh Edomim? The riddle has never been solved, but there were obstinate rumors that they had been executed. The leaders of the community now had an opportunity of verifying the truth of that rumor, or finding some clue leading to a solution.

Claiming that the area was dangerous and a threat to anyone unarmed, the Authorities refused the family permission to search there. When one of the Rubovitch brothers produced a license to carry firearms, the police officer changed his tune and told them that a troop of cavalry had already seached the place and found no trace of a body.

In the meantime the *Lehi* was unremitting in its acts of retaliation. Major Farran was finally forced to emerge from hiding and give himself up to the authorities. The latter immediately brought two famous attorneys from England for his defence. The trial opened with Farran pleading: Not guilty!!

Farran looked calm and collected as the prosecution presented its evidence. There was the famous cap by means of which the Rubovitch family had been able to trace him. Evidently an attempt had been made to rub out the name inscribed inside it and, despite the clear signs of erasure – the judges refused to regard the cap as incriminating evidence. Another piece of evidence which everybody had been waiting for was not even produced before the court. This was Farran's notebook, which he had given to his commanding officer before escaping to Syria. The court refused to demand this notebook and Colonel Fergusson, Farran's C.O., refused to give evidence, for fear he himself might be incriminated. And so ended the blitz trial as everybody had predicted; Farran was acquitted and declared innocent. The soldiers and policemen who filled the court applauded the judges and the sentence. Early next morning Farran was whisked away to England.

The *Lehi* found him there. In May, 1948, a package containing the Works of Shakespeare reached Farran's home. His younger brother, Rex, who was there on a visit, opened the package and paid with his life.

The British finally realized that they had failed in combatting the insurgents with the "Special Squads", so famed for their cruelty and violence, and were now hated as never before. There was no bridging the chasm that now divided them from the Jewish population...

The mysterious disappearance of "Ha'im," the Freedom Fighter, has remained unsolved to this very day, his body undiscovered, his last words unknown...

But we do know the things he did not tell his torturers – those they most wanted to hear. Not a word did he say about his comrades or leaders, their plans and operations. It was for this silence that he was tortured to death.

As many others have been martyred for their last words so has "Ha'im" joined the company of our sacred heroes and martyrs by virtue of his silence, and he but a boy, sixteen and a half years old. My dearest, most beloved of friends.

"You are needed in the 'Youth' Division."

Some time after Ha'im's disappearance Tanchum tried to tell me something, hemming and hawing as if uncertain how I would take what he had to say. It was during a walk in one of the Succat Shalom lanes, and I looked at him sharply, tension rising. "Nu," I encouraged him, "What is it?"

"We have to separate."

"Separate?"

"Yes... You're being assigned new duties. Ha'im is gone, and there's no one to take care of the younger members. The leaders think you're the right man for the job."

My reaction to the idea was ambiguous. On the one hand, I was overjoyed at being offered the chance to deal with the youngsters, but that would mean I would have to leave the Division. If only I could be in both places at once... It had always been my wish to inculcate the young members with Ya'ir's *Principles of the Revival* – the guiding lines of the *Lehi*. Now, with Ha'im gone there was no one with whom I could share my feelings and problems, and the work with these youngsters who had joined our ranks could be just the thing for me. Yet it suddenly occurred to me that this activity would bar me from any combat operations – something I could not accept.

"Nothing doing!" I declared. "I'm staying in the Division."

"First of all – it's an order," replied Tanchum. "And secondly, you'll go on taking part in the Division's operations."

Operations... Much as I wanted to participate in them all, there was one special operation in which I was particularly interested, in Wauchope St... If the Center was really taking it seriously, would they have tranferred me to the Youth Division at this particular time?

I decided to be frank with Tanchum: "Tell me, won't this new task harm my chances for the MacMillan operation?"

"There's no connection," he promised. "Right now you're needed in the Youth department so we're transferring you there. As to MacMillan, you can rest easy, we haven't given up on him. I give you my word that your work with the Youth will not interfere with the plans."

I was now under Avner's orders, and the first thing he asked me to do was to change my name as "Datan" was by now too well known and there were some men no longer in the *Lehi* who were familiar with it.

There were so many "good", meaningful names, that it was quite a problem what to choose. Avner came to my rescue and suggested "Elchanan", code name of Avraham Yehudai, one of our best men, who had fallen in action. Elchanan had been badly wounded and lost an eye in the attempt to blow up the Haifa refineries. Then, several months later, he took part in the attack on the Railway Workshops and was killed, together with ten other comrades.

Avner introduced me to Efrat who then led me to the place where two new members were waiting for me. These were my first charges, introduced as Elchanan, Nachshon and Datan...

"Datan? You must be mistaken. I am now called Elchanan," I whispered to her, "Not Datan."

"I knew you'd be surprised," she replied. "Don't you understand? As a mark of honor to Freedom Fighter Datan we decided to give your old name to one of your charges."

"Nachshon" was well known to me - Moshe Hazan who lived quite close to us in our neighbourhood. His family had immigrated in the twenties from Munster in Yugoslavia and lived at first in the Old City. When Moshe was six years old, his father died, and his two elder brothers had to leave school in order to help their mother support their family of seven.

They came to live in our quarter in the early thirties taking a house in the Tachkimoni lane. When Moshe finished Primary School he, too, began working as a carpenter's apprentice in a mechanized carpentry workshop, spending his evenings at a Boys' Night School. The owner of the workshop liked the serious youth who was so good at his work, and paid him a relatively high wage of 1½ pounds a week. But this soon came to a stop. The *Hagana* people discovered, as was their way, that the boy spent his time in suspicious circles, and ordered the carpenter (who was himself a *Hagana* member) to dismiss him forthwith.

Nachshon had had some experience in "conspiracy" even before joining the undergound. This was long before he began trying to find his way to us. One day he found a package of proclamations abandoned on a street corner. Asking no questions he took them and distributed them all over the city. When he finally succeeded in becoming a member he brought with him a list of young sympathisers whom he subsequently helped to recruit.

Two days later I met some more boys: Aviram (Datan's brother), Amnon, Michael, Zichri and one girl - Nurit.

From the very first day I cracked down on the group, leaving them no time for idleness. And there was plenty to be done. Three times a week we went out on "pasting" operations. Our posters were bursting with information as operations were becoming increasingly frequent. Besides the weekly poster *The Deed* there were proclamations of different sizes announcing various operations and explaining the need for them. Sometimes it was painful work. Precious comrades lost their lives and our boys paid them a final tribute by putting up notices of their deaths.

Operations continued to increase. Again and again our comrades succeeded in laying their hands on the Barclay's Bank safes – a veritable horn of plenty, which helped finance our activities. It was necessary to distribute explanatory proclamations and notices.

Most of our work was done in the evenings at that time. Conditions had changed since I myself belonged to a "pasting" group and we worked in the early hours of dawn. The streets of Jerusalem were now full of policemen patrolling at all hours, day and night, so it was found better to paste while the streets were crowded with people. As darkness fell, it was easier to hide in the crowd and if they caught sight of you one could get lost among the passers-by. The public was no longer hostile to us, as they had been in the past, nor were they indifferent. We now had their sympathy, in spite of the unremitting incitement waged against us by the *Hagana* and the "Organized Community."

It was the atrocities perpetrated by the British that had brought about this change. There was now a feeling of understanding and appreciation of the fighters who showed such heroism in prison, in court-rooms and on the gallows. Most people were no longer prepared to betray us.

On "free" days, with no pasting or guard duty, I taught my boys the ideology of the underground; not omitting the rules of conspiracy, but devoting much time to its history and its tenets of faith leading to the salvation of our people. The kids sat in a circle around me, drinking in every word.

If ever it became necessary to cancel a group meeting – either because I was called to the Division or was busy meeting new members who had just joined – the boys would be sadly disappointed and said so. I took this as a great compliment, as in other cells drop-outs were not unknown. After all, it is not every boy who can withstand the pressures of worried parents, nor can they all prove capable of displaying the complete devotion demanded of our youth.

There's A Pasting in the "Triangle" This Evening

The "Triangle" was virtually swarming with police and military, and no place could be more dangerous. Whereas in other places we had to be on the look-out for them appearing unexpectedly to surprise us in our work, here we had to be the ones to surprise them. We had to hang around in the streets, moving this way and that, waiting for the precise second when we were out of their line of vision. Then to spread out, paste, and move on, waiting patiently for the next opportunity.

We reached the Triangle and found ourselves stuck there. A full half hour had passed since I had whistled the warning tune of the "Poppies" song and was about to whistle the all-clear with "Aunty, give us your O.K!" when I took another quick look around. At that moment two civilian cars pulled up along side of me, brakes shrieking, and about ten Britishers sprang towards me, about half of them in civvies and the others in police uniforms. It came to me at once that they were part of the special squads for combatting insurgency. They tallied with the description given by witnesses who had seen the Farran gang that had kidnapped Ha'im.

Before I realized what was happening, two of them grabbed hold of my arm, which held a leather bag. "What's in there?" The bag was empty, and the proclamations it had contained just a short while before had been given to the boys. When they ordered me to open it and saw that it was empty, they wanted to know why I was

215

carrying an empty bag. I told them I was going to borrow some books from a friend.

The rest was routine: identification card followed by a body search, during which time my boys were all a few meters away from me, trapped by the ring of policemen and detectives, unable to get away. I knew that they had managed to get rid of the paste and the proclamations, hiding them somewhere in the vicinity. But what if they were asked to produce their I.D. Cards, their hands dripping with glue?

It transpired that, against my express orders, the boys had brought along a harmonica. Datan, our musician, pulled it out of his pocket and started playing on it. The others, all happy and nonchalant, joined him in the song and even began dancing in the middle of the street, thus hoping to divert the attention of the police from me. Although I had been carefully searched with no result and my I.D. passed, the other one called me back just as I began moving away. "Wait a minute!" he cried, peering around behind a near-by fence, the one that served Mr. Stein as a newspaper stand during the day. Could the proclamations be there? I hadn't seen where the boys had hidden them, but as this fence was so close I assumed that this was where they had put them. In that case I would find myself in the hands of the Farran gang, something which I was by no means ready for. I decided to shove aside the two Tommies holding me and to start running. If they opened fire from where they were standing there was a chance they would miss me and I would get away, just as I had gotten away in Chancellor St. But should they decide to give chase, they would surely catch up with me without too much effort. The advantage here would be that the boys could get away. I had to decide when to start running and delayed it for a moment to see if they had actually found the proclamations. There was still a chance they had been hidden behind the gate or some other fence.

They returned. "You may go," the first one said. His companion, more suspicious, stopped me again and returned to inspect the stone fence going up as far as the iron gate. "Run!" I told myself. "The package must be there. All is lost! Run!" I looked at them intently, waiting for them to relax their vigilance for a moment so I could begin running madly.

Again and again their companions bent to examine the whole length of the fence, the gate, and the stairs at the entrance, going up and down the stairway. I was certain they were waving the incriminating package to show their friends who were holding me, and was about to start on my mad flight. But wonder of wonders! They returned empty-handed. They had not found the proclamations! "You may go!"

I went, and the suspicious one didn't call me back. I wanted to run and hug the kids but felt that I was being followed,. As I went up Ma'alot St., there were two shadows sticking to me. In Shmuel Hanagid, corner of Ben-Yehuda St., there is a building with two entrances. Entering one of them I went up the stairs to the roof then down again through the other entrance in the street where I saw, to my relief, that I had lost my shadowers.

I had gotten away but what about my boys, were they safe? Heavy-hearted with worry I walked for hours in the alleys of Zichron Yoseph, hoping to meet one of them who lived in the quarter. Not one of them showed up and I was almost in despair when suddenly Nachshon appeared. His home was in a different part of the city and only chance had brought him there at that hour. He couldn't understand why I was so worried – the British had given them no trouble at all, the merry dancers having aroused not the slightest suspicion. "And where were the proclamations?" – I asked. "Where? behind the gate, of course!" As soon as the British had gone away, the boys picked up the package and hid it in a safe place.

The next cell meeting was held in the empty lot near Dr. Ticho's Opthalmic Hospital, and there I asked them why they had disobeyed me and brought the harmonica to the pasting. My rebuke failed to make any impression this time and they all grinned with pleasure. So, to "punish" them, I taught them the *Song of the Harmonica,* written by our comrade Moshe David Eichenbaum. The lads sang it with much emotion:

Song of the Harmonica

My good friend he got him a harmonica,
And he always played it, the harmonica.
At a feast or at a wake, a success or a mistake,
This is what it had to say, the harmonica:
"Winning is no victory, losing – not the end,"
So forever sang the harmonica.

And it never changed its tune, the harmonica.
Ever fresh the melody of the harmonica:
"Winning, never lose your head; failing – try again,"
Always listen well to your harmonica.
Never lose your nerve man, it may mean your life.
Guard it with a tune on your harmonica.

Then it met with evil days, the harmonica,
By its enemies pursued the harmonica,
But surrender it would not, the harmonica
And it kept our spirits high, the harmonica,
Never did it cease the enemy to mock,
Kept us safe and sane, the harmonica.

What was the evil that has silenced the harmonica?
Where the merry melodies of the harmonica?
In a dewy vale we dug our comrades grave,
By a bullet felled, man of the harmonica.
Locked inside its box it mourns, the harmonica,
Orphaned now, alas, the harmonica.

Though you're heard no more, O harmonica,
In our hearts you throb, dear harmonica.
Enemies will fall and the land be freed.
Zion will be raised on high, O harmonica.
Ever remembered will be our merry friend, a hero,
Who fighting wielded both his sword and his harmonica.

With the "Triangle" guarded by the Farran gang, I thought it better to give up all pasting operations there. Instead we would shower the proclamations from above, under cover of the gate of a building in King George St., throwing them over the heads of the crowds around the movie theatres before the beginning of the show. I called Zichri and he hid the proclamations inside his shirt before we set out for the entrance of "Shieber" House in King George St. Luckily no one paid any attention to Zichri's "belly." I showed him the window that looked out over the street below, and we fixed the time for letting the sheets fly. Then we went down together so I could show him the back way through which he would leave when his job was done. As soon as we came out into the street our eyes were blinded by torches and we were ordered to stop, in English. Suddenly we were surrounded by police and soldiers, who dealt with me first, ordering me to produce my I.D. Card and then going on to search me thoroughly. Then came Zichri's turn. "Your I.D. card!" they demanded. "I'm too young to have one," he replied, with complete truth, as any-one could see. Nevertheless they proceeded with the search feeling his arms, legs, pockets, everything that is, except his belly...!

Elnakam

I did not keep my code-name, Elchanan, very long.

We had a room in a shack in Agrippas St., near the Eden cinema, where those in charge of the Youth Cells often met for ideological discussions and task assignment. One day the British happened to discover an *Etzel* storeroom in the vicinity of our shack, and proceeded immediately to carry out intensive searches in the whole area, during which our room was broken into and searched. A quantity of proclamations as well as a list of names fell into their hands. The names, of course, were all in code but for the sake of security it was decided to change them all. From Elchanan I now changed to Elnakam. Datan became Yfrotz and for Nachshon I suggested Samson. To be honest about it, I just said what first came to my mind, not considering for a moment whether the name fitted the boy or not. On second thoughts I regretted my hasty suggestion because Nachshon was skinny and frail looking, the shortest in the cell. It seemed a mockery to call him Samson. But, as the Hebrew saying has it, "What the brain can't do, the name can do."* Before many weeks had gone by the boy began to grow taller, his shoulders broadened and soon he was the Hercules of the cell (Years later he was to win the title: "Mr. Israel").

Not satisfied with looking so manly, our Samson began to behave like a man. One day he came to the meeting, carrying a parcel in his hand, which he offered to me. When I took off the wrapping a Colt pistol was revealed in all its glory. "Where did you get it?"

It transpired that he had emulated the Samson of old, famed for his habit of using his enemies, the Philistines, to provide all his needs. One evening as he was sauntering with Aviram in Yellin St., they saw a British paratrooper staggering along in his cups. Not hesitating for a moment, our Samson darted towards him and grasped the gun that was attached to the leather belt. In a split second he cut the tie with his pen knife, grabbed the gun and escaped. Oh, what a boy!

They were all dear to me. As I had grown to love Ha'im and Israel, my brothers in arms in my first Youth cell, so was I now deeply attached to the boys entrusted to me. This feeling was fully reciprocated, and they regarded my word as law.

My circle of friends was steadily widening and now included others who, like myself, were in charge of the Youth Cells, as well as my own superiors, who were changed from time to time. True, we spent very little time together but there was a deep bond between us. For myself, I admired their devotion and selflessness, their readiness to risk their lives while still no more than children under their parents'wings. Each one was different in his ways and personality but I have never, not then or afterwards, had such wonderful comrades.

* The actual proverb is: "What the brain cannot do, time can do."

What a joy it was to look at Efrat's ever-smiling face and childish figure, her plump baby cheeks rounded and pink as apples. And that was what indeed we called her affectionately: "Little Apple." Then there was Dvorah, our liaison who supplied us with proclamations for pasting – always running non-stop, always there when needed. And who could fail to be impressed by Itamar, so tall, serious and ever ready to listen. Even at that time we foresaw a great future for him as a scientist, nor were we wrong. Then there was fair-haired Michael, so shy and unassuming and Kochava, so gentle and soft. My feelings for her were very special, this quiet girl with her calm, luminous face. She had come to us from Rehavia Gymnasium, the prestigious high school of the well-to-do part of the community, the better educated, richer, more disciplined part, for whom the word of the establishment was law, to be blindly obeyed. Very few of us had come from "Over there." I would see her glancing shyly at me and my heart turned to water. In her company all my courage disappeared, I was no longer the hardened man of the underground. I would stand beside her like an embarrassed child, with not a single clue as to how to show her my feelings towards her.

*

Our meeting place with Dvorah, who brought us the material for distribution, would be changed from time to time. Michael, Kochava, Dvorah and I decided to meet in one of the yards of the Nachlat Zadock quarter. As Dvorah began handing out the packaged proclamations we were surprised by some British police marching towards us, their guns at the ready. I jumped over the fence dividing us from the yard next door, calling to my friends to do the same. The yard after that had two entrances, through one of which I managed to get to Ussishkin St.

In vain did I wait for them, for Michael, Dvorah and Kochava. All three were caught and imprisoned. It was a heavy blow and I, the only one to escape out of four, was left bewildered and miserable. Never had I felt so guilty, though I realized that this was unjustified and one did not submit to arrest out of a feeling of solidarity... Yet, rationalize it as I may, my heart was heavy when

I thought of them: Michael, Dvorah and Kochava, especially Kochava! She, too, was under lock and key... my Kochava!

I met Avner, now the only one in the cell, without Michael, Dvorah or Kochava...

Some days later I went to another meeting and suddenly my heart stopped: There was Kochava, and she had a fantastic tale to tell: like all the other pupils at the Gymnasium she was a member of the *Hagana,* and to avoid suspicion when she joined the *Lehi* she continued with her activities there. When her superiors in the *Hagana* found out that she had been arrested, they decided there was some mistake, used their C.I.D. connections and had her released forthwith.

Ariella

The appearance of a new Division Leader was the cause of great excitement among us. It was a woman this time. Her original code name, Avihail, had been changed to Ariella. She was a beautiful woman, so beautiful I could not tear my eyes away from her, especially when she smiled. But Ariella rarely smiled. Obviously something was bothering her, and it was said that she found it hard to be separated from her family in the plains.

This did not deter me from trying to bring a smile to her lovely face by making jokes and playing the clown generally. My efforts sometimes proved successful, to my delight. Her lips would open in a smile and her gloomy features light up. That is how we were always to remember her: beautiful and smiling.

Ariella was idolized not just for her beauty. She was an ideal member of the underground who, from the moment she came to Jerusalem, became active in many different areas: organizing courses, public relations, physical training. Once she told us to come to Tel-Aviv in scouts' uniforms. We met on the banks of the Yarkon river where she gave us two days' training in field manoevres, and in day and night tactics. We crawled along the dunes, between bushes and thorns – nothing was too difficult for us in her presence and we outdid ourselves for her sake. How proud I was when I found myself the first to reach the target after a long and difficult crawl! But there was Kochava, her mouth full of sand and my pride turned to helplessness. What wouldn't I have given then to take her in my arms and comfort her. But I was too shy...

All that time, for a period extending over many months, I was bothered by two things. The first was the way Ha'im had disappeared, leaving virtually no trace. Even though it was so horrible, the fact that his body hadn't been found still left us a shred of hope that he might still be alive somewhere, imprisoned in some secret place from which he might one day escape or send us a sign of life...

Sometimes I would dream that I was waking from some nightmare and there was Ha'im before me, alive and merry, argumentative as always – the Ha'im I loved. How terrible to awake in the morning and find it had been just a dream! Walking in the street I would imagine meeting him casually, talking about this and that. Interesting what he would have to say about Kochava and Ariella... Suddenly I would see a youth of a build similar to Ha'im's, and my heart would start beating wildly. Ha'im! Ha'im! I would rush towards him, trying to quell the wild hope rising in me, fearing I was mistaken, afraid of being disappointed...

The second thing that gave me no rest was the Center's attitude to my plan for MacMillan. There he was, every morning at eight-thirty sharp, completely at my mercy. Yet this man, whose bloody hands had sent my friends to the gallows, was still alive!

The men in charge of the Operations Department were never free for long from my constant pestering. Again and again I would demand their confirmation to act, and again and again I was put off with promises that "the affair was being duly considered." Only after the British had left the country for good did I learn that my plan had actually been rejected at the outset because, although it ensured the liquidation of MacMillan, the chances for my subsequently getting away were practically nil. I had not been informed of the rejection for fear I would decide on a suicidal mission regardless...

223

"They hang Them..."

I respected my brother Avraham no less than my parents, for was he not my older brother? I never argued with him on principle, even though he was an active communist. At one time in the past things had come to a head between us. Avraham, a successful artist, painted a portrait of Stalin and hung it on the wall at home. It was undoubtedly a fine work of art but I couldn't accept the fact that the image of Stalin, at that time the god of the communists and *Hashomer Hatza'ir* (Israeli extreme leftist party), would hang on the walls of my home. I made up my mind to tear it up and tried to think of something that would make such an action justifiable – in his eyes as well as mine.

A portrait of Herzl on a calender I saw by chance gave me an idea. I knew that if Avraham found it hanging on the wall he wouldn't hesitate to tear it down. Sticking the portrait of Herzl on a piece of cardboard I hung it on a nail right next to Stalin. Avraham behaved just in the way I had predicted, tearing Herzl to shreds. So, pulling down the portrait of "The Father of Nations," I treated it in exactly the same manner. Result: a ringing slap in the face and some painful kicks in the backside. But I had achieved my target!

Avraham arrived at his communist convictions not in the conventional way of ideological influence. The process began when he was serving in the British Navy in Salonica during the Second World War. As he was walking along in the Greek port, he came upon an enormous demonstration of men and women, half starved and in tattered clothing. The demonstration had been organized by the communist party. As he stood looking at the pitiful sight, the British Army opened fire from machine guns and many were struck down. Avraham was deeply shocked by this slaughter and as he stood there, burning with anger and sympathy, a man approached him, asking him to bring some food for these people who were dying of hunger. Avraham managed to steal some conserves and biscuits from the Army Stores and gave them to the man, who happened to be an active member of the communist party. It was his influence that turned my brother into a communist.

224

One day while the boys were busy putting up the sheets and I was patrolling the area as their look-out, it happened that I met my brother Avraham. He saw me first and came up to me, offering to take me home as the area was dangerous. He had seen some youths putting up proclamations, but had failed to make the connection between them and me. While he was trying to persuade me to come along my boys appeared, and seeing me deep in argument with a stranger, interpreted the situation in their own way, as experience had taught them. They decided that the "stranger" was a *Hagana* man trying to hinder us in our work and began pushing him around and threatening him unless he made himself scarce. Turning to me, they asked: "Should we hit him? Should we beat him up?" I asked them to let him go and told him to go quietly.

Avraham was upset. So his little brother Zuri was mixed up in these "fishy" affairs and he had known nothing of it? He should be separated from these people without delay.

He hurried home to tell our parents what he had seen. They heard him out and sighed. He begged, importuned them to do something.... to save me... they remained silent.

"The British have no mercy for them... they hang them..." Avraham was trembling his face wet with tears, but they had nothing to say...

My parents had long been aware of my dangerous activities, yet did nothing to stop me, realizing instinctively that it would do no good. Like many other parents they looked on helplessly as their child deliberately courted danger... What could they do but pray for my well-being and that of my companions? And pray they did, from the bottom of their hearts.

I returned home, steeling myself to resist the storm which was bound to follow the unfortunate meeting with my brother near the Sick Fund, but surprisingly enough not a word was said. Later, when I found myself alone with Mother I asked her if Avraham had told them anything about me.

"Yes, my son. We are all worried about you. I told Avraham that you believe in the way you have chosen and we have to accept it..."

Some days after my encounter with Avraham, as the boys were pasting in the Mahane Yehuda market, with me serving as their look-out, Yfrotz and Aviram came up to me, upset and scared. Their father had caught them at their pasting and now they didn't know what to do, as they were afraid of returning home. "Our Dad isn't like all the others" – they muttered - "He's young and very strong. He'll break every bone in our body! On top of everything else he is a *Hagana* man and he'll never forgive us for joining the dissidents."

"Tonight you don't go home!" I told them.

"Where'll we sleep? What'll we eat?"

"Sleep? You can find yourself some stairs. As for food, you'll survive for a few days on *pitta* and *falafel*. Hey, fellers, let's have a collection". I drew out my own pitiful coins and so did the others, altogether enough to provide the brothers with some *pitta, falafel,* tomatoes and cucumbers for a few days.

As for me I wasn't too happy with the "solution" I had offered them, knowing well how difficult it was for pampered children to make do with stair cases... Neither was I unaware of the suffering of the parents when they realized the children had not come home. But I knew there was no alternative and I was asking nothing more from the boys than I had demanded of myself.

Next morning the father of Yfrotz and Aviram appeared at Amnon's house, as I had felt sure he would. He knew Amnon was in the underground, having seen him with his own sons during the pasting the day before. He demanded to know what had happened to his children and why they had not come home to sleep. On hearing that they were safe and well, he threatened to beat them up the moment they returned. "You won't see them so soon," Amnon told him, following my directions how to deal with the father when he came making inquiries about his offspring. "As of today they won't be going to work or returning home. They've become regular soldiers and will take part in the action every day."

The he-man was broken. He begged that his children be allowed to return, promising not to touch a hair of their heads. All he wanted was to have them back at home.

Amnon's father also intervened. "There's nothing you can do to make them leave the underground. Believe me, I've learnt this the hard way, with my own son."

"O.K. Let them stay in the underground, so long as they return home."

In order to make sure that the father kept his word it was decided that the two would stay away for another twenty-four hours. This was a terrible strain for both parties. The pampered boys had not slept a wink for fifty hours; indeed, how could they on the hard, narrow stairs? If they did manage to drop off for a moment they were roused by the bitter cold. As for the ubiquitous *pitta* and *falafel* – all that did was to arouse their longing for their mother's aromatic cooking.

I, the cause of their suffering, suffered with them, knowing that there was no other way but to do as I said. When they returned home their father made no bones about wanting to beat them within an inch of their lives, but the boys let him understand that if he laid a finger on them they would leave home forever. The father was "persuaded."

★

I was invited to the "hothouse" – a room in Anteby St., in Nachlat Zadock, one of whose walls was made of glass. I was assured that the meeting would be extremely interesting. When I arrived I found Dror, an intense young man who – jointly with Ariella – managed the Youth section. I liked working under Dror's guidance and I knew he liked and depended on me. He and Ariella always welcomed any suggestions I made and did their best to implement them. Had the "Division" been like them, MacMillan would have long been dispatched by now...

I went to the "hothouse," leather bag in hand. It contained a small spade which I would use that night to dig a pit big enough to hold a milk container filled with pamphlets. Such pits, dug in abandoned fields often served us as emergency store-rooms, and I wanted to teach the kids how to make one.

Entering the "hothouse" I found some comrades who had arrived before me, among them one called Igal whom I had never met before. He seemed to be fascinated by my bag, staring at it with barely suppressed excitement. Finally he could restrain himself no longer and cried: "May I... May I just touch it?" "Touch it? What for?"

But then I understood. The glitter of the tin can in the bag had made him think there was a pistol inside. The lad was hungry for some real fighting, but in the meantime would content himself with simply getting the feel of a real weapon. In those days carrying arms meant the death penalty. No wonder a pistol was so attractive...

★

Dror told me I was to take some psychotechnical test. I had never heard of such things before, and now there he was, presenting me with sheets blotted by coloured inks and asking me to tell him what I thought they represented. To me they were no more than just ink blots, but I realized that I was supposed to "see" all kinds of things in them. My replies might even determine my fate in the underground – if I would see active fighting or be assigned to less dangerous work. I decided therefore to lie without mercy and began inventing all kinds of gory scenes bathed in fire and smoke - anything, so long as I was found fit for action. Dror just laughed and told me I had a vivid imagination.

The Youngsters of Ra'anana

Acting on information obtained from Beduin informers, the police arrested a group of young trainees, aged between 16 and 17, in a course in Ra'anana. We were all indescribably shocked.

This is how it happened: The morning's work began as usual: after the lecture the weapons were taken out of the store. The boys squatted down on their mattresses and began cleaning the weapons, in the same way we had done during our training in the past. The group comprised five boys and three girls, all belonging to Youth Cells. Igal was in charge and Hemda acted as nurse.

While Hemda was busy in the kitchen and Igal demonstrated how to clean the pistols, one of the boys was on look-out duty at the window – much the same procedure we had followed in our course. Two hours had passed when the look-out gave the warning cry: "Gentiles!"

Everybody froze in his place. Igal ran to the window and ordered them all into the back room, lowering his voice to a whisper. Silently they obeyed him. In the back room there was a window with detachable wooden bars which could be lowered to the ground, forming a ladder by which to escape.

There was a loud knocking on the door and, still in a whisper, Igal ordered the ladder to be lowered: "When I tell you, jump outside one by one and run to the orange groves." The knocking was growing louder by the minute. Should they put up a fight?

This was out of the question. The youngsters barely knew one end of a gun from the other... He signalled to Hemda to open the door and saw a sergeant in a red beret outside. The front room was empty. At that moment Igal peeked in from the other room and the sergeant, seeing the slight movement at the door, instantly opened fire, at the same time calling out some orders in English. Igal, too, gave the order: "Everybody out! Run to the groves!"

One after the other the youngsters jumped outside but they didn't run far... Fire was opened on them from different directions and they fell one by one. One of the girls, Nimroda, thought her friends had thrown themselves down to avoid the shots and followed their example. Hundreds of soldiers emerged from the grove. They collected the bodies of Igal, Ruth, Hemda and Ariel. Ora was badly wounded, received first aid and was hurried to hospital, only to die on the way. Nimroda, who was lying there unharmed, was arrested together with four wounded boys. The five of them were imprisoned in Jerusalem.

The loss of the house in Ra'anana was a serious setback in itself, but now we were in mourning for the group leader Igal (Itzhak Moskovitz), aged 19 and the four trainees – Hemda (Sara Belsky, aged 18), Ruth (Leah Gindler, aged 16), Ora (Yehudith Cohen aged 16) and Ariel (Shalom Macharovsky, aged 17). We raged at the arrest of the four wounded, who were taken prisoners.

None of the fallen were known to me personally, yet I felt as if they were my own flesh and blood. Like them I had spent some time in the orange groves of Ra'anana. Like them I had had to surmount the difficulties of worried parents and forged "sick" reports for presentation at work or at school; like them I had known the joy and pride of being chosen to take part in such a course – the initial step to actual combat in the underground. But for the grace of God it could have been me and my friends!

It had become clear to the British that they could no longer rule our country unchallenged. Their hopes of making Palestine the center of power over the Arab states that they had created – the focus of control over the sea-ways and the oil – were doomed. Britain had been forced to send enormous numbers of police and soldiers, all placed behind protective fortifications, which – in their turn – became nothing more than the targets of the insurgents.

Even London was not immune from the underground.

Bombs exploded in the foreign office and in Farran's home.

The traditional allies of Britain, Europe and America, did not condone its policy. The "Special Squads for Combatting Insurgency," formed in order to crack the network of conspiracy protecting the underground, by means of kidnapping and torture, had set the whole world against the British. The disappearance of Alexander Rubovitch, who had kept silent to the very death, made them an object of fury and contempt by the Jewish population, so that any chance of bridging the gap with the community had practically disappeared. Even the staunchest supporters of British Rule were by now hard put to justify its behavior.

The British were faced with a choice between two extremes: Leave the country or destroy the Jewish community.

England asked the U.N.O. to send a Commission of Inquiry to find a solution to the Palestine problem. One of the steps taken by the British in order to demonstrate just how indispensable they were in keeping the peace between the two warring nations, was to incite the Arabs to attack and massacre the Jews. Arab villages were turned into arsenals of British-made weapons, and hundreds of Arab youths were trained in their use and in that of explosives, the instructors included many Englishmen. All this was done openly, in the light of day, but the British Government was "blind" and "deaf" – it knew and saw nothing...

The Trans-Jordan "Border Legion" that had formerly been under British command was now transferred to that of King Abdullah, a British puppet. This Legion was now alerted to attack the Jews in case they managed to overcome the Arab bands, and all the necessary preparations were made for the day the U.N. would decide the fate of the country – "the day of the long knives." But there was some difficulty in restraining the incited gangs, and for several weeks before the U.N., Assembly began its discussions regarding the fate of Palestine, the former were already busy shooting and murdering. Not a day passed without its dead or wounded. One night they attacked and killed the guests gathered for the evening in the Hawaii Café on the banks of the Yarkon River.

THE DEED (HA MA'AS)

Organ of the Freedom Fighters
January 3, 1947

The Stench of the Abbatoir

After slaughtering the body of the Jewish people it is now the turn of the Hebrew homeland to be dissected.

The land which is one and undivided by its destiny, its nature, its history and economy, is about to be cut up.

No one listens to the moan of its wastelands that lie to the east, to the deserts of the Bashan, the Gil'ad and Moab.

Hebron – Jerusalem – Nablus – Samaria, iron core and heartland of the ancient fathers, the prophets and kings – all are ignored as if they had never been.

The voices rising, *de profundis,* from the past, are unheeded, as are the thundering warnings of the millions of exiles in the diaspora.

Minds and hearts have become hardened, rejecting the laws of nature, of history and the impending future; aware of nothing but the ephemeral needs of the present.

Cold and impartial are the dissectors – uncaring strangers.

And in that house of slaughter, standing beside the operating table on which is spread the body of our homeland, are the aliens, sticking in their pitchforks, knives and drills, ruthlessly cutting and tearing up in an orgy of destruction. Nor are the betrayers of Israel absent – the collaborators, the traitors, aided and abetted by the pious Rabbis of Israel as they whisper their approval: a kosher slaughter.

The aliens are just that – aliens. The flesh they are cutting up is not their own...

Never in all the saga of suffering to which this land has been subjected has it known such searing shame. The sons tearing up the flesh of their mother are an obscenity and their sacrilege can never be expiated.

The skinners are ready nearby, panting for their loot.

The wolves and hyenas are on the prowl, impatient for their part of the spoils.

And the sinning sons of Eli the High Priest, Hofni and Pinchas, are there as well, the pronged forks of their lust held ready, eager for the choice bits of the sacrifice.

An appalling stench is rising from the slaughter house: the stink of scorched earth, of a homeland indiscriminately torn apart, of the poor man's ewe slaughtered for prey.

And there is another smell:

The rivers of blood that will inevitably follow the slaughter.

And the worst one of all:

Their garments, are bloody with the evil deed, with the perfume of the "State." Oceans of perfume will not drown the stench of their betrayal.

It will follow them always.

PROCLAMATION

The Recruits:

Ora

Hemda

Ruth

Ariel

Fighter-Instructor, Igal

Overwhelmingly outnumbered, they fell in the fields of the Sharon on January 29, 1947, during a surprise attack. Young recruits, they were learning how to join the fight in their people's struggle for survival.

Their innocent blood commands us:

DEATH TO THE ENEMY – FREEDOM FOR THE HOMELAND

The Underground – Lehi – February 1, 1947.

LEHI PROCLAMATION

Where is Alexander Rubovitch?

On the 6th May, 1947 Alexander Rubovitch, aged 17, living in Jerusalem, went to a meeting with his friends.

He was stopped at 7p.m., at the corner of Keren-Kayemet and Aharon St., by an Englishman in civilian clothes carrying a pistol.

The youth began to run, was chased and caught again. Passers-by tried to intervene and extricate him from the Englishman, who then produced a Detective Warrant.

Alexander Rubovitch was dragged by force into a car waiting at the corner of Keren Kayemet and Ussishkin Streets. Two more Englishmen were sitting in it, one of them wearing a policeman's cap.

Alexander Rubovitch refused to go into the car, and in the ensuing struggle one of the Englishmen lost his cap. The car left at high speed and the cap was picked up. It had the name "Farran" inscribed inside it.

As the boy failed to return, his family went to the offices of the C.I.D.

The C.I.D. officers pretended to investigate the boy's disappearance, permitting his family to search all the prisons and "legitimate" places of detention in the country.

He was nowhere to be found – all traces had vanished.

Three weeks have passed since his disappearance.

A thorough investigation of the case leaves room for only one conclusion as to his fate:

ALEXANDER RUBOVITCH HAS BEEN TORTURED TO DEATH BY HIS KIDNAPPERS AND HIS BODY DISPOSED OF.

If the enemy rulers fail to reveal the boy's whereabouts within the next few days the above conclusion will be taken as proven.

IN THAT CASE THE BRITISH CRIMINALS WILL GET THEIR JUST DESERTS.

**THE UNDERGROUND – ISRAEL FREEDOM FIGHTERS – LEHI
JUNE 1947**

PART III

"OUR EYES ARE TURNED TOWARD ZION"

Let there be no Division!

November 29, 1947. The General Assembly of the United Nations Organization has decided to form two states in the western part of Palestine, between Jordan and the sea.

This was in keeping with the demands of the official Jewish institutions, and as soon as the decision was publically proclaimed the streets were filled with the celebrating masses. As for us, we watched them with anxiety, praying that the evil would not materialize. Not for this had we prayed over the long years of fighting – not for the creation of another Arab State in our land did we struggle against the British giant. We were reminded of the woman in the Judgement of Solomon who demanded that the child be cut up, for well she knew it was not hers. We watched the dancing crowds with apprehension, for the enemy, both in town and village, was sharpening the long knives...

Our people were celebrating in the streets and the Arabs were making ready for an all-out attack throughout the country. Even before the State had come into being, its sons were forced to fight for its survival and their own. The frenzy of joy quickly passed, to be followed by the rude necessity of deployment of forces, of guard duty and of war.

In Jerusalem it began in the commercial center. According to the papers crowds of incited Arabs left the Jaffa Gate via Mammilla Rd., and overflowed the Jewish commercial center,

235

stabbing and killing any Jew who had not managed to escape. Many were wounded and the excited mob looted the shops, tore up floor tiles, doors, windows, water pipes – anything that could be carried away. Three buildings belonging to Arabs had been specially marked beforehand and were untouched.

Moshe Kan–Dror was a merchant in that center, owner of a textile store. He was a decent, patriotic Jew, a member of the *Hagana*, who also helped the *Etzel* when necessary, but kept this a secret from his two sons, Yfrotz and Aviram, who were active in our Youth Division. We now heard from the two boys that their father had come home bleeding and bruised in his whole body, cursing the *Hagana* for abandoning the commercial center. His story was that many Jews, upon hearing that the Arabs were organizing riots, tended to stay away from their stores in such a dangerous area. But the *Hagana* insisted that they go about their business as usual and not let the Arabs dictate to them, at the same time stationing armed *Hagana* men at strategic points to deal with the rioters. But, just before the mobs arrived, some British armoured cars appeared in the streets and the *Hagana* men were ordered to get out.

The *Hagana* men resented the order bitterly, as did the merchants there. When they asked for an explanation they were told that it was considered better for the world to realize that the Arabs were the first to break the law. Furthermore, as Jerusalem was now supposed to be an international city, the legal situation was extremely complicated and no one knew if its defence was the responsibility of the *Hagana* or of the U.N.

Meanwhile the mob, its roars growing louder by the minute, was converging on the quarter from two directions. To their consternation the shop-keepers realized that the first angry wave was already upon them when they were struck by a hail of stones directed at them and at the truck containing most of the members of the *Hagana*. The truck driver let in the clutch and drove off, putting as much distance as he could between himself and the raging mob. One of the *Hagana* men didn't make it to the truck and was immediately surrounded by the rabble who stabbed him to death with their knives, and nearby a British armoured car was parked, full of armed soldiers who showed some interest in what was going on but made no move to intervene.

Moshe Kan–Dror had a pistol hidden inside a flower pot. Taking it out he released the safety catch and waited. When the mob reached his store he fired some shots, hitting a few of the rioters and clearing a path for himself to one of the positions nearby, beside a pile of rocks. He kept on shooting as long as his ammunition lasted and then resorted to throwing rocks, helped now by another Jew who had somehow managed to join him. They were both excellent shots but hardly a match for such a huge, excited mob, among whom were many women who had come prepared with donkeys and sacks for bearing away the expected loot. These women encouraged the men by a sustained wailing. Moshe Kan–Dror and his companion were badly stoned and growing weaker. The first armoured car had in the meantime been joined by another one, and the wounded men begged the soldiers to take them into the vehicles and save their lives. The British laughed at them. In desperation Kan-Dror and his friend jumped onto one of the cars, beating off the soldiers who tried to push them out. Somehow they forced their way in and escaped with their lives.

When I returned home there was much weeping in our court-yard. Itzhak Penso, cousin of our neighbour Avraham Penso, had been the man murdered in the commercial center. Itzhak had been a sturdy, handsome man, just recently married! What a bitter, cruel end!

I, too, grieved for him for I knew him well. He was the brother of Goel, the *Lehi* man famed for exploding booby-trapped vehicles in the Sarafand Military Center and in the C.I.D. in Haifa.

As soon as Kan–Dror had recovered from his wounds, the *Hagana* gave him the task of guarding an ammunition store in the Bayit Vegan quarter, "so that the *Etzel* won't steal it." At this Kan–Dror lost all his patience: "You don't permit the use of these weapons against the British, and insist on 'purity of arms'? This didn't prevent you from abandoning the Jewish commercial center to the mercies of the Arab mob... These weapons you want me to guard – what do you need them for, for fighting against Jews? No,

I've had enough of your orders!" Kan–Dror severed all ties with the *Hagana* and joined the *Etzel*. His friends, who like him, had been put in charge of the arms, left with him.

A popular slogan in those days was: "The whole land is the front." It was also the unvarnished truth. Jews who were anywhere within the range of Arab guns immediately became living targets. The enemy was everywhere; any Arab, whether old, young or just a boy – and any British policeman or soldier. The Arabs had arms in plenty, generously supplied to them by the British.

The initial attacks were spontaneous, with no organization behind them. Seated behind their windows, the Arabs would sit and stare into the street, holding their guns with the safety off. Any Jew who came within range of their sight was immediately shot at.

As there were hardly any streets in Jerusalem not within shooting distance of the Arab guns, the whole city quickly turned into a shooting range. Sheikh Jerrach quarter shot straight in the direction of Shim'on Hatzadick, Shmuel Hanavi and the Bukharin quarters. Katamon fired at Rehavia and Kiryat Shmuel; Bak'a and Tzur-Bakher at Talpiot, Arnona and Ramat Rahel. Mekor Ha'im was the target for snipers in Beith Tzafafa, Kiryat Moshe for those snipers of Deir Yassin, who also tried their hand at Beit Hakerem and the road to Tel-Aviv. There was constant sniping from Sheikh Bader in the direction of Mahane Yehuda, Zichron Ya'acov and Nachlat Achim. Yemin Moshe was fired at from the walls of the Old City. The lists of dead and wounded grew from day to day. Women on their way to buy bread and onions, children playing ball, men on their way to prayers, peddlers in the street – all were in mortal danger.

Barrels and sacks packed with sand were placed at improvised borders put up between streets and quarters. There were even those farsighted enough to begin digging trenches and fortify positions.

The British were still in the country. Not till the last moment of their ignominious departure would they stop being the "guardians of law and order," that is, see to it that the Jews would find it impossible to protect themselves. No Jew could go armed into the streets, though these were by now veritable death traps. On seeing a pile of sand bags they would immediately search the position and "confiscate" all available weapons. Impotent to rule, they were yet capable of inflicting much damage. But the underground organizations no longer feared them as in the past, for the C.I.D., their most formidable instrument of power, had been practically disbanded. The way things were, it was hard to find a Jew willing to betray his brothers to those who were unashamedly aligned with our enemies in seeking our destruction, advising them and giving instructions.

Though the habits of conspiratorial behaviour were still adhered to, things were not the same. The collapse of the C.I.D., encouraged a certain relaxation of discipline among us, even carelessness. We now dared to approach certain institutions with requests for help.

As for me, I was no longer wary of keeping my membership in the underground from my colleagues, the postmen. I went so far as to ask them to bring me any mail intended for certain Arabs and Englishmen.

Hundreds of letters would pour daily into the underground, so that we had to open an extra "censorship" at Sneider's Drug Store in Ben Yehuda Rd. Nehemia, a native of Iraq, was in charge of the Arabic department of the censorship. The letters he read yielded much information about the plans and intentions of the Arabs. One day we received an envelope containing documents sent to Jamal Husseini, cousin of the Mufti, that infamous Jew-hater Haj Amin El Husseini. We sent the envelope to our "Technical Department" in Tel-Aviv so that an explosive device could be included among the papers in the envelope. Luckily for Jamal, Jerusalem was by then under siege, all postal services were stopped, and the envelope was never delivered.

The End of King George!

The British were still with us, even though their power diminished from day to day. Many of our streets still bore the names of their rulers, statesmen and peers, a symbol of their mastery in the land. One day Ariella brought me a tin of liquid tar, a wooden pole and paper signs with "King David Street," written on them. The orders were to replace the street name "King George St.," as one of Jerusalem's main streets was called, with the new Hebrew name. Actually this was a repetition of what one of our cells had done several months before.

Beginning at the corner of Jaffa Rd., near Yampulsky's Pharmacy, we covered the pretentious stone slab bearing King George's name with tar, smeared the tar with glue and stuck the new sign, "King David St.," over it. In this way we went from corner to corner, putting up the bright new signs.

Next day at the Post Office, where they were classifying the mail, I found the two men in charge of mail deliveries in that street and told them to cross out the words "King George St.," on the envelopes and replace them with the new name: "King David St. It's the end of King George!" I told them. They took this to be an order from the underground, to be carried out without too many questions as to who had issued it exactly. They immediately set to crossing out the old address and putting in the new.

The public liked the change, and even the newspapers, which were still subject to British censorship, dared to "dethrone" His Majesty and in his place crowned David, the sweet psalmist of Israel.

But that was not the end of the story. Long after that symbolic change of name, after Israel was declared a State at the end of a vicious, bloody war, and recognized by Britain itself (though just de facto), Moshe Sharett the then Foreign Minister, was asked by the British Ambassador to reinstate the name of King George V in the most important street in the eternal city. Sharett consulted with the Mayor, Daniel Auster, who agreed to make this "gesture to friends in the past." The signs were changed, and the street has been called "King George St." to this very day.

240

★

All during the struggle against the British, the *Hagana* kept its weapons buried in sliks or hideouts, insisting that its "unsullied" arms were intended for "a real emergency." Then, when the crisis reached its peak, it was realized that part of the "sliks" could not be found at all, and those that could be located, contained weapons that had rusted away and were practically useless.

There was a very serious shortage of weapons. Arms available to *Etzel* and *Lehi* were anyway, always in short supply. The underground organizations were centered mainly in the towns, where hiding places were few and far between, always at the mercy of repeated surprise searches. As a last resort, the weapons would be hidden in private homes in the various suburbs. Holes were dug underneath the floor tiles or in the walls, big enough to hold the milk containers in which the guns were packed. But a milk container was barely large enough to hold a dismantled sub-machine gun...

Besides the shortage in arms of all kinds, the *Hagana* was also handicapped by other factors that contributed to the Arabs' superior position: During the first few weeks of the joint Arab attacks, the *Hagana* issued an order to its people to refrain from firing at the enemy, except in case of an actual attack. This meant firing at enemy positions that were preparing to launch future attacks. Furthermore, there was to be no confrontation with the British patrols that always showed up after firing had been heard, confiscating the weapons of the Jewish defenders. The *Hagana* order was clear and concise: Give up the weapons without any resistance! This policy was frequently a cause of tragedy, and the now helpless underground fighters were abandoned to the mercies of the barbarous enemy.

The *Etzel* and *Lehi* held that the lives of the Jewish community could not be protected from behind walls of concrete and sandbags. Thus began a series of operations inside the enemy's population and commercial centers. Utilizing their past experience in catapulting barrels of explosives at the British, they now bombed the Damascus and Jaffa Gates of the Old City most effectively.

The *Lehi* concentrated its efforts in bombing tall buildings wherever they served as sniper bases for the Arabs. It also initiated operations for sowing panic among the Arabs who lived in mixed-population areas and had been known to harbor enmity against the Jews, in order to force them to flee the neighbourhood, thus ensuring the safety of our people.

★

After the Commercial Center had fallen into Arab hands, the inhabitants of Rommema, a mixed-population quarter, informed the *Hagana* that their Arab neighbours were speaking openly of their preparations to massacre the Jewish inhabitants. The reply of the *Hagana* was like a thunder bolt: "There's no alternative but to pack your things and evacuate the quarter." The representatives of Rommema were totally bewildered. It was inconceivable that the *Hagana* commanders failed to grasp the fact that to evacuate Rommema meant the complete isolation of Giv'at Sha'ul, Kiryat Moshe, Beit Hakerem and Bayit Vegan from the town center. Didn't they realize that Rommema must not fall into Arab hands controlling as it did the road to Tel-Aviv, the rear of Jewish Jerusalem? That cutting off this life-line meant putting the city under siege?

A few hand grenades were thrown by the *Lehi* into an Arab coffee house in Rommema. Panic stricken, the Arabs evacuated the quarter that very day.

★

The only places in the city where Jew and Arab met now, in spite of general hostilities, were the British Security Zones – which were mostly located between the Jewish suburbs and commercial centers – and those of the Arabs. Here it was still a common sight to see Jewish and Arab officials working together under one roof.

But the atmosphere was now completely changed. Entering the Post Office Building, we would be confronted by inimical eyes expressing such hatred as we had never seen before. Former colleagues, with whom we used to have friendly talks from time to time – during which they would give us flattering smiles and blame the British for all the woes besetting the country – now smiled somewhat differently: their lips would grin and the forefinger would move back and forth across the throat... Just wait, they seemed to be saying, we'll get you in the end and you won't escape our knives... Jews were murdered every day by hidden snipers or by gangs attacking the convoys on the roads. On such days the Arabs would walk proudly erect, conscious of their superiority... Their impudence knew no bounds. If before they had only dared to suggest obscurely what it was they really wanted, nothing could restrain them now: "It's a State you want, isn't it? But just you wait! You have no idea what we have in store for you! You'll be praying on your knees for the British to come and rescue you. Who do you think you are, compared to the mighty Arab powers? What will your *Hagana* do when seven Kings of Arabia will come at you simultaneously?"

They had no scruples in telling us that they had already planned the distribution of our houses and women. Now they were just waiting to get what was theirs...

These were not just empty words. The story was still being told of how, during the Second World War, when the armies of General Rommel were advancing in the Western Desert, the Arabs in Palestine had been busy dividing the houses of the Jews and their property among themselves. One day a terrible quarrel broke out backed by crossline shooting, between the Arabs of Sheikh Bader and those of Ein-Kerem, triggered by the question as to who would get Kiryat Moshe when the time came for dividing the spoils..

Gradually we began to see our "colleagues" for what they really were. Esau to our Jacob. But we restrained ourselves, trying to hide our real feelings. But one can take just so much and then....
An Arab "colleague" of mine, one Bader, got the surprise of his life when I gave him a stinging slap in the face after he came up with the friendly suggestion that I come and hide in his house when the rioters came to kill and loot in our neighbourhood. There was just one condition attached to his generous offer: I wasn't to forget to bring my sister – (not omitting a salacious wink)...

243

They were obsessed by the thought of our women – our sisters, wives and daughters. Sexually excited, they would hold forth about rape and sadism, not lowering their voices when passing us and openly weighing the merits of our girls. Which were better, those who were of European origin or those coming from the East?

Let the Sabre Speak!

There was a new hit song endlessly played on all Arab radio stations, calling upon every pure-blooded Arab to take part in the "Holy Massacre." *Ad nauseum* the refrain could be heard: *"Hali el seif Yakul!"* – let the sabre speak! Our Ishmaelite colleagues in the Post Office sang, hummed and whistled this song constantly.

We were now engaged in fighting on two fronts – from within and the rear. This protracted struggle against both the British and the Arabs wasn't easy, and we worked at a high pitch never known before. I was still occupied with the Youth Department, but Dror told me to get together with Yankele and Zamir to discuss some action against the Arabs.

Our first anti-Arab operation was in Lifta. A group of freedom fighters met late at night in the Elite Sanatorium in Rommema, each of us carrying a satchel containing 20 kgs. of explosives. After a short march we placed the satchels close to the walls of two buildings known to be central bases of the gangs. Lighting the fuses, we ran behind a fence, seeking protection against the stones and rocks that were about to fly in all directions. After a few seconds the whole area was lit up as though by a flash of lightening, and our ears were deafened by the thunder of the explosion. The two buildings had become a pile of rubble.

The Lifta operation caused the enemy heavy losses, but, more important still, it triggered a hurried evacuation of Upper and Lower Lifta. This provided a partial solution for the lack of apartments needed to house the Jewish families who had been forced to flee from the Shmuel Hanavi quarter by snipers in Sheikh Jarrah.

244

Lifta and Rommema were now cleared of Arabs but the snipers of Sheikh Bader (today Givat Ram, site of the Hebrew University) still endangered Jewish lives in the area. The quarter, built on a high hill near Rommema, overlooked a large part of the city, and its houses sheltered the sharp-shooters sniping at the inhabitants of Zichron-Yoseph on their way to the Mahane Yehuda Market.

A unit of ours penetrated the Sheikh Bader quarter one night. At its very center they placed a load of explosives near the walls of a two-storey house which towered over its neighbours and through whose windows so many lethal bullets had passed. The house collapsed, burying all its inhabitants. Next day an unnatural quiet settled over Zichron Yoseph which was quickly and correctly interpreted. Sheikh Bader had been abandoned immediately following the explosion. The abandoned houses were quickly filled by Jewish families and the quarter, famed for its rioters, was now a Jewish quarter.

We kept one of the buildings for ourselves and in time it became the *Lehi* Training Center.

The Katamon quarter was another source of trouble. Lying next to Kiryat Shmuel and Rehavia, it housed the killers of many Jews. Unlike Sheikh Bader, Lifta and Rommema, which were surrounded by Jewish quarters, Katamon had a strong Arab backing – Bak'a to the North and the East, the German Colon and Abu-Tor to the West.

Sappers sent by the *Lehi* to Katamon blew up many buildings and the dwellers of Katamon, some of whom were among the richest people in the country, thought it a good idea to go to Beirut, capital of Lebanon "for the time being." But many still clung to their houses and the Arab gangs stayed on. There was still nothing we could do about them.

I was called to Harari's in Mekor Baruch for a briefing before an operation in Katamon. And there was Yankele, his usually smiling face serious and gloomy. "You won't be joining us in this operation," he told me. The room grew silent. Yankele was well aware of how this hurt me, though this was not, I hoped, apparent to an outsider. Only someone who has been in the *Lehi* can understand what it means to plan taking part in a combat operation and then be summarily ordered to stay behind while his comrades did the fighting. I felt a constriction in my throat and my eyes clouded with tears. It was a great effort to stop myself from crying. Everybody looked away from me as I left the room hurriedly for fear that my grief would become a burden to them all.

Two hours later I was called to Yankele and found him smiling as usual. "The operation's been put off," he told me. He had wanted to commiserate with me. When the Katamon operation did finally take place, I was there.

Dror and I went up to one of the roofs in Kiryat Shmuel. His job was to cover the sappers who had penetrated into the Katamon quarter with his Bren gun, while I stood beside him, loading the magazines. From our vantage point I enviously watched our boys, who by now had reached the center of the quarter, Dror letting off his rounds of ammunition, I regarded my own task as menial. Still – someone had to do it. My help was needed.

The sappers went in deeper, running from fence to fence. Then they attached themselves to a wall and busied themselves with the charges in their satchels. Next we heard the loud explosions and Dror opened fire at the enemy positions, keeping them busy and enabling our boys to retreat. When they came back they had an amusing tale to tell: when they had finished placing the charges near the target building, just a few minutes before they were about to light the fuse, they heard a scared voice from inside calling: "*Min Hada?*" (Who is it?) The man must have heard a suspicious movement and come to the window to call to his friends for help, but in reply his friends called him "a coward, scared by every passing rustle," and begged him to let them rest in peace.

Our comrades, clinging to the wall, heard every word, and kept as quiet as possible for fear of discovery. Finally the "coward" calmed down and they went on to light the fuses. The building, a central base of the enemy gangs, went up in the air.

After that I took part in all the operations.

Twice a week we "took care" of Katamon, led by either Dror, Zamir or Yankele. Our sappers were mostly of Kurdish origin, famous for their physical strength and powers of endurance. Having worked in the quarries all their lives, they were quite familiar with explosives. Among the sappers was a girl, Yehudit, capable of marching many kilometers with the men while carrying, as they did, a rucksack loaded with twenty kilograms of explosive materials, her face beaming with pride and joy at being allowed to fight side by side with them.

Why I couldn't draw my Gun!

The British lion, cowed and beaten, was finally forced to slink out of our country and – like the proverbial wounded beast – did not balk at using its last reserves of strength to perpetrate as many cruel acts of revenge as possible. An example of this was the case of the men who held the Mandelbaum Gate.

The strategy of both the *Hagana* and the *Etzel* was based on holding defence positions. They would establish themselves along the length of the front, thus preventing any chance penetrations into our quarters. The Mandelbaum Building held just such a position, its importance lying in the fact that it overlooked the quarters of Mea Shearim, Beit Israel and Shmuel Hanavi. Its loss would have been irreparable, leaving these areas open to attack. The British, hoping to force the Jews out of there, would come repeatedly to conduct their searches, confiscating weapons that had not been hidden in time. Yet, in spite of the continual harrassment, the area was not abandoned. This time, though, the British were not content with confiscating the weapons. They dragged the four defenders into an army truck and drove them over to the square opposite the Damascus Gate, where they delivered them into the hands of the inflamed mob. The four men were torn to bits, then the crowd, thirsty for blood, danced its macabre dance around the pitiful remains.

A similar case happened to thirteen *Hagana* men who were taken from their posts at an alcohol factory in Jaffa–Tel-Aviv and delivered into the hands of an enraged mob in the center of Jaffa.

The *Lehi* reacted in kind. A group of us was sent to take retalliatory measures. Prepared to cut down any soldier we met on our way, we entered the center of town. But the British, realizing we intended to take revenge on them, took to their heels and disappeared from the streets of Jerusalem. A number of turns around the center convinced us that it was empty of British soldiers. The next day we met again, five of us: Israel, Shmuel, Arnon ,Yoram and myself, each armed with a revolver. I also carried a sack for collecting British weapons as well as a hand grenade and a flash bomb for cover in case of retreat. Our instructions were as follows: If we encountered any British, Yoram was to draw his gun immediately, tell them to put their hands up and drop their firearms. Anyone who refused was to be killed on the spot.

As my left hand was faster than my right, I put the grenade in my left pocket and the flash-bomb – about half a finger of gelignite – in my right one. Then, finding this arrangement uncomfortable for some reason, I decided to change pockets – the flash bomb in the left pocket and the grenade in the right. As I was doing this, I told myself I was acting unwisely. Then, angry at myself for bothering with such unimportant details, I told myself to forget it, and left things as they were.

We set out, Yoram and Shmuel about five meters ahead. We followed them to Jaffa St., turned to Ben-Yehuda, then to King David St., and back to Jaffa St. So we walked round and round the Triangle and not a British soldier in sight for our trouble. It began to look as though they wouldn't show up at all that day.

Suddenly we spied two of them coming up Ben–Yehuda from Zion square. At last! Approaching them slowly and carefully, we saw that they carried Thompson machine guns of good quality. As the distance between us lessened, Yoram and Shmuel by-passed them, intending to confront them from the other side. So far everything was going according to plan, but they must have smelled something, because even before we managed to draw, they opened fire on us. My friends pulled their guns out at once but for some reason I could not move my left arm whose fingers lay on the butt of my Webley. I was unable to pull out the gun that was tucked into my belt under cover of my jacket.

One of the soldiers began to run into the alley behind the Alno Cafe and I saw Israel, Shmuel and Arnon chasing him. The other soldier stood quite near to me and, if I could have drawn my gun, would have been easy prey. But my hand was nerveless and I couldn't. I saw Yoram grabbing hold of the soldier's Tommy-gun and pulling it with all his strength. The two fell down to the pavement and began rolling around in the struggle, as if in a movie. Again I tried to draw but couldn't. The two men were about equal, but there I stood, my hand paralyzed. Finally the Englishman managed to rise, freed himself of Yoram and started running. He reached the corner of Ben Hillel St. about fifteen meters from me, where he could turn the corner and disappear. Suddenly I felt my blood beginning to flow again. In a flash the right hand moved, I drew the gun and fired. He crashed down and when I reached him I saw he was dead.

As I was about to get away people came out of their shops and called me in to hide. I continued running but they still called me to stop, though I couldn't understand why they persisted. After I had run some distance I noticed that I was limping. Was I wounded? At that moment I felt a sharp stab of pain in my left thigh, near the groin.

I continued running but had to stop near the Orion Cinema, completely exhausted. Gavriel, the gateman, caught hold of me and drew me inside. At first he put me in the ticket booth, where I took off my pants and saw a red stain inside my crotch. I went on examining my leg, trying to pinpoit the exact spot where I had been hit. It appeared that the bullet had pierced the groin and come out on the other side, which was indeed blood-stained and wet. That must have been the cause of my momentary paralysis, when I wanted to pull out my gun.

I looked again at the point of entry and could have shouted with relief: the bullet had passed within a few millimeters of the flash bomb. A few millimeters lower down and I would have been blown to kingdom come. It was then I was reminded of the strange impulse to change the places of the grenade and the flash bomb. If the grenade had been in that pocket it would certainly have been hit by the bullet and then... who knows if even one of the five of us would have been spared.

Knowing that the British would soon be scouring the area, and not wishing to endanger my good Samaritan, I asked him to help me into the cinema hall, into the last row. If they found me there, I could say I had sneaked in without anyone's knowledge. Meanwhile Gavriel went to find a certain taxi-driver friend of his who sympathized with the underground and would take me where I could get medical aid.

The movie went on, and he stood outside, waiting. Suddenly the street was filled with furious Britishers, who asked Gavriel if he hadn't seen some terrorists fleeing. He answered that he had, showing them in what direction they had gone. They took off at once, but the taxi driver decided to wait till the end of the show, so as not to draw any untoward attention. I sat there looking at the screen, not seeing a thing. When it was finally over the crowd streamed out till I alone remained. One of the attendants supported me as we made our way to the waiting taxi.

The driver wanted to know where to take me: To *Hadassah,* which was also a first-aid station, or to *Kupat Cholim* (a sick fund clinic). At first I decided on *Hadassah* but then, after a while I changed my mind. One policeman, I knew, had been killed, but what had happened to the other one? If he had been wounded then he, too, would be brought to *Hadassah* and I would fall right into their hands. "Drive to *Kupat Cholim!*" I told the driver.

My decision proved to be the right one, and probably saved my life. The other British policeman had also been killed and the two bodies had been brought to the Department of Pathology by a whole squadron of policemen and detectives, all waiting there for the autopsy to determine the cause of death.

As we drove to *Kupat Cholim* I was again beset by doubts, as it was a branch of the *Histadruth* (the General Workers' Union) and its doctors were certainly not known for their sympathy to the underground. Not that they were likely to throw me out or give me insufficient treatment, but it wasn't pleasant, putting yourself in the hands of a doctor whose ideas were opposed to yours. There was our private doctor, Dr. Heffner – certainly a sympathiser, though not a member of the *Lehi* – but I had no right to put him at risk. Then I remembered seeing a doctor's sign in Agrippas St., one Dr. Orenstein not far from Mahane Yehuda. I felt sure he would treat me.

"Go to Agrippas St.," I told the driver, who then wanted to take a short cut through Ben-Yehuda St. This wasn't such a good idea, as it was there we had confronted the Britishers and the place would by now be crawling with detectives, police and the military, who would not leave a stone unturned. I therefore asked him to turn right into Lunz St., but he either failed to hear me or decided that I didn't know that this would make our trip much longer. He didn't do as I asked, and drove straight into a roadblock put up by the police. We were trapped.

There was a row of cars before us, and each one was stopped and searched, the passengers being asked to step outside. When our turn came I was expecting the worst, but miraculously they let us through without searching.

Dr. Orenstein received us warmly and treated me with great kindness, giving me first aid and bandaging my wounds. He thought I should let a surgeon see me at once and suggested Dr. N. in King David St. Thanking him, I returned to the center of town and climbed the stairs leading to the surgeon's apartment with great difficulty, leaning on the driver's shoulder.

We rang and the door was opened. "What happened?" he asked.

"I've been shot."

"Come in, then. How did it happen?"

It never occurred to me to lie and I told him about the shoot-out with the British police. He wouldn't let me finish. "Sorry!" he said, his voice cold and hostile. "I can't help you." He held the handle of the door, waiting for me to leave so he could slam it behind me.

The driver refused to accept such an answer. "What do you mean, you can't?" The doctor seemed to hesitate: "I haven't got any instruments."

He hadn't examined me, didn't know if there was a lethal bullet lodged in my body. All he wanted was for us to get out immediately. He was still holding the door handle, impatient for us to go.

The driver lost his temper and would have hit him if I hadn't begged him to leave him alone. All he could say was: "But why, why?..."

Why indeed? I wish I knew. The C.I.D. had long disintegrated, and he could easily have helped me without any danger to himself. But the man's hatred must have overcome his reason. We left and went to the *Bikur Cholim* Hospital where I was finally admitted to a surgeon and tended by experienced nurses. They chattered in Russian and I smiled to myself, thinking of all the events of the night, the narrow escapes...

"Do you speak Russian?" they asked me pleasantly.

"Me? Russian? Can't you see I'm a Sephardi of oriental origin ?"

"We saw you smiling... and in the circumstances... we thought you understood what we were saying."

And indeed, how could I explain why I was smiling, in spite of all the pain.

After receiving an injection in the area of the wound I asked for permission to go home, as I didn't wish to frighten my parents, and the wound wasn't too serious. My faithful driver was still with me and I asked him to help me up the stairs of our house. I apologised for not asking him in but I wanted to enter quietly without waking everybody up. He was very understanding.

I entered on tiptoe and turned on the radio very low, hoping to hear something about the other cell members whom I had last seen running away. I was also curious about the fate of the second Englishman.

There was a news bulletin in Arabic, and I liked what I heard. Two British policemen had been shot down in Ben–Yehuda St. by unknown killers. Thank God, none of my comrades had been caught. I did not know then that Yoram was in hospital, a bullet in his breast.

"Why are you limping?" Mother called from her bed.

"It's the new shoes. They hurt a little."

Mother fell asleep again and I breathed in relief. They would sleep well that night for they knew nothing.

In the morning I asked Father to go and get a "sick report" from Dr. S. "What's wrong?" he wanted to know. I decided to put off telling him as long as I could and said I had a blister on my seat, which made it hard to get up. Later when I told them the truth, that I had a bullet wound, they found it very difficult to believe me.

Then I asked Father to contact my friends and let them know my condition. Shortly afterwards, Nehama of our Medical Corps came and changed my bandages. Dr. Heffner, too, came late that night, telling us that he had been stopped by police who asked where he was going. "It's a secret!" he said. When they insisted, threatening arrest, he agreed to tell them, provided they didn't tell his wife. "I'm going to my mistress," he whispered in their ear. Much amused, they let him go, clapping him on the shoulder in encouragement.

I stayed in bed for a week, and it took me yet another week to regain my strength and walk normally, without limping. That was the reason I had to miss the daring attack waged by my friends on the Tannous Building.

A Meeting in the Hospital

The Tannous Building stands in the middle of the commercial center, in the eastern corner facing the Old City Walls. Housing the Regional Headquarters of the Arab Legion (Jordanian army under British Command), whose men had attacked the Ben–Shemen convoy and murdered fourteen Jews in cold blood, it stood in a totally Arab area – a fact which did not deter the underground from carrying out a punitive operation against the Arab Legion after the terrible crime. Goel, whose brother had been killed nearby, was wounded in the foot. Zefania, whose father had been shot in the belly by an Arab sniper a few days ago, was now lying in the same hospital as his father.

253

The father, luckily only slightly wounded, lay in a room quite close to Zefania and was in the habit of wandering from room to room, chatting with the patients and the nurses. Whenever he entered Zefania's room, his son would quickly cover up his face with his blanket, reluctant to be recognized. The father wondered at this strange behaviour of the unknown wounded man who never let him see his face, so obviously avoiding any contact with him. Oh, well, he thought, one must respect another's wishes and he would certainly not force himself upon him..

One day the father entered the room quietly, catching the son unawares. He couldn't believe his eyes! The wounded man always hiding beneath a blanket was actually his own son! Never had the doctors and nurses known such a difficult time as he gave them that day. How could they do this to him, he shouted at them in abusive terms. Never would he forgive them for conspiring against him and hiding the fact that his beloved son lay suffering in the very next room and he was kept in ignorance...

★

At the height of the bitter struggle being waged here the American Government gave us a "gift:" an embargo was declared on all arms supplied to this community that was fighting for its life. The Americans were well aware of the dangers facing us for the British made every effort to convince them that the Arabs could and would sweep us off the face of the earth. This premise was also confirmed by their intelligence sources. The Americans did not let themselves be swayed by these facts in any way, nor were they moved to help these 600,000 Jews doomed to annihilation. They remained "neutral" and indifferent, forbidding American citizens to volunteer for this war even as private individuals. The British never tired of warning the world that if they left Palestine nothing could save the half million Jews here from genocide. Not content with these Cassandra-like prophecies based on intelligence reports, they did whatever was in their power to see that they did not fail to materialize: supplying the Arabs with arms, and turning a blind eye to the organization of the gangs in their bases, at the same time doing their best to disarm the Jews of their "illegal" weapons wherever they could and destroy their strategic positions. Nor was this all!

A police truck loaded with explosives was brought to Hasollel St., in the center of town by two British policemen and an Arab, and abandoned near the office of *The Palestine Post.* One man was killed in the blast, twenty wounded, and the whole editorial system destroyed.

Encouraged by this "success," the enemy struck again:

I was eating the omlette Mother had just given me for breakfast, when a terrific explosion was heard. When I ran outside I heard people saying; "Ben-Yehuda!" so I hurried there. Never had I seen such terrible destruction. An enormous high-rise building in the middle of Ben-Yehuda street had been demolished, with tens of families buried under the rubble.

The facts were by now common knowledge: three trucks driven by British soldiers and accompanied by an armoured car arrived at the *Hagana* road block in Romemma and requested permission to pass. One of the guards wanted to examine the truck, but the man in the armoured car assured him everything was O.K. The convoy was allowed to pass uninspected and drove into the center of town, near the *Histadruth* House. As the road there was blocked by barrels they went to Ben-Yehuda street parking close to the tallest buildings. The drivers abandoned the armoured car, and left quickly.

As I stood there, gazing at the shocking sight, I saw Zamir in the area, "We're going to pay them back for this," I thought, "and soon." And nothing would make me miss that operation.

"I'm not going to work today!" I told Zamir. "I've got to be there when we take revenge."

"You go to work, do you hear?" he spoke with a bitterness, the likes of which I had never heard before. "Go there and stay there. We'll meet at four, just as we said we would." I saw that there was no arguing with him while he was in that mood, and by now I was well aware of the benefit derived by the underground from my work in the Post Office.

"When I shout 'Moshe!' You shout too!"

At four o'clock on the dot I was in our safe room in the Beit-Ya'acov quarter. It seemed that no punitive operation could be launched because.... there were no targets! The earth seemed to have swallowed up all the British, and in their daily patrols of the city neither the *Etzel* or the *Lehi* encountered a single one... Someone suggested that we launch a frontal attack on the Mustashpha, a British base in the heart of Mahane Yehuda. I recalled that at one time I had been posted for observation near the Italian Hospital on the way to Ramallah and had counted tens of military vehicles on the road.

"They don't dare to use the Jerusalem–Tel-Aviv road now, as it passes through Jewish territory," I said. "But they may be using another route, the Ramallah–Latrun road. If they are, then they will have to pass the Batei Ungaren quarter, and that's where we'll nail them."

Zamir heard me out: "You wait here," he told me and disappeared.

Together with Arnon and Michael we waited on tenterhooks for his return.

A full half hour went by, and no Zamir. Instead, Yochanan came in to fetch me. "They're looking into your idea," he told me.

Michael took us in his car to the Batei Ungaren quarter where, at long last, we saw some British! Every few minutes a truckful of soldiers went by.

Returning to our Beit Ya'acov room we took out a mine, two tins containing forty kilograms of explosives, some electric wiring, an electric battery and a switch. We carried it all into the car and, just before setting off, Arnon and I were each given two Mills hand grenades.

We chose a suitable spot for the mine. At the edge of an empty lot, just touching the road, a barrier of empty barrels had been put up. We placed a tin of explosives inside one barrel, hiding the other tin behind it. We connected the tins to the wire and to a detonator, then stretched the wire to the other side of the empty lot, where Yochanan held it in readiness.

The British fortifying and defending themselves

Firing position defending government offices

Rolls of barbed wire to defend government offices

Field Marshal Montgomery (right)
advises the British High Commisioner

The murderer Roy Farran

From where we stood, we could see only a few meters of road, so it was hard to know what vehicles were arriving. We therefore went into the adjacent lot where there was a long building. From the terrace facing the road we saw that here, too, visibility was limited and there wouldn't be enough time to activate the mine before the vehicle disappeared from view.

I therefore knocked on one of the doors and asked the people in the apartment if they had a window with a good long view of the road.

There was a war on, and people didn't ask too many questions. They saw we were fighters and they were ready to do anything within their power to help.

They admitted us into their home and led us to a kind of French window with an uninterrupted view of hundreds of meters, as far as Sheikh Jarrah. The only drawback was that I couldn't see Yochanan, who was somewhere below, waiting for a sign from me. I said to Arnon: "Wait for me outside next to the railing of the yard. When a British car comes along I'll shout 'Moshe! Moshe!' You'll take off your cap and wave it at Yochanan as a sign to activate the mine."

I stood by the window. The road was completely empty. Suddenly an armoured car appeared, but it carried some Jewish Supernumerary Police who were patrolling the area. All we needed was that Arnon would err and think I was shouting 'Moshe!' If he took off his cap and waved it at Yochanan we would be guilty of killing our own people. To my intense relief the armoured car passed, only to return in a few minutes on the road beneath me. And what if Arnon didn't hear my cry of 'Moshe!'? I turned to the owners of the apartment and asked them to join me as soon as they heard me calling out.

As we were talking, the children milling excitedly around, promising to shout their loudest, I noticed a truckful of British soldiers approaching, followed immediately by another one. I wanted to raise the cry at once but thought better of it and decided to wait until I could see the soldiers' faces better. Yes! There was no doubt about it, they were British!

"MOSHE!" I yelled.

"MOSHE!" came the outcry of the whole family.

I pulled out a grenade, drew the pin and waited for the explosion down below. There was a flash of lightening and then we were all flung into the air, almost to the roof. When I was back on my feet I saw that the blast had, for some reason, removed the lever. We were all in mortal danger, particularly the children... I sprang to the window, my body between the grenade and the children, and flung it out upon two masses of flames that, less than a minute ago, had been British trucks. I then drew out the second grenade and another rain of shrapnel followed that of the first.

I left. Arnon told me that the blast had thrown him high in the air. It was only by a miracle that he had managed to grasp the iron railing and save himself from falling some fifteen meters to the ground below.

The seven o'clock news revealed that seven British soldiers were dead, killed by a mine, and twenty were wounded. How twenty men could have survived that conflagration was beyond me.

The same evening our men attacked the Mustashpha Building, inflicting heavy losses on the enemy. This was followed, several days later, by an explosion of a military train near Rehovoth, where twenty-eight British soldiers were killed and thirty–five – wounded.

Two of the Englishmen who had perpetrated the Ben-Yehuda atrocity were also made to pay, by some strange quirk of fate. It began with the decision taken by the *Lehi* to infiltrate a booby-trapped truck into Nablus in order to destroy the Headquarters of the gangs camped there.

Avraham Cohen (Shmuel) – who had gained some experience in a similar assignment when the Sarayah in Jaffa was demolished – loaded 500 kilograms of explosives on a truck and covered them with oranges. Taking an Arab with him, he left for Nablus, but was betrayed by the guide who handed him over to the gangs. Avraham Cohen was tortured and executed. Dismantling the truck was another story. The Arabs dared not do it, fearing it might be booby-trapped, so they brought some British sappers who had specialized in such jobs. As the Arab mob looked curiously on they proceeded with the task. There was and explosion and many were killed, among them the two British "specialists" who had often bragged of the fine job they had done in the Ben-Yehuda explosion.

The Whole Land is a Frontier

There was fighting everywhere, in every town, village and house. No target was too small for the Arab gangs; every road with Jewish traffic using it was under fire. The roads became death-traps for anyone driving a Jewish vehicle, the major attacks being focused on the strategic segments controlling the Jerusalem–Tel-Aviv Rd., and that of Jerusalem – Gush Etzion (approaching Hebron). The whole nation had turned into an army: there was hardly a youth capable of handling arms who was not fighting by now, within the framework of one organization or another.

But everywhere there was a serious shortage of fighting men. The Jews were a minority in the country, while armed Arabs flowed in to every front from all the lands of the Near East. Fully-armed battalions arrived from Iraq and Syria. It was total war and the front-lines were long and tortuous.

It was no time for tactics based on the "Purity of Arms" ideology, where one fired only under attack and at the place and time of hostilities.

The advocates of the "Purity of Arms" doctrine, if they wanted to remain alive, had to emerge from behind their fortified positions and attack those Arab villages and towns which served as bases for the gangs – something which entailed the killing of citizens, among them women and children. Yet even now they did this as if under duress, always seeking excuses, and hiding behind the fact that there really was no other alternative. In other words, for them this was no War of Liberation which they had determined to fight, but something forced on them from outside, leaving them no choice but to defend themselves. Even now the *Hagana* still had no final goal to strive for, as we had had from the very beginning of the conflict: the ultimate liberation of the land and declaration of a Jewish State. They were still hoping for some foreign guardians who would do the dirty work for them. When it was suggested in the U.N.O. that Scandinavian forces be dispatched to Palestine, the Jewish leaders were eager to accept. When they despaired of the "chance" that the world would serve us a divided and truncated state on a platter and fight for us – they never gave up hoping that some international power would be found that would undertake to rule Jerusalem.

For these reasons, even though we were in the midst of a cruel struggle which did not distinguish one Jew from another, the time was not yet ripe for uniting the various underground organizations into one fighting force.

As for me, I was still an employee of the Post Office. Between one "sick" and another – that is to say between one operation and the next – I would show up at my place of work.

Among the Arab postmen, too, there were many "sick" on leave, some of them known as active gang members. The others, too, appearing after a prolonged absence, were full of innuendos regarding mysterious acts of heroism in which they had been involved.

My erstwhile "friend," Mr. Sherrif, who was always hinting at the fabulous strength of the Arabs – and who, out of the depth of his friendship for me advised me to ignore the promises mentioned in the Bible – was usually absent from work. He himself did not belong to any fighting gang, but many of his kin and friends did and were usually in mourning for someone who had fallen in the *Jihad* (Holy War).

Our Ishmaelite cousins were well aware of the fact that our losses were heavy. Anything which caused us pain was for them a source of rejoicing, encouraging their insolence. Proud of their victory, they would hurry to tell us and their colleagues of the deeds of valour of their heroes.

One day the insolent Khativ came panting into the classification room breathless, to report a wonderful act of bravery that had just taken place in the very next street. An Arab hero, prince of princes, threw a grenade at a woman who had been walking along, one hand pushing her baby's pram and the other holding her little child. The three were blown to bits! "Well! What can you say to that?" Khativ challenged me, drunk with this fabulous victory. "And you dare to talk of a Jewish State? Wait, just wait. When Haj Amin comes he'll show you, if there's still anyone of you left to watch…"

Haj Amin El Husseini, Mufti of Jerusalem, fellow traveller of Hitler and his collaborator in initiating the "Final Solution" of the Jewish problem, was now the idol of the Arabs and his call to a *Jihad* was driving them into a state of ecstasy bordering on hysteria.

Another popular hero was Fawzi Ka'ukji who, with his soldiers, had penetrated the country from Syria. At the mention of his name they would give an evil smile, looking askance to see how we reacted to the "terrible name" which was calculated to strike the fear of death in all who heard it.

One day they celebrated the massacre of the convoy that left Gush Etzion and was ambushed in Nebi Daniel and we were privileged to watch a veritable "bourse" for the exchange of pictures of the cut up bodies of the victims, beheaded and the genitals cut off…

We did not let ourselves be provoked by their barbarism. All of us, the Jewish members of the Post Office staff, were convinced that the only answer to this terrible madness of theirs was to crack down on them within an inch of their lives. Only a formidable strike which would reduce them to a state of abject resignation could return them to some semblance of sanity.

The Slogan – A United Front

Don't go to work tomorrow," said Zamir. "Be at the Girls' School in the Even Yehoshua quarter at 9a.m."

An order from Zamir to stay away from work could mean one thing only - a major operation.

The following morning thirty of us, boys and girls, were gathered in one of the class rooms of the Even Yehoshua school, near the Mea Shearim quarter. Like diligent pupils, we squatted on the small seats and concentrated on Dror as he stood by the blackboard, chalk in hand. "Tomorrow," he announced, "We're going to capture an Arab village."

Though he spoke quietly we were electrified by his words. His announcement signified a new stage in our campaign. We had been active for some time in Arab villages all over the country, often causing the villagers to abandon their quarter or hamlet – a method also favored by the *Etzel* and the *Hagana,* which served to shorten the lines of fire and improve our positions. But never before had we embarked on an operation aimed at capturing territory. This was a real innovation. "The target is Deir Yassin," continued Dror, sketching a map on the board. The village lies on a hilltop, west of the Giv'at Shaul quarter and north of Kiryat Moshe and Beit Hakerem. It overlooks and controls the Jerusalem–Tel-Aviv road, as well as the inner routes connecting the above districts to the city and the western zones.

"We've been in touch with the *Hagana* Command and they have assured us that the occupation of Deir Yassin will help in controlling the Jerusalem–Tel-Aviv road, many parts of which are now under Arab control, a fact which brings the danger of a siege on the city so much closer. We have also been informed that Iraqi volunteers are entrenched there, so the plan to take the village fits fits in perfectly with the over-all strategy of the *Hagana.*"

At first we weren't too sure we could take the place by means of a frontal attack. We were few in number and most of our former operations had been based on stratagems, on maximum concentrations of power at a single point for short periods, and on hit-and-run methods. Such operations were well suited to very small units, but would we be capable of taking a large village filled with hundreds of armed men?

Before we could voice our doubts, Dror hastened to reassure us that we would be operating in conjunction with the *Etzel* – a refreshing change indeed! "The *Etzel,*" he added, "insisted that everything be done so that women and children will remain unharmed, and we have agreed to stand by this restriction."

Someone rose and asked how anyone could guarantee this,

when it was well known that the enemy was hiding in the houses, among the women and children? How could we overcome them, shoot inside, throw grenades etc., without harming the citizens?

"We have decided to forego the element of surprise in order to ensure the safety of the civilians. Loudspeakers will call for the evacuation of all women, children and the aged before we attack."

★

That evening we marched in groups to the meeting place, the Giv'at Shaul Beer Factory, where we were briefed again, formed into small units and given arms. The plan was as follows: an armoured vehicle mounted with a loudspeaker would leave Giv'at Shaul in the direction of Deir Yassin, with Nechemia of our "Arab Division" and Yankele carrying a Bren. A group of men would march along beside the armoured car. Another force would approach the village from the north. Simultaneously, the *Etzel* would march into the village in two columns, from the direction of Beit Hakerem. The *Lehi* leader of the operation was Yo'ed.

The pass-word: "A United Front."

It was indeed an affirmation of a united front. The *Etzel* was short of explosives – we supplied their needs, as we manufactured them ourselves and had enough for all. On the other hand we lacked weapons, which they had in plenty, having just inaugurated a plant for the production of Sten guns. Just before the operation we were sent a quantity of shining new weapons, straight off the production line. They looked far superior to the original British Stens we had been using so far. We were filled with pride as we prepared to use these first "made by *Etzel*" guns, but they were to cause us some trouble later on. These machine guns had not been tried yet in actual combat and afterwards, when we used them under actual fire, we discovered not a few defects resulting from the fact that their officers wanted to economize on ammunition, which we were all chronically short of. Before the battle they had changed the mechanism of their gun, limiting them to one shot at a time instead of a full volley of fire.

Zero hour was 2 p.m., and Dror suggested we take a short nap, as no one could say how long the battle would go on. We tried to take his advice but who could sleep at such a time?

Tense and expectant, we whiled the hours away in talk and speculation. Most of all we were pleased by the creation of the United Front, that is, the joint operation with the *Etzel,* after all, what difference was there now between us?

The *Etzel* had long been trying to unite the two organizations, and as far back as two years ago we were asked to give our opinion of such a consolidation of forces. We were all for it. The ideological differences of the past had diminished over the years of fighting, sacrifice and suffering. But, on the other hand, there were advantages to our operating as an independent group. As a small active organization bringing off one impressive coup after another, we posed a challenge to the larger organization – a challenge which the *Etzel* accepted and met in a way commanding our deep respect. Its strikes at the enemy were painful and debilitating. One might say that if we, the *Lehi* were the nails in the coffin of British rule, then the *Etzel* had supplied the timber. One reason for our hesitation was the fear that it would be difficult to observe the strict laws of conspiracy necessary for our survival if the organization over-extended itself. The larger the unit, the more difficult it is to know each individual fighter, a fact which would facilitate the infiltration of enemy agents. A large organization requires large units, thus endangering the element of secrecy so essential for our survival.

All this had been true in the past, but things had changed beyond recognition. Combat strategy was completely different, and we were now fighting openly instead of striking from the underground. There was now a need for larger units, in military formations headed by a single command. The united front was no longer wishful thinking but an absolute necessity.

Truth to tell, we had hoped that the *Hagana* would also join us, in spite of the bitter memories and the ideological differences. The *Hagana,* though it avoided taking the initiative, was forced to adapt itself to the new realities, and in the final analysis weren't we all involved in the cruel struggle for survival which had been forced on us by the British?

The mask had been stripped off, to reveal the real, ugly face of the British, so that even the *Hagana* could not but acknowledge the fact that they were the real enemy.

The hours passed slowly and there was time to ponder over many things. I found myself thinking about my "friends" at the Post Office, Kativ, Bader, Bakir and Udda. What would their reaction be after we had taken Deir Yassin? I would have given much to see their faces with the insolent smirks wiped off...

Then I imagined my neighbours at home, the old men going to morning service and meeting the fighters returning from the battle, crowned in victory – most of them striplings who had grown up before their eyes. I saw the mothers, aproned and toiling for hours at the primitive Primus stoves; and the girls, just awakened from sleep, their hair awry, emerging from their homes to watch the warriors back from the battle-field.

It was time. Not waiting to be called, we got up and prepared to move in.

I marched with my group beside the armoured car, according to plan. We left Giv'at Shaul behind us and were now on the path leading to Deir Yassin. We knew there would be road-blocks on the way but had no idea how difficult it would be to remove them.

First road block: a long pile of rocks and rubble cutting across the whole width of the road, backed by a deep trench. The armoured car came to a halt, and – lacking spades – we used the few helmets we had and our bare hands. We dismantled the barrier and filled up the trench, an operation consuming much precious time. That done, we came up against a second road block, thirty meters from the first. Again we used our helmets and hands, removing the stones and filling up the trench. Time went surprisingly fast and the darkness that was to have sheltered us slowly faded. Would we get to the village before dawn?

The night was rapidly waning and the sky lightened. The shadows of the village houses began to emerge and we were faced with the third road block. Dismantling it would delay us, forcing us to enter the village in full daylight. The only alternative was to abandon the armoured car there, beside the trench. That meant that we couldn't use the loud-speaker to warn the women and children inside the houses.

We chose the second course and went on on foot. It wasn't far and there was a chance that they would hear us from where we were.

In the meantime the other forces had already reached the village on foot and we could hear the sounds of battle.

Nechemia addressed the villagers but his voice was drowned in the sound of fire coming from all directions.

"I've been shot!" came the cries of Ben-Zion, Shmuel and someone I couldn't identify.

"Eldad's been killed!"

We were now joined by the *Etzel* force that had come from south-east of the village. Their leader, Ben-Zion Cohen, was wounded.

Taking his Bren, Yankele left the armoured car in order to cover the men who were dispersed throughout the area, easy targets for the snipers.

We had to reorganize and destroy the source of fire.

Dror, a superlative sniper, asked for a rifle to eliminate the Arab snipers, something his Sten couldn't do. I took his Sten and gave him my carbine, not without regret. The exchange of fire went on and we began to seek cover. Our snipers were now hunting theirs. This went on for a long time; it could go on forever.

We had come to take the village, hadn't we? When would we begin to move and how?

"Who's ready to come with me into the village?" asked Dror. "We have to assault the block of buildings in the center and take them." That was more like it and I went with him, as did Giora – who had escaped a short while ago from the Central Prison in Jerusalem – and two *Etzel* men.

With a spurt we ran towards the buildings on the hill in the heart of the village. Actually I had no idea how to "capture territory." In the underground we had learnt how to steal up to a target, lay the explosives and make ourselves scarce. But to "take" a target, I thought, the very opposite would have to be done. We would run forward in the open, shooting all the time, which I proceeded to do. I ran forward, drawing all the snipers' fire towards myself.

They shot from every direction.

"Are you crazy?" Dror shouted, pulling me down behind a fence. "Wait a while. Let me finish off some of the snipers around us before you start running. Don't make a move before I tell you to run, and even then take care. Jump from cover to cover!"

He jumped and threw himself down flat on one of the roofs, shooting in the direction from which the fire had come.

"You two," he turned to the two *Etzel* men who had joined us. "When I give the word, break into those two houses at the entrance of the lane. Stay there. When we run forward keep an eye on us, see we're not outflanked."

"Now," he told me, "Try to make a run for it!"

I ran into a twisting alley and saw an Arab cocking his gun. It was either him or me and the first to shoot would live. I squeezed the trigger and my heart seemed to stop. No shot! I jumped backwards, pressing myself to the wall. A shot. I felt a sharp pain in my right thigh. I'd been hurt and the pain made me afraid it was serious this time, for when I'd been shot some weeks before I'd felt nothing.

"I've been shot," I told Dror, showing him the place where my assailant was hiding. Dror shot him in the head and he fell down dead.

When I examined the wound through a hole in my pants all I could see was a blood stain. I could move the leg freely and realized it was just a scratch. Running towards the dead Arab to take his gun I saw another one kneeling fully armed beside him, taking his gun and pulling away the ammo belt. Seeing me he ran away and I took the gun, which had wounded me just a moment ago, and the belt. The dead man was wearing an unfamiliar uniform and some insignia showing his rank (I learnt later he had been an Iraqi officer). Then I rejoined Dror, who had just saved my life, and would do it again and again that day. He was shooting indefatigably, hitting the snipers one after the other. I was worried by the fact that they had discovered his position on the flat roof by now and were firing at him from every position.

Giora ran from house to house, shooting inside and forcing the Arab fighters to emerge. When he saw me carrying a gun as well as a Sten he asked me for the latter. I told him it was out of order and he fired a trial shot with it. It didn't work. He went on squeezing the trigger. Sometimes it fired and sometimes it didn't. I went on running from door to door, taking cover behind the walls. Finally the block of buildings in the village center was in our hands, and under their cover we fired at the snipers' positions. Though we controlled the buildings we refrained from entering them for fear of an armed ambush. We had no grenades or effective automatic firearms. We decided to wait for our friends in the rear to take our place so that we could go on attacking.

It was a long and difficult wait. We controlled the village center but were practically cut off from our own forces.

The two *Etzel* men who had joined Dror, Giora and myself, now reached us. They told us that there were many killed and wounded and our reserves had been exhausted. Our comrades who had stayed behind because there were no weapons for them were now in the thick of the battle, replacing the killed and wounded. Some buildings had been taken, but only after very heavy fighting. A woman came out of a house, drew a gun and wounded two of our men. When she was shot it transpired that "she" was an Arab in disguise. The village was apparently full of Iraqi volunteers with unlimited quantities of weapons and ammunition. We, on the other hand, had almost run out of what little we had. Our officers were discussing the possibility of stopping the fight and retreating from the village.

Dror asked one of the *Etzel* men to contact Yo'ed and tell him that a great part of the village center was in our hands, hoping that this information would encourage Headquarters to go on with the operation. The ploy succeeded, and shortly afterwards our men began to shoot heavily. We afterwards learnt that when our messenger reached Headquarters he was in time to witness the arrival of fighters bringing in whole cases of ammunition found in the captured buildings. The cases were marked: "Palestine Police."

By midday we had captured the village and cleaned it up. The fighting continued. Arab snipers continued shooting from the surrounding hills, and as I sat with Gideon in one of the houses we could hear the ping of bullets hitting the wall above us. Gideon wanted to look out of the window and pin-point the troublesome sniper.

"Wait!" I pushed his head down roughly, not wanting the snipers to discover us. "They'll get you before you can even see where they are, and then – no Gideon." There was no doubt in my mind that at least one gun was fixed on that window, with a man's finger on the trigger just waiting for the opportunity.

Pulling his helmet off his head, Gideon stuck it on the barrel of his gun and lifted it up for a second. At least one bullet hit the gun itself and a number of them riddled his helmet.

It was late at night. Twenty four hours had passed since we left Giv'at Shaul for Deir Yassin. The shooting had finally quietened down and, together with some other fighters, I had been sent to the rear base for a short rest and a quick nap in the Giv'at Shaul beer factory. It was there I heard more details of the battle. In some parts of the village the Arabs had fought obstinately in every street and house and on every roof. Even when forced to retreat and abandon their women and children in the houses that had fallen to us, they continued shooting. Many of them escaped to the mountains and hid among the rocks, from which they went on firing at us for many hours. They shot at every moving object and caused us many casualties. It was not only our men that they got but also some of their own women and children. The targets were hard to identify from such a distance, having the setting sun behind them. To this was added the hysterical behaviour of the women who were running back and forth in the crossfire between us, turning themselves into targets in what was practically indiscriminate shooting. Arab fighters, finding themselves trapped indoors with no way to retreat, hid behind the locked doors and brought down many of our men. This left us no option but to toss grenades into the houses in order to silence them and that, too, caused the death of many women and children.

When we finally forced our way in we discovered many women and children hiding in the cupboards and under the beds. Some of the "women" were still unshaved.... All the survivors were collected and transported behind the Arab lines in East Jerusalem.

Finally I slept, only to awaken to a cacaphony of terrifying screams filling the air: "Hear O Israel our Lord, the Lord is one!" I was totally confused. Had the Arabs launched a counter-attack and were by now slaughtering the inhabitants of the quarter? Remembering the tales of pogroms in Europe I grabbed hold of my rifle and ran outside. Such a thing could not be permitted here.

It was a false alarm and the screaming women were the unhappy inmates of the adjacent insane asylum. I went back and slept till morning.

When I returned to Deir Yassin I heard the good news that the *Hagana* had taken the *Kastel* (A vital lookout at the entrance to Jerusalem), Abdul Kader El Husseini, the popular hero of the Arab rioters, had been killed and his body abandoned by his men as they fled in panic.

This was more than good news, as much blood had been spilt to capture the peak of the *Kastel* and many lives had been lost in the effort to get control over this position – which, because of its elevation, gave whoever held it control over the road leading to Jerusalem and its environs. It had often been taken by the *Hagana*, only to fall back into Arab hands. The night we took Deir Yassin the *Hagana* captured the *Kastel* position once and for all and established its men there permanently.

From our vantage point in Deir Yassin we could see the flames rising from the Kolonia School above Motza. The *Hagana* had set fire to it after the place had been abandoned by the Arabs, following the capture of the *Kastel*, and Deir Yassin.

The tide had now turned, and the Arabs, having lost their initial advantage, were now put on the defensive. This fact was doubly significant as the 15th of May was approaching, the date on which the British were scheduled to leave the country, and the surrounding Arab States were ready to invade us and crush the Jewish community totally.

Yet even then, at a time when the whole country was at war and there was not a man among us who was not fighting the common enemy, the official leaders of the community persisted in their animosity towards us, not to say praise. Still, for the first time in many years we did feel that we were part of a fighting fraternity. In Deir Yassin, where there was still sporadic fire, and we were busy cleaning up the village, we were approached by some *Palmach* men positioned in the area who congratulated us on the success of our operation and offered to help in the final stages.

Experienced as we were in the bitterness of internecine hatred, there was something very refreshing in this new attitude. We desperately wanted to believe that it signified the breaking of the ice; that this time the *Hagana* leaders and the rest of the community would be forced to admit that the *Etzel* and the *Lehi* had done a fine job and, after some hard and bitter fighting, had captured a strategic point of major importance. And for the first time this operation had been planned in complete co-ordination with their Headquarters. We were badly in need of some such recognition on their part. Personally I, too, expected a sign of appreciation and friendship. As in the days of the Rebellion Movement, we were hungry for any sign of sympathy...

Our disillusion was not late in coming...

Deir Yassin village had been in our hands for several days when we learnt that the British were planning to bomb it from the air in order to kill the *Etzel* and *Lehi* men who were holding it! As we had no anti-aircraft artillery we informed the *Hagana* that we were leaving the place, but, much to our astonishment, they tried to stop us by force, going so far as to threaten to open fire on us. Fortunately, their own people refused to obey such an order to shoot and their officers had no option but to let us go. It later transpired that the British had fully intended to bomb the village in order to destroy us, but when they learnt that the place was now occupied by the *Hagana* they gave up the idea.

We passed through the streets of Jerusalem in convoy, singing "Deir Yassin is ours!" The passers-by, among them many members of the *Hagana*, clapped and cheered us. But even before we had entered our homes the city was rife with terrible rumors about the atrocities we had allegedly perpertrated against the "helpless" inhabitants of the village. The Arabs, the British and the leaders of the Jewish Community outdid themselves in spreading hair-raising tales and inciting the people against us.

One couldn't blame the Arabs, who had sustained heavy losses and were in a general state of shock. They had never hidden their lust for mass killings, rape, cutting up our corpses and generally humiliating and desecrating our living and dead. Now that we had overcome them they were quick to accuse us of all those crimes they had intended to commit against us. Their wild charges actually meant very little to us. Let them scream, weep and wail! This was only further proof that they had been hard hit. We had no intention of convincing them that we were really "humane." In their eyes, all the talk about the "purity of arms and humanity" was nothing more than an expression of weakness, encouraging them to believe that they could push us back into the sea by means of barbaric terrorism.

Nor was it hard to understand the British, who had also been hit where it hurt most. For them the Jews were nothing more than traitors, who had given up all hope of redemption – had they not been taught as much in England at their mother's knee, suckled on the milk of antisemitism? The damned crucifiers of the Redeemer were capable of anything...

What really caused us pain was the incitement of our people by the Jewish leaders. Such venomous expressions of hatred had not been heard since the explosion in the King David Hotel. At that time we had been persecuted and held up to public shame, but we took it in our stride, knowing that the time was not far off when the people would realize who were its true friends and who its enemies. But now? After such a victory? With the best of our comrades lying dead or wounded, some of them crippled for life? How dared they – now that we were united with our whole people in this bitter and desperate struggle for survival – incite and revive the old hatred? It was almost more than we could bear.

Islands of Hebrew Government

Once more I was back at my job in the Post Office. For some days after the capture of Deir Yassin some of the Arab staff still showed up, walking around in a daze, their whole bearing expressing fear and shock. Encountering one of the Jewish workers, they would lower their eyes in humiliation. I must confess it did me good to see them so. How could I pity them in their plight after all they had done to us: the cunning provocations, the insolent threats of annihilation while we were grieving for our brethren they had just massacred. It was to our credit that we refrained from taunting them with their weaknesses, with the truth, as compared with their empty boasting. Yes, we were happy to see them humbled and cut down to size. Gone was the bombast of the past, the taunting finger pretending to cut the throat from ear to ear.

Soon they stopped coming to work altogether, and as soon as the Jewish staff took over the responsibility of running the Post Office, the British officials too, failed to appear. The post office had become Jewish!

After *Lehi*'s retaliatory action following the Ben-Yehuda explosion, the British began to retreat more and more into their strongholds. They became a rarity in the Jewish zones, where they dared not show themselves, and it was then that independent Jewish government began to take shape.

With the fall of Deir Yassin and the *Kastel,* members of the British civilian administration, too, stopped going to work, preferring the protection of the military barracks and preparing themselves for the rapidly approaching evacuation. They were replaced by Jews, and a new reality was created: the Jews administered the civil workings of their city, unaided and acting under the orders of their own institutions. Though argument was rife whether an Israeli State should be declared or not, small nuclei of independent Hebrew government were forming, such as *The People's Administration* – a temporary government until the time when the British left for good. Then only did this government solemnly declare the inauguration of the State of Israel. Most of the country, it was true, was in enemy hands; the majority of our population was totally dependent on our brethren in the diaspora; our community leaders here were ready to relinquish Jerusalem, the heart of our nation, to foreign rule domination. Yet in spite of all this, here and there small islands of independent Jewish rule were emerging. The Jewish State was a fact, whether officially declared or not, and what we had taken as the spoils of war would remain ours.

The "Anonymous" Soldiers emerged from the underground.

Lehi and *Etzel* put up their military camps for all the world to see. They served as training camps and bases for the organization of military operations. The *Etzel* men wore an identification pin bearing a hand holding a rifle, with a map of the country in the background and the slogan *"Rak Kakh!"* (There is no other way). Our fighters, too, wore a pin depicting a hand raised as in taking an oath, and the slogan: "If I forget thee, O Jerusalem, let my right hand wither."

★

We used one of the abandoned buildings in Sheikh Bader as a training center, naming it "Yoav Camp," dedicated to the memory of a *Lehi* man who had met his death while engaged in assaulting a British armoured vehicle. It was there that I took part in a comprehensive course in the use of firearms. No longer hindered by the restraints imposed by the underground, we could enjoy decent training conditions and target practice with real guns. I was pleased to see that I was still a good shot, even though my head was slanted at a somewhat queer angle when taking aim because of a weakness in my right eye.

I also discovered another talent, one I never suspected I excelled in, when someone organized a competition as to who could hold a drawn revolver hand raised high, the longest.

We drew. I watched my friends doing their utmost to keep the hand holding their revolver at a steady height. One by one they tired and their hands began to droop. The best of them could only keep it up for six to seven minutes. Israel, who managed to hold his gun up for fifteen minutes, became the object of general admiration. Surprised at myself, I kept mine up as long as he did. The gun was heavy but my hand was steady. Twenty minutes. My hand felt as if it were made of lead. I'd reached my limit!

Twenty five minutes. It was certainly difficult, but still not

274

impossible... Thirty one minutes and twenty seconds. My hand fell, to the loud cheers of my friends.

I felt a small satisfaction at this victory. It wasn't that I craved praise or wanted to be outstanding among my peers, but I realized one need not be a Hercules to overcome grave obstacles. It was will-power that did it. Most of my friends – though not all – were husky types, much stronger than myself. Zamir, seeing me standing there with my hand stretched out said: "You could stand the worst torture without opening your mouth!" I agreed with him.

★

A block of buildings we renovated in the abandoned village of Lifta served us as another camp. We named it "Eldad" for another one of our friends who fell in Deir Yassin. It was there that I became aware of the fact that many acquaintances of mine were *Lehi* members. Who would have thought that the brothers Yankele and Benjamin Shalom, my close neighbours, were active in the *Lehi?* How good it was to renew our friendship that went back to the days of hide-and-seek and "hit the stick." And who could have guessed that Yehoshua, the Eldad Camp fighter, was none other than Nissim Helber, my former class mate at Ratisbonne?

Just a few days earlier I had seen him kissing his mother and father goodbye. I stood there watching him: an upstanding youth, dressed in khaki and in full military equipment, barely hiding his impatience to go. But his poor parents were crying! It must be hard to send a beloved child to war. Later I discovered that my neighbour Nissim had been on his way to the "Eldad Camp." He had been in the *Hagana* before that, but after the leaders of the community agreed to hand Jerusalem over to international powers – refusing to initiate a campaign to take the city – he left the *Hagana* to join us. But first he completed a course in the use of machine guns, after which he took a Bren and joined the *Lehi*. We talked, he told me about his brother Simon and I told him about my own brothers. We remembered our days at school and wondered at the great number of Ratisbonne pupils who had joined the *Etzel* and the *Lehi*. Could it have been the Principal – a Fenchman well known for his love of the Motherland and his dedication to the idea of liberty – who had influenced us in our childhood?

Or perhaps it was that, unlike the pupils of the Hebrew schools, we did not belong to any youth movement, and had not been brain-washed to hate the "Revisionists". Or had we been drawn to the underground because we were just poor, working class children who had never been spoiled or pampered from the day of our birth, and knew instinctively that liberty had to be won the hard way?

In the process of organizing into military formations, my cell was incorporated into a combat unit. Amos of the 6th Division asked me to be liaison for him. I agreed, provided I could participate in all combat operations involving my own unit. Amos agreed and was to keep his promise.

Things began to improve on all fronts in the country. *Hagana* units began to take the initiative and attacked the bases of the Arab gangs right in the heart of Arab villages. Following these attacks the Arabs packed up and left, abandoning their homes and property, and the Jewish settlements which had long suffered from the gangs entrenched in their neighbourhood were finally relieved of the constant harassment and could return to normal.

Jerusalem alone knew no relief.

True, many quarters were now free from the menace of Arab snipers, but these had been replaced by mortar and cannon fire. The Arabs had managed to lay their hands on a number of such guns and positioned them at *Nebi Samuel* – said to be the burial place of Samuel the Prophet – an excellent observation post, from which they fired daily at the Jewish quarters of Jerusalem and at the road leading down to the plain.

The mortars fell at all hours of the day, bringing in their wake death and destruction.

Our house was struck by two such mortars, but luckily only a few bricks fell from the wall and no one was harmed.

There was hardly a house in the city that had not been hit by mortars. Fortunately for Jerusalem, its houses are built of stone, and a mortar striking a wall can only make a hole in it, not destroy it.

Between one burst of mortar fire and another I would rush round the beleagured streets, bringing messages to Amos. Coming upon some victims, wounded and crying for help, I would stand there helplessly, waiting for some vehicle to pass by and take them to hospital.

The number of casualties increased daily.

Not a day passed but some acquaintance of mine would be reported killed. A shell hit the Aboutbul home in our lane, killing four and wounding two of the family. Two of our milkman's children were badly wounded by shrapnel. In Bagdadi's house across the road, a girl was killed. Yehuda Hayun, a boyhood friend of mine who had been slightly wounded in the hand during one of the skirmishes he had been engaged in as a *Hagana* member, was killed by a shell on his way to the Sick Fund for first aid. Issachar, one of the six who comprised our Youth Cell, left the camp for a short leave and had reached the door of his home when a shell hit one of the walls. A flying brick hit him in the head and killed him.

But worst of all – the city was under siege. No water supply, no electricity. Public traffic was at a stop and there was an ever-growing scarcity of food, water and fuel, for which the people would have to queue up patiently in the street while shells exploded in the close packed line, killing and maiming.

Slowly hunger became widespread. The roads were blocked and the meagre stores of foodstuffs were allocated in small rations. Distribution stations for food and water were opened sporadically, between shellings, and the inhabitants, hungry and thirsty as they were, were forced to wander through the streets in constant danger, searching for the distribution depots. There were also those who dared to venture into the fields, there to pick what edible plants and grasses they could find.

Many times the *Hagana* tried to break the siege and bring food into the city. These attempts, for all that they cost many precious lives, were mostly unsuccessful. The capture of Deir Yassin made a tiny crack in the ring closing in on the city and the *Hagana* built a small airfield near the village. But the "air force" of the embryo State was made up of just a few piper cubs – planes so small that the amount of food brought in by them was negligible, when compared with the needs of 100,000 inhabitants.

This airfield was the source of much speculation in the city. There were those who said, whether cynically or in anger, that the real function of the Deir Yassin field was not to bring food and arms into the town, but to take out those community leaders who had not managed to leave Jerusalem in the good days before the siege...

Dr. Bernard Joseph (known as Dov Yoseph) was nominated Governor of Jerusalem. The nomination was "temporary," holding good only until a U.N.O. force would take over administration of the city. The *Hagana* was now under the command of David Shaltiel, who had gotten his military experience as a sergeant in the French Foreign Legion. As a counter-balance to this meagre experience in all things military, Shaltiel was rich in other qualities which were much valued by Ben Gurion, foremost among them was his unadulterated hatred of the *Lehi* and the *Etzel*. As head of the *Hagana* Intelligence Service (*Shai*) he had been very active against these underground organizations.

The *Etzel* launched an assault on Jaffa, which had become an active base of the Arab gangs who fired ceaselessly at the border districts of Tel-Aviv. Jaffa at that time was the largest Arab city in the country and a major center of power. But in this attack the *Etzel* also had to confront a regular military force – the British army. The latter did everything within their power to ensure an Arab victory, rejecting totally the possibility that Jaffa could fall into Jewish hands. Their soldiers, who had been confined to their barracks in preparation for the coming evacuation, came out in full force to join the fight. The *Etzel* blocked their tanks and continued to advance in the streets of Jaffa, the British retreating before them. Orders came from London to throw in more forces and go on fighting, but the *Etzel* would not retreat. With a heroism that has by now become legendary they blocked the British in their steel monsters. General MacMillan was forced to admit that he was unable to force them out of Jaffa nor was there any point in attempting to do this as the local population was fleeing in panic and no force could stop them. Jaffa had become a ghost city and who was there to fight for? Even if he beat the *Etzel* back, to whom could he hand the city?

Using the *Hagana* as intermediary, the British contacted the *Etzel*, promising not to interfere in Jaffa on two conditions: 1) The *Etzel* must promise not to harm the British forces camped in the Manshia quarter in Jaffa. 2) The *Etzel* must undertake to leave British patrols in the vicinity of the police station strictly alone.

While Menahem Begin was conferring with his men at *Etzel* Headquarters, discussing the British offer, a terrifying explosion was heard. "What is it?" he asked, turning to "Gidi," who was in charge of operations. "Gidi," (Amichai Paglin) replied: "It's our reply to the British offer. That was the explosion of the Manshia police station."

At the beginning of May there seemed to be some improvement in the general situation on the different fronts in the center of the country. Our luck appeared to be turning.

Not so in the *Gush Etzion* area, the isolated Jewish settlements on the way to Hebron. These settlements, clinging to the barren rocks of the Hebron mountain, had been cut off for a long time, and no mechanized convoy had been able to reach them. An attempt to infiltrate a *Palmach* platoon on foot, along paths in the mountains, ended in catastrophe. The men, 35 in number, were discovered and surrounded by hundreds of villagers of the area. They fought in desperation for many hours to the last man.

The *Gush Etzion* block was still cut off, with no reserves, insufficient ammunition and no supply of food or medicine. Clearly the settlers could not hold out much longer, but they refused to leave, choosing to die rather than give up their land.

On the 4th of May, the bloc was attacked by an armoured force of the Jordanian Legion, reinforced by four British tanks. The ultimate goal of the attack was Jerusalem. Again and again they shelled the settlements in the attempt to force their way in. The defenders, isolated and worn out as they were, nevertheless succeeded in repelling the attack. But the cost was heavy – the fallen could not be replaced.

The Legion attacked relentlessly, day and night, and on the seventh day succeeded in breaking through the defences. Next morning, the day before the declaration of the independence of Israel, the Jordanians, followed by hordes of villagers from Hebron and the area, burst into *Gush Etzion* and proceeded to massacre the settlers who had capitulated, taking no more than a handful of prisoners.

The settlements were annihilated, the houses destroyed, the gardens and the trees torn up and burnt. Only one old oak tree was left where it stood on the hilltop, watching the devastation below.

A time would come when the oak would be comforted: after the Six Days' War the sons of those who had fallen in defending Gush Etzion returned to rebuild their heritage. The weeping oak was now the oak of redemption.

Grieve for the Jewish Quarter!

May the 15th, when the British were scheduled to depart, was rapidly approaching. The British High Commissioner, whose life we had so often attempted to take, was packing up. He had good reason for satisfaction: his prediction that blood would flow here if Britain were forced to leave was amply fulfilled. No one had worked harder than he to achieve this end! Many Arab states threatened to join the war and wipe the Jews off the face of the earth. These were no empty threats but backed up by the unsheathing of swords. Rows of armoured vehicles, representing seven Arab states, stood waiting for the order to proceed with the holocaust.

We had to move fast: acquire territory, improve our positions and get control of strategic points before they arrived.

In Jerusalem the front line passed right through the heart of the besieged city, the Jewish quarter beleaguered within it.

To reach this enclave it was necessary to break through the

ancient city walls and the crowded Arab quarters now amply reinforced by "volunteers" from other Arab lands. Between us and the walls were still the British, refusing to surrender their strategic positions and acting as a wedge between us and the Arabs, letting it be clearly understood that these positions would be transferred into Arab hands when the time came for the British departure. Knowing this, the *Hagana* was busy planning ways and means of gaining control over these important places the moment they were abandoned, and all plans for forcing our way into the Jewish quarter had to be put off.

This quarter meant more to us than any other. We identified with its inhabitants who fought so bravely without any proper weapons, on starvation rations and hardly any water. How could we forget the women, the children and the aged, whose homes had been turned into defence positions. The Western Wall; and the Temple Mount – symbol of our faith, life and struggle.

No one could remain untouched by the unbelievable courage displayed by the defenders of the Jewish quarter. But how long could they hold out against such numbers? We had good reason to fear that if we delayed too long in coming to their aid by breaking our way in, they would suffer the same fate as *Gush Etzion.*

Some time before the 14th of May the leaders of the *Hagana,* and *Etzel* conferred and drew up a detailed plan in preparation for the British evacuation. But the *Lehi,* mistrusting any agreements with the *Hagana,* stayed away from these meetings.

The *Hagana* and the *Etzel* divided the city into zones and it was decided that a maximum effort be made to gain control over the most critical ones in the north and the south. According to the plan, the *Etzel* was to attack from the Russian compound, advancing northwards towards Sheikh Jerrach and the Police Academy. The *Hagana,* also coming from the Russian compound, would move in the southern direction, towards the Allenby Camp.

The *Lehi,* without co-ordinating with the other two organizations, decided to force its way into the Old City. Then, realizing that without additional support the whole project would be jeopardized, we turned to the others for help, using every means in our power to convince them of the absolute necessity of such an operation at that time.

The *Hagana* procrastinated: the situation in the Old City was satisfactory; there was no lack of men or supplies and there was nothing to get desperate about.

It was different with the *Etzel*. They were as eager as we were to liberate the Old City, but now found themselves obliged to adhere to the agreement reached with the *Hagana* Command.

Though we were well aware that such an operation was beyond our meagre capabilities, we could not stand by, passively watching the desperate struggle put up by the people of the Jewish quarter. Something had to be done, whatever the cost, and in our hearts we wanted to believe that when the time came our brothers-in-arms would not withhold their assistance.

A State is declared in Tel-Aviv

On the 14th of May, 1948, a Friday morning, the State of Israel was born. In Jerusalem there was nothing to distinguish that day from any other, and fighting went on as usual. Well-armed we set out from the "Eldad" and "Yoav" Camps and marched towards *Bevingrad* (a notorious British stronghold in the center of the city). It was hard to believe that there was no one there, that the "Dragon's Teeth" (cones of reinforced concrete with which the British encircled their strongholds as protection against the insurgents), were now nothing more than empty facades hiding buildings and forsaken firing positions! We still found it hard to believe that the British lion had left his barbed-wire cage, retreating ignominiously to his proper lair and leaving behind him, as a reminder of his past iniquities, the stone lion on the roof of the Generali Building!

But they were well and truly gone and there was no turning the clock back.

My comrades and I entered the Central Post Office building, where I had spent five years of my life, beginning as a teenager in the telegram room and going on as a postman. For five years I had managed to hide my true identity and the vocation that gave meaning to my existence – my membership in the *Lehi*. But that day I walked in, upright and confident, the symbol of the *Lehi* on my cap for all to see.

As I walked up the stairs I was beset by memories of what now seemed to be my distant childhood. It was on these walls that I had written the slogan: "Freedom or Death."

How many of my comrades had given their lives without realizing the dream of a free Israel! Would I be among those privileged to see it come true in my own lifetime?

"Has anyone got a pencil?" I asked, and when it was handed to me, my colleagues were astonished to see me cover the whole width of the wall with the words "Freedom or Death."

"So it was you who did it then!" exclaimed one of the workers, remembering the "cheeky" slogan daubed there in the time of the British. "Good for you!"

From the Post Office we went to the Anglo Palestine Bank, there to deploy for the coming battle for the Old City.

Once again we turned to the *Hagana* and the *Etzel,* practically begging for a positive reply. In the meantime our boys went down into the storeroom and changed their clothes, for British uniforms. I was the only one who couldn't find a size small enough to fit me, so I remained as I was.

We waited till after noon and as no reply was forthcoming – decided to act. Dror called me and five other men to join him.

"Wait here!" he ordered.

In the meantime our men came out of *Bevingrad,* group by group, each one with its special assignment: to capture a number of buildings that stood between us and the Walls of the Old City.

I wished I had been among these first groups, but it was good to know that Dror wanted me to fight beside him.

We had fought together many times; shoulder to shoulder, in Katamon as in Deir Yassin, and now, finally, in the City of David. As always, Giora was there and I prayed all would go well with us as in the past.

The target of our group was the Barclays Building, the

outermost among the houses we were to take that day – (the Jerusalem Municipality has its offices there now). This building overlooked the Old City and the Arab positions inside its walls.

Once the building was in our hands, we went up to the roof and kept up a steady barrage of fire, aiming at any Arab in sight. We kept this up till dark. The Arabs, for their part, shot at us indiscriminately, whether they saw us or not, and it was obvious they suffered no shortage of rifles or machine guns, and simply wasted their ammunition.

We, on the other hand, had to economise on every bullet, saving them for the next day when we planned to take the walls. So as soon as it was dark we stopped shooting, even though they kept at it all through the night. Then there came an unexpected lull and someone looked at his watch. "Midnight" – he said.

May 15, 1948

Exactly at the moment of the formal termination of British Rule in Palestine there we were, sprawling on a roof facing the walls of the Old City. "Listen, everybody," I cried, pulling out a grenade, "this is the moment we've been waiting for – the end of British domination!" They looked at me and it was hard to say whether they were jubilant or mocking.

"Put your head down, brother," I heard a voice in the dark saying, "Don't use it. We still need it."

"In God's name, forward!" I shouted and, rising above the balustrade I cast the grenade with all my power at the walls.

The quiet of the night was shaken by the explosion, to be immediately followed by a "concert" of lead and fire. "There's their answer for you," came Giora's dry rejoinder. Where the hell had they obtained so much ammunition? "If we had only a tenth of what they've just wasted on us we'd have reached Jordan by now" said Giora.

All night they fired at us non-stop, and some of the bullets fired that night can still be seen, buried in the walls of what is today the building of the Municipality of Jerusalem.

Tired as we were, we couldn't afford to sleep for fear the enemy might try to cross the square which separated us.

Finally came the dawn – the morning of May 15, the first Independence Day of the State of Israel.

"Skinny Jacob" (Gershon Levy) and I were asked to lead two units in storming the mass of buildings behind the square. My unit was to take the old Post Office Building, and Jacob's – the Fast Hotel. The two units swooped across the square together and in a few seconds, before the Jordanian Legionnaires could get us within their sights – we were on the other side and out of range of most of the enemy snipers stationed on the walls. The square was an inferno of rifle and gun fire. Now the main trouble came from the snipers in Notre Dame Church. We had to find cover immediately and by means of a detonator, broke the lock on the gate of the old Post Office and rushed inside.

We progressed from room to room in a constant exchange of fire. This time I had a Tommy-gun that could be depended on, unlike my erratic Sten at Deir Yassin. It didn't take us long to clean up each floor and get full control of the building. "They were shooting at us all night," said Michael, as we stood looking at the corpses. I saw that he was grinning wryly with one eye. The other was covered in blood.

"Michael, you got it in the eye! Go to the doctor immediately!"

"Leave me alone," he answered indifferently, as if we were talking about someone else. "Just let me go on! I'm fine, I tell you, so don't call the orderlies before we've cleaned the place up, or they'll get hurt on the way here."

"Orderly! A stretcher!" I shouted.

"Be a sport and wait a while... let me go on." he went on begging me, training his gun on some target outside with his one good eye.

I refused to listen to him and went on calling to my friends in the Barclays Bank Building to hurry and send us the orderlies with a stretcher. The stretcher bearers were fully covered from all our positions as they crossed the square. Protesting vehemently, Michael was taken to the hospital.

Michael (Benyamin Shalom) was a neighbour of mine and I not only knew his parents well but thought very highly of them. They must have taken great pride in Michael's beauty, the most handsome of their sons. Would it make them proud that he had given his eye for the walls of the Old City? If I had a son who made such a sacrifice I would surely be proud of him, I thought. "Dear God," I prayed silently, "If the same thing should happen to me and I get it in the eye, let it be my right eye – it always was the weaker. Don't let it be my left eye – it's made me a champion sniper!"

We went on firing from the old Post Office building till we had captured and cleaned up the adjacent structure, with the enemy meanwhile letting loose a rain of fire on our heads. We, on the other hand, were careful of every bullet. As we stood there, taking careful aim before each shot, our men assaulted the church.

Someone came in, fresh from a meeting with the *Hagana*. "Ben-Gurion," he reported, "has declared the establishment of a Jewish State at a meeting in Tel-Aviv. The *Hagana* men told me they heard it on the radio."

From our point of view, independence had begun two months ago, with our emergence from the underground. In any case, we didn't believe there was anything to celebrate yet. Most of the country was in the hands of strangers, even the Old City of Jerusalem. It was here that the future of the State would be determined, here and in every place where Jewish youths were fighting, so what was the good of declarations?

Like my comrades, I was indifferent. The ceremony in Tel-Aviv meant far less to us than the sharp-shooters on the walls.

With the capture of Notre Dame Church and its outlying buildings, we were at long last face to face with the wall. Our positions on the roof gave us the advantage over those of the Arabs stationed on top of them particularly in that segment through which we were planning to force our way inside in order to join up with the men fighting in the Jewish quarter.

Again and again we turned to the *Hagana,* asking for reinforcements to enable us to hold on to the houses we would take on our way into the Old City. Our forces were insufficient, but still the *Hagana* hesitated. Meir, who was in charge of the *Lehi* in Jerusalem pleaded for help and did his best to convince them, explaining that the armoured forces of the Jordanian Legionares were approaching the City and the defenders, hungry and lacking ammunition as they were, would fall into their hands. Shaltiel, Commanding Officer of Jerusalem, thought otherwise, arguing that there was enough food and ammunition and that there was no valid reason to fear the Jordanian Legion, particularly as it was a well-known fact that armoured units could do nothing in a highly built up area.

The *Etzel,* when we turned to them, told us that they were bound by an agreement with the *Hagana,* and "a contract is a contract."

It was inconceivable to us that the *Hagana* and the *Etzel* would persist in their refusal, would ignore the uniqueness of the opportunity and the fact that we might never have such a chance again, but they were adamant.

We went on fighting in the meantime, not evacuating our men from the church in the hope that confirmation of help would arrive at any minute. In a very short time two of our friends were killed and others wounded. Yehoshua – no other than Nissim Helber, who only a few weeks ago I had watched kissing his parents goodbye on the doorstep of their home – would never return alive. Ya'akov, our Yankele, forever laughing and joking – was gone. He who was so strong that he held a Bren gun as lightly as a pistol; he who, together with Jimmy, had managed to drive a Post Office Vehicle to the Sarona Police Headquarters and blow it up – was no more. The Government of Israel had today established its administrative offices in that same Sarona, on the first day of its official inauguration – but Yankele was dead. We called that roof "the Roof of Death."

Ophra was killed! I had always looked forward to meeting her, but now this would never be. My friends told me that she had been a *Hagana* member for many years but joined us to fight for Jerusalem, the Capital of Israel. She had begged to be sent to join the battle for the Old City, only to be killed there while waiting for the sign to attack from the Fast Hotel.

Sha'ul, Achino'am and Kochava were wounded, among many others. There was nothing for it but to inform the *Hagana* that we would have to relinquish some of the buildings we had taken. It was a question of either breaking into the Old City at once or retreating.

They did not come.

One of our Brens was useless, with one barrel simply worn out and the other pierced by an enemy bullet. We were growing weaker, and things went wrong with one weapon after another. Half of us had been killed or wounded and the others were beginning to lose confidence. The tension and the superhuman efforts of the last few days were beginning to take their toll.

An Arab unit from Musrara managed to penetrate Bible House and, once there, threw a grenade at a group of our boys who were waiting to be briefed in a public garden. Again there were wounded, forcing us to shorten the lines and retreat, abandoning Notre Dame we recaptured Bible House and consolidated our positions there.

My orders were to evacuate the old Post Office building and return with my men to the Barclays Bank. With a heavy heart I thought of all my fallen comrades. If only we had made it to the Old City... But to have given the ultimate sacrifice in order to retreat...?

Once again we had to cross the square lying between the Barclays and the Post Office buildings, but this time it was more difficult. Snipers shooting from the direction of the Nablus Gate kept up a constant volley of fire. We had run out of grenades and there were only a couple of flash-bombs left.

I asked one of the men, Amatzia, to take a quick look at the Damascus Gate and pin-point the source of fire. As soon as he raised his head it became the focus for endless bursts of fire. Luckily he was unhurt.

Cursing myself for having endangered him so, I began to wonder why I hadn't looked out myself. I knew that I was responsible for the unit and couldn't do everything myself. It was only logical that orders had to be given, but it seemed to be wrong somehow. I realized I would have to stay till the last man had left

The British evacuate Eretz Israel

The British flag is lowered

British soldiers board ships and evacuate

The municipality building, Barclays Bank

The old Post office building

the building in order to provide them with cover as they crossed the square, yet I had the nagging feeling that I should take all the risks myself.

After a flash-bomb was thrown in the direction of Nablus Gate there was a few seconds' quiet and three of my men jumped out and crossed the square. I was now alone and the fire intensified. Something told me that I wouldn't make it in safety but there was no alternative. I was alone in an abandoned building... I began to run, bullets whistling past my ears. The magazine containing the ammo for my Tommy gun, that was tied to my belt, got undone and fell off, but I made it unscathed.

Glancing backwards I saw the magazine lying in the middle of the square and instinctively began to run back to retrieve it. Ammunition was too precious to be abandoned... Bullets were screeching all around me and I could hear the terrified screams of my friends on the roof of Barclays Bank calling: "Maniac! Let it be! Madman!"

Again I returned, untouched. Avramico showed me some bullet holes in the magazine, which was now rendered useless. "Look!" he said, "Was this worth risking death for?"

I was stationed at one of the windows of Bible House and handed an English rifle. My job was to watch the walls, on the other side of which I observed an Arab carrying sandbags to the roof of the *Freres* School. They were putting up a look-out and a fortified position at that point which would put our own in danger. I took aim and, before I had time to cushion the butt well into my shoulder – there was his head right within my sights. I immediately pressed the trigger and was hit smartly on the chin by the recoil. I had to bear that pain for a fortnight but it was worth it. The Arab fell on the sand-bags and lay there dead, his hands spread before him on the balustrade.

Dan, who commuted from one position to the other, came to see us, carrying the last Bren gun that was left. I showed him the position on the roof opposite us. We both took aim – Dan with his machine-gun and I with the rifle – and waited.

Another Arab appeared but I told Dan to wait, thinking that there might be more coming up and the Bren could deal with them all together. In a few minutes two more of them appeared on the roof and we liquidated the three. "Let them have a Roof of Death too!" said Dan.

We remained at our posts till midnight and only then the Hagana men who were supposed to relieve us showed up.

I left then but not to rest or sleep. I was sent to the *Bikur Cholim* Hospital to join a guard of honour around the bodies of our comrades. Again I saw Yankele, a smile on his lips even in death. And I met Ophra, a privilege denied me when she was alive. Then there was Gabriel, someone I had never heard of. I wanted to look at Yehoshua but was quite blinded by tears.

The *Hagana* men who had come so late to relieve us paid a heavy price when they recaptured Notre Dame after we had been forced to retreat. There were four dead and many wounded in this battle. Sometime later we heard that the attacks we had waged against the buildings near the wall had engaged most of the Arab forces in the Old City, among them the notorious Iraqi volunteers. This eased the pressure somewhat on our positions in the Old City. The *Hagana* leader there, Moshe Rosnak, informed Shaltiel by radio that he was in a location to attack the enemy positions, now greatly under-manned, and widen his radius of control. Should the momentum of our attack continue, he might even be able to attempt to join the outside force, thus breaking the prolonged siege.

Shaltiel refused Rosnak permission to attack but the latter nevertheless decided to capture some places of strategic value the Armenian quarter, which was still free of Arabs at the time. Shaltiel demanded that he retreat at once. "Otherwise," he told Rosnak, "Our relations with the Consular community will deteriorate!"

The Jewish fighters left the Armenian quarter, thus losing a precious opportunity which may never return. Next morning the Arab Legion sent additional reinforcements to bolster the volunteer units from Syria, Iraq and Egypt.

Five separate Arab Armies invaded the country and combat conditions were completely changed. The Lebanese and the Syrians attacked in the Galillee; the Iraqis in Samaria; the Arab

Legion marched on Jerusalem from Trans-Jordan and from there to the center of the country; and the Egyptians attacked from the south.

The situation in Jerusalem again became intolerable. There was fighting in the whole country and every settlement found itself on the front line - Jerusalem however was in a state of siege, completely surrounded by two regular armies – the Egyptians who had marched from the direction of Hebron and *Gush Etzion* to Ramat Rachel, and the Trans-Jordanians (as they called themselves then) who helped by the British, attacked the besieged Holy City of Jerusalem from the north and the east. The irregular Arab forces that had already been shelling Jerusalem long before May 15, were now strongly reinforced by the Egyptian and Jordanian artillery, and were harassing us from the west and the south.

Every day I would drive over on my bike to the Press Bureau in Ben Yehuda to get Amos a copy of the official news bulletin issued to the press (reading it myself, of course, as soon as I got it). One morning I was shocked to read that the Egyptians had taken Ramat Rahel and the sixty *Etzel* men who had been stationed there were missing.

At first I couldn't take it in. Sixty! All ours! For me the *Etzel* and the *Lehi* were one by now. I knew and liked many of the *Etzel* men, admiring them whole heartedly for their courage and devotion.

A whole day passed before we learnt what had actually happened. That the situation was much better than announced. It was true that the Egyptians had penetrated Ramat Rahel and all communications were cut off between our fighters and Jerusalem. The *kibbutz* members had been evacuated some time before and the *Etzel* men who were garrisoned there put up a brave fight, surrounded as they were by enormous enemy forces with unlimited supplies of heavy artillery and ammunition. The ensuing battle was long and hard, but finally the *Etzel* courageously repelled the enemy, saved the *kibbutz* and blocked the Egyptians' progress to Jerusalem. Later on I learnt that Shlomo Lombrozo, a good school friend of mine, had shown remarkable courage and escaped death by nothing less than a miracle, Tragically several months later he was killed while fighting in the Israeli Defence Force (I.D.F.)

Until the Arrival of the U.N.O.

With the inauguration of the State of Israel, Dov Yoseph's nomination as Governor of Jerusalem was confirmed, much to our consternation. Tel-Aviv and Haifa had no need of a Military Governor. Jerusalem alone, the Capital of Israel, was regarded by our government as foreign territory, temporarily captured and held until it could be handed over to its "legal rulers," the U.N.O.

Ben-Gurion was quite explicit about this: It was the Governor's duty to provide for the needs of the Jewish inhabitants until the United Nations Organization arrived and took over. Dov Yoseph was also warned to do nothing that could be interpreted as opposition to this takeover.

Dov Yoseph followed orders willingly, stressing *ad nauseum* to the "Consular Committee" how willing he was to discuss the internationalization of Jerusalem!

We were familiar with Dov Yoseph from the time he had been held in detention at the Latrun Camp. His attitude towards the British was, if not slavish, at least one of appeasement, so what could we expect of him now? A brilliant lawyer and a speaker, he used his gifts to protect the rights of the Jews of the City... He succeeded in digging up obscure *Articles of the Law* proving his claim that he was within his rights in providing the hungry inhabitants with food... His appearance before the Consuls in the guise of a talented lawyer automatically turned them into a panel of judges with whom he would argue about the number of calories each citizen had a right to. The Consuls were finally convinced that every Jew should be given the same number of calories enjoyed by the average Indian, while Dov Yoseph demanded a quantity equal to that consumed by the average American...

With the opening of the Burma Road, Dov Yoseph was able to

bring a fresh flow of food into the City, free from the supervision of the U.N. But this brought the fury of Moshe Sharett, the then Foreign Minister of Israel, upon his head. Sharett demanded that the supplies arriving via the Burma Road be placed under the supervision of the U.N., thus conserving our image of a people who "honored" their contracts...

But it was not Dov Yoseph who formulated national policy – this was done by the Government in Tel Aviv. He himself appeared to be an excellent administrator and a firm, honest man. He succeeded in arranging convoys of supplies from the Plains and saw to it that these supplies were justly distributed among rich and poor alike. For that, at least, Jerusalem owes him its gratitude.

★

Our organization was growing fast, particularly as there was now no difficulty in joining us. The Eldad Camp was overflowing with fresh, enthusiastic youngsters who quickly proved themselves to be intrepid fighters. There were now four Combat Divisions, three of them named after those who had fallen during the assault on the Old City walls: the Ya'akov, Yehoshua and Ophra Divisions. The fourth one, the Zion Division, consisted of orthodox youth and was much admired for its prowess. Most of the men there came from Mea She'arim, from the Yeshivot (religious academies) of Agudath Israel and Netorei Karta, and preferred to fight in the framework of the *Lehi* which held Judaic tradition and religion in high regard. Its members, they realized, submitted wholeheartedly to the ultimate value of martyrdom and selflessness. The organization as a whole consisted mostly of free-thinkers, men who generally neglected to observe the religious rituals and tenets, but one and all, we appreciated the fact that these ultra-orthodox youths had cast their lot with us and were treated with affection and respect. We knew that by volunteering to join us they had incurred the disapproval of their spiritual leaders, so we did everything within our power to enable them to follow all those customs and precepts enjoined by their beliefs. It was the least we could do for them.

Giora, Commander of the Orthodox Division, offered me the

post of Second-in-Command but I refused, regarding myself as unsuitable. It was always a terrible strain for me to send others into actual fire. I would willingly charge a fortified position and assault it with grenades, but sending others to do it was something else. I shall never forget the day when I ordered Amatzia to risk his life in order to ascertain the source of enemy fire.

Dror has been killed! A bullet inadvertantly discharged from a rife during target practice, killed this outstanding fighter!

It was hard to accept that Dror should die like that – the man who had been an inspiration to us all, our leader in the Battle of Deir Yassin. It was he who had prevented me from running blindly into the enemy cross-fire and had saved my life time and time again. Dear Dror, who never hid the fact that he wanted to have me beside him, always worrying about me and protecting me. There never was anyone like him for teaching the finer points of weapons and their usage. And how he loved to sing! It was his songs we used to sing on our way to and from training, or when relaxing in the camp. We all loved him dearly, but I more than anyone.

On May 16 we were informed by the defenders of the Jewish quarter in the Old City that the situation was hopeless. On receipt of the communiqué, *Hagana* headquarters promised to send reinforcements within "an hour and a half."

May 17 was a black day indeed for us. The enemy succeeded in breaking through the defences in the Street of the Jews and was not pushed back till evening. Using loudspeakers, the Arabs called the Jews to capitulate and many of the inhabitants gathered in the synagogues to pray.

In their desperate appeals for help the defenders warned that any delay would render help useless. "Your 'hour and a half' has by now become thirty six hours," they said. "What kind of clock are you using?"

On May 18 the Arabs launched a general offensive against the Jewish quarter. They issued an ultimatum: "if you don't capitulate at once you'll end up like the corpses of *Gush Etzion.*"

The defenders continued transmitting their desperate cries for help, and were promised by the *Hagana* that the attack on the Old

City would begin within an hour.

Many hours went by but no attack. Breaking again into the Street of the Jews, the Arabs began demolishing house after house. Again the message was delayed: "If you don't send help it will be too late!"

There were those among the civilians who wanted to demand protection from the Red Cross, or to carry out a white flag, and the defenders had to use force to restrain them.

Finally they informed us that the Old City would fall in a few minutes. Shaltiel promised that his forces would enter the Old City from the south that very night.

At 2.40 a.m., March 19, a *Palmach* force headed by Uzi Narkiss penetrated the Old City, going quickly through the Armenian quarter into the Jewish quarter. The exhausted inhabitants welcomed them with hugs and kisses, rejoicing, as they believed, that the siege was finally broken. But their joy was premature.

The *Palmach* force, too, was in a state of exhaustion after fighting on so many fronts, and Narkiss informed Shaltiel that they could not hold the quarter. He insisted that more men be sent immediately to hold the alley he had taken and also to provide reinforcements for the defenders of the Jewish quarter. Shaltiel delayed his decision and Narkiss announced that if such a force was not forthcoming at once he would leave with his men immediately.

Shaltiel "capitulated" and sent a group of middle-aged men from the Civil Guard, whose main occupation had been, till then, the putting up of earth-work fortifications. They didn't know one end of a rifle from another and burst into tears when they realized that they were to stay in the Jewish quarter... The problems of these oldsters the defenders had to deal with was now compounded by this "force."

Uzi Narkiss did as he had theatened, ordering his men to leave. They obeyed him, even though some of them did so under protest. A young woman who had spent the last few months fighting in the quarter was asked to join the retreating force but she refused, saying: "What, leave now? I'm used to it here, and the devil himself won't make me."

That morning the abandoned positions in the Armenian quarter were relinquished without a shot and passed into Arab hands. The siege was resumed and the days of the quarter were now numbered.

Only some hundreds of meters separated them from our positions on Mount Zion but help was not forthcoming. The defenders held on to every house, fought on every roof and in every yard, and most of their officers were killed. On May 25 they announced that there were no officers left and on the 26th, that they had only 170 machine gun bullets and no grenades.

All that night the Arab loudpeakers called for surrender, adding that all the Jews in the New City had already done so and the old City's Jews had better follow suit....

On May 27 there was no bread.

On the 28th the oldsters of the quarter walked out towards the Legion's positions, a white flag in their hands.

The Old City had fallen. When the Commander of the Arab Legion took a good look at the "surrendering force," he couldn't believe his own eyes. "I should have been able to take them with clubs," was his reaction. There were no more than forty able-bodied men and no ammunition.

Count Falke Bernadotte of Sweden was delegated by the U.N., to mediate between the warring parties, and at the end of June, 1948, this go-between published his plan for the final solution of the Palestine conflict, which included the following: Abdullah, King of Trans-Jordan would be given all Arab territories in Palestine, including Jerusalem; Arab refugees would return to their homes; Jewish immigration would be cut down to a minimum and the Negev was to lie outside the jurisdiction of the Jewish State.

By the end of May of that year, Israel had won victories on all fronts. The territory allocated by the United Nations for the Jewish State was by now in our hands and there was little chance that the Arabs would succeed in pushing us into the sea. The U.N. Security Council decided, therefore, that the time was appropriate for a cease-fire in order to prevent the possibility of "chaos." Unwilling to give up the practice of fishing in murky waters, the great powers thought they could continue to meddle with the Jews with the help of the "Consular Committee" and Count Bernadotte, the mediator. Israel accepted the offer at once and Bernadotte took it upon himself to explain to the Arabs that a temporary cease-fire would help them improve their positions, but to no avail. They would not agree. Only after the Old City had fallen into Abdullah's hands did they accept a four weeks' cease-fire, the time needed to reorganize their armies, co-ordinate their forces and then, with one fell swoop, bring the young State to its knees.

★

The cease-fire, we decided, would be a useful respite during which we could strengthen our forces.

A great majority of our members in the Plains had joined the Israeli Defence Forces and sworn allegiance, but not a few came to Jerusalem to join us in the coming struggle for the future of the capital. Their arrival created the problem of additional barracks and "Camp Dror" was opened in some abandoned houses in the Talbieh quarter. All during the cease-fire, Yanai (Yoseph Menkes) worked our Jeep Squardon day and night, supplying Jerusalem with great quantitites of ammunition, explosives and weapons from the Plains below. Many new faces also appeared. Names that had grown into veritable myths suddenly became flesh and blood, walking and breathing among us – our men released from Latrun, our exiles returned from Africa. When the legendary Yehoshua Cohen appeared I couldn't resist telling him about the night of enchantment, long ago, when Yehezkel, our group leader taught us *From the Depths of the Underground,* his, Cohen's haunting song. Much time had passed since then. Shortly after that meeting in the Valley of the Cross, Yehezkel had been caught and detained in Latrun, from which he succeeded in escaping without any outside help only to be caught outside the town of Ramleh in a state of complete exhaustion. This time he was exiled to Africa. Returning with the rest of the exiles, he immediately volunteered to join a combat unit even though he was a sick man, unfit for any kind of military service.

I would have given anything to see him again but it was not to be. Some time after my meeting with Yehoshua, Yehezkel was killed by a shell in the course of a battle near Beit Guvrin.

Then who should show up but Uzi! "Ginger" Uzi! What a re-union! He told us that he refused to serve down there in the Plains while Jerusalem was being abandoned by the Government, and had come to join us in the coming battles that would determine its fate.

★

Artillery! Jerusalem was bereft of guns!

Month after month the Jewish quarters were inundated by mortars, our homes demolished, our brothers and sisters, grandparents and children, torn to pieces before our very eyes.

The days spent in underground shelters, the fighting, the constant thirst and hunger – all these only strengthened the determination of the Jerusalemites to win. Now, with the respite afforded by the cease-fire, the city had a chance to relax a little and catch its breath. But of course it was only an interlude drawing to a close, the shelling and the fighting were not too far off...

If only we had some artillery with which to give the enemy a taste of their own medicine of fire and brimstone!

The rumor spread like lightening! A ship-load of arms was being brought by the *Etzel* to the shores of our country, carrying eight hundred men especially trained to fight for Jerusalem, with them 5000 guns and ammunition. 250 machine-guns, mortars and, most important of all - cannons for Jerusalem! tanks and mortars for Jerusalem!

The horrifying sequel is well known by now. At a time when the whole Jewish people was fighting for its survival, with Jerusalem in ruins, bleeding at every pore – an evil hand struck at the precious weapons. Shells that were so desperately needed in Jerusalem were fired at the *Altelena,* the arms' ship and freedom fighters, some of whom were survivors of the holocaust in Europe coming to join us in our struggle, were shot down by misguided and misled brother Jews.

Certain as we were that the fighting would be renewed, we

remained confined to barracks. The Arabs, on their part, were ceaselessly reinforcing their old positions, putting up new ones and transporting artillery from Jericho to Jerusalem. This did not prevent them from indulging in occasional sniping at passers-by, killing and wounding many. Dov Yoseph, Governor of the City, would lodge complaints with the U.N. Inspectors, who duly made out a report... On July 24 he was said to have lodged 34 complaints of breaches of the cease-fire in Jerusalem, but this was almost the daily norm. The Arabs did not take the cease-fire too seriously and were further encouraged by the indifference of the U.N. – an attitude that led them to believe they were permitted to increase their military preparations in order to ensure their advantage when firing was renewed.

Both the *Etzel* and the *Lehi* continued holding their forces in the City with the express purpose of preventing any attempt to transfer its control to others, whoever they may be.

The fighting in the Plains was over, and most of the former members of the *Lehi* were now serving in the I.D.F. But in Jerusalem things were different and we were still an independent military force, for we believed that so long as the Government of Israel did not recognize Jerusalem as the country's capital, we would not disband.

When the cease-fire expired the I.D.F. initiated a major offensive. In Jerusalem, too, an attempt was made to harass the Arab positions in the New City as well as in the surrounding villages. The *Hagana* approached the *Etzel* and *Lehi* with the suggestion that we clean up the areas to the west and south of Jerusalem and get rid of their troublesome inhabitants. This task was divided amongst the three organizations: the *Etzel* was assigned to clean up Malcha; we, the *Lehi* were to attack the fortified look-outs above Ein-Kerem, and the *Hagana* – the look-outs of *Hirbat-el-Hamama* (today Mount Herzl).

The operation was set for midnight, Friday night.

Meeting in one of the Bayit Vegan buildings and its surrounding grounds, we had a long wait before finally moving towards *Beit-Mazmil* (today Kiryat Yovel) and our objective: a hovel and some houses.

Kochava, who had by now recovered from her wounds, walked beside me, in charge of our first-aid kit which she carried in a rucksack while I had the stretcher on my back. My love for her, always kept secret and hidden inside me, was still as strong as ever, but I was too shy to reveal it to her. Enough for me that she was there beside me and I could carry the stretcher for her. Nothing could have made me happier!

In the heavy darkness we climbed up perpendicular terraces, stumbling on sharp rocks and slipping down as we went, the stretcher I was carrying struck Kochava badly as she followed me. We seemed to have been walking for ever and my hands were turning to lead under the weight of the stretcher. Uzi's order to halt came as a relief. We were all breathing with difficulty, for it was all uphill, and could barely see a thing. It certainly wasn't easy to feel your way along the rocky terrain with one hand holding a gun and the other a stretcher.

Uzi failed to return. Much later, just before dawn, we decided there was no alternative but to begin without him. At sunrise we were visible to the enemy. It was then that we discovered that the miserable tin hovel was heavily reinforced with concrete on the inside, and effective protection against our fire. Behind the hovel was the enemy, ready and shooting. As the darkness receded, a few of us were wounded and then more and more. We were given the order to retreat quickly and did so, some carrying the wounded on their backs. I collected the guns they couldn't carry and began crawling in the direction of Bayit Vegan, when I came upon Aviram, a member of my cell, trying hard to crawl along but badly impeded by a wound in the leg. He proved too heavy for me to lift so I asked him to climb upon my back. Some rounds were fired at us so I climbed with him over a terrace fence. I felt a queer sensation in the neck. It wasn't painful but experience had taught me that one could be wounded and feel no pain. Touching the place, my hand came away dry, no sign of blood. It was only later, back at the base, that someone noticed a bullet hole in my collar.

Once back at the base I snatched up a stretcher and hurried back to the line of fire. There were many wounded there, carried by comrades on their backs for lack of stretchers.

300

I found Elida, badly hit in the belly, carried by two comrades. Putting him on the stretcher, we tried to get away from the range of fire, at the same time doing our best to shelter him. We began to crawl through some trenches and I was so exhausted my hands dropped from time to time and the wounded man was covered with earth from the walls of the trench. Not far from us I noticed Tamir crawling along, carrying a load of guns he had collected from the injured. I called out, asking him to change places with me.

Back at the base we were informed that five comrades had been killed, with Uzi among them.

Uzi, who had taught the British to fear him, was dead! The man who, when he realized that Jerusalem was about to be abandoned by the Government, gave up all thought of joining the I.D.F., and hurried to join us in our campaign for the capital. Uzi who had taken me, still a boy, to activate a mine under the wheels of MacMillan's car, the leader under whose tuition I had become a man and a fighter. Uzi!

And Amnon – one of my boys in the Youth Cell entrusted to me, who never stopped begging me to let him join the "real" fighters. I could still hear his every word, trying to convince me: "You'll see... you'll find out how good I am"... It was after he had committed some childish misdemeanor in a matter of discipline and I had had to chide him, that he promised he would prove his worth and had indeed done so, paying the ultimate price...

That day we also lost Barzeli, Itzhak and Arnon. Altogether five of our best comrades...

Shattered in body and spirit we boarded the vehicles taking us back to the base. On our way we drove past our friends in the Orthodox Division, returning on foot. They told us that there was great virtue in driving to war – so great, in fact, that one was permitted to do it on the Holy Sabbath. But returning empty-handed – that could be done only on foot.

The atmosphere at the base was gloomy and morale was low. Men and weapons had been lost, and all for nothing. The enemy positions had remained intact. Our depression was also aggravated by a rumor that the *Hagana* had promised us artillery fire during the operation but had not kept the bargain, turning us into nothing less than cannon fodder.

The *Etzel* attack on Malcha also resulted in heavy losses. At first everything went well, the village fell at the first charge and the men decided to take a short break, putting their trust in the *Hagana*'s Mortar Unit which was positioned at the entrances to the village. Then, without warning, the Arabs began shelling them heavily. The look-out and artillery men of the *Hagana* disappeared, for some reason, leaving the fighters without cover. The wounded, who were many, were bandaged and waiting for help in a near-by cave, but in the meantime the enemy had succeeded in taking back a part of the village. They even reached the cave where the wounded were lying, stabbing all but one of them to death.

The battle was protracted and finally the *Etzel* got the upper hand. But they paid a heavy price – seventeen men killed and many injured.

★

Our camps were rife with bitterness. There was talk among the official politicians of another cease-fire and every passing moment was precious, unredeemable. True, we were in constant action, capturing vital positions in the environs of Jerusalem, and God knows every strip of the homeland was precious to us all, but why, we were all asking, why was nothing being done about the Old City? Wasn't this the most essential operation of all? Our men and those of the *Etzel* had been pressuring Shaltiel constantly to break in through the walls. The *Etzel*, which during the last cease-fire had obtained many reinforcements in men and arms, was becoming more and more insistent, and finally went so far as to threaten Shaltiel with independent action if the *Hagana* went on with its shilly-shallying. Then and only then, was an agreement reached that *Lehi*, *Etzel* and the *Hagana* would act jointly in the attempt to free the Old City.

This Night the Old City will be freed!

On July 15 the word was out: Get ready! We're about to begin an operation of major national importance.

We all began to speculate about the nature of the target. What could it be? Was it Beit Tzafafa? Sheikh Jerrach? Could it be Bethlehem? Or perhaps... but no, the name of that place was taboo, not to be mentioned after all the negative answers we had been given in the past. We could not bear to be turned down again.

The men in charge insisted that the target was secret. On the night preceding the action we tried to catch a few hours sleep but the "secret" made us all restless. What kind of target was it, that had such "national importance"? Was it possible that we were finally on our way to take the Old City? How could it be anything else?

Hopeful and expectant we rose that morning to prepare our equipment, when we got a message: "Early tomorrow morning, on the Sabbath, at 5.30 a.m., a new cease-fire comes into force. This has already been agreed to by our Government but the Arabs have promised nothing yet."

Strange that we were prepared to accept a cease-fire at a time when our soldiers were penetrating the enemy front-lines everywhere. Why did we need a cease-fire at a time when the Arabs were fleeing the field? Why should we be interested in their confirming such an agreement while the Old City was still in their hands?

These questions put our forthcoming action, the one "of supreme national importance" in a somewhat questionable light: Would there be time to carry it out before the ceasefire came into force, or would it be scratched at the last moment?

We were called for a briefing. Meir (Yehoshua Zetler), *Lehi* Commander of Jerusalem, announced that we were going to free the Old City. It was enough. We asked for nothing more. Our hearts overflowed with a happiness such as we had never known before, an emotion so profound that we might almost have been in a state of shock. All we could do was murmur: "Tonight we're going to free the Old City!" When we finally came to our senses we burst out in wild singing.

Then it hit us: a cease-fire! We crowded round our leaders, bombarding them with one pertinent question after another: "What about the cease-fire, will it come into force? And if it does, how can we finish the job between 11 p.m. (zero hour for the operation; and 5.30 a.m.?'

We were told that Ben Gurion, and Shaltiel, the *Hagana* Commander in Jerusalem, were now talking of the Old City as the "Hope of Ages"... Did they really mean it? We found it hard to believe them, after all they had done to us – the fighters of the underground – and to the inhabitants of Jerusalem.

The leaders were overwhelmed by our questions, and Meir tried to calm us down: "What they think and how far they are ready to go to keep their word is not important. We'll break into the Old City and in the heat of battle, time has no meaning! We will go on till we take the town!"

We believed Meir, or rather, we wanted to believe him. We could not bear the thought that he might be mistaken or that he had been misled tonight!

Till then – jubilation, hope and increasing tension. The joy was more than we could bear; the tension – a great strain.

How well we knew that the wall of stones, fire and lead would have to be broken by our own bodies; that many of us marching to the battle would never return; never live to see the greatest victory of all, the victory to which all our lives, our dreams, our sufferings and tribulations, our hopes and rejoicings had been dedicated.

We had long made ourselves worthy of this holy mission, and our hearts were full, though there was little of the heroic in our appearance. My friends and I, men of the 3rd Division, envied those of the 1st who would be the first to charge. They, in their turn, envied the sappers who would precede them.

We examined our weapons, trusting them to bring us to the Holy Mount of the Temple. Meir seemed to have changed – or perhaps the change was in us. It was as if Judah Maccabee was facing us there, and our friends of the Orthodox Division with their bearded faces had become the priests and levites accompanying us to war.

304

But we had let our imagination carry us too far. It was time to return to reality. The briefing was as follows: At 22.00 hours the *Hagana* would begin shelling the Old City with *Davidka* mortars in an assault, so they promised, stronger than anything ever seen before. Zero hour for breaking in was set for 23.00 hours that night. First the sappers would lay an enormous load of explosives at the foot of the walls, behind the old Post Office. The first target would be the *Freres* school to be immediately followed by the Jewish quarter, the Western Wall and the Holy Mount of the Temple. Simultaneously with this, the *Etzel* would storm the New Gate, moving in the direction of Damascus Gate, and the *Hagana* would force its way into Zion Gate, moving in the direction of the Jewish quarter via the Armenian Gate.

Tonight!

★

We assembled in the great square at the heart of Camp Dror – the Fighters for the Liberation of Israel, each Section headed by its leader. Mine was headed by Ariella and other girls could be discerned here and there among the men: Drora, Achino'am, Yehudith and Kochava.

Blessed indeed is the nation that can number such women among its daughters!

We couldn't restrain our excitement; it mounted by the minute and the slightest cause served to stimulate it. You looked at your friends and the jubilation in their eyes excited you; you caught a glimpse of a girl and your heart beat faster. There was Old Hillel, the bearded old Yemenite and a veteran fighter, and you felt like hugging him and kissing his red beard... And little Uzi, Hillel's son who had followed in his father's footsteps – you looked at him and your heart overflowed with pride, pride in your tribe – the tribe of fighters for the liberation of Israel, and pride in this beloved child of a father's old age, obstinately following his old parent to battle!

Then the wounded arrived to shake hands, to bestow a blessing and to wish us success. In their eyes could be seen a profound love mixed with a burning envy. Tears were swallowed in embarrassment and the girls were crying openly.

And there was Meir. A deep silence filled the camp as we waited for him to speak. His words were simple – the same words that had caused us to leave our loving homes in order to struggle along the Via Dolorosa. On this night. At this hour. "The generations of two thousand years have been waiting for you" – said Meir "They have been waiting for this night."

"Tonight we go forth to liberate the City of David."

It was enough. We felt as though we had suddenly grown in stature. The longings of generations of our people had given us wings. Countless martyrs had dreamt of such a consummation, but to no avail. This night had been given to us!

Suddenly the square rang with the cries of children: "Good luck!" "Good luck! Go in peace and return in peace!" We turned and saw that the place was crowded with youngsters, five and six-year olds. They had come from the orphanage near-by. Some of them were orphans whose parents had died of some illness or at war. But there were those whose parents had entrusted them to this institution until they themselves returned from the fighting.

And here they were, taking leave of us with their innocent prayers.

There was not a dry eye among us, not even the hardiest.

In silence we took to the trucks.

Orders were strict: No lights, no singing, no talking. Nothing should be done that might give our presence away to the enemy. One could easily go crazy, choking down all that pent-up emotion.

There was *Bevingrad!*

Two platoons, the one I belonged to and the Orthodox one, marched into the building above Artzieli's the watchmaker. The religious comrades began chanting the Friday evening prayer before the Sabbath (*Ma'ariv*), gradually to be joined by all of us, even those who had forgotten the last time they had said a prayer in their lives. There was no need to look for head coverings this time – we had been provided with steel helmets.

Dov and Shimeon, long bearded and with side-curls coming down to their shoulders cried out bravely: "And the saviours went up Mount Zion to pass judgment on Mount Esau." Before leaving camp we had already been speculating on the part to be played by them in this operation. Now we knew...

It was almost time for the "formidable" shelling we had been promised. We went into Bible House.

We waited till after 22.00 hours. The sounds of heavy shelling filled the air – bombs and mortars exploded, lighting up the skies of Jerusalem. They came from the enemy lines to explode in the New City. Were there any of ours falling on the other side of the walls? Had the *Hagana* started the promised offensive?

After 23.00 hours we were still unsure. Shells without number were exploding but were they ours or theirs?

"Could it be that the *Hagana?*... "The same doubt and bewilderment was in all our minds, but who dared express aloud such monstrous thoughts?

A message arrived from the *Hagana:* "There have been some technical difficulties... They promise to begin the operation in one hour."

Another hour passed. The enemy mortars were now falling closer and closer to us. The house sheltering us seemed about to disintegrate, burying us all in the rubble. Then suddenly there was the sound of heavy shooting and a series of shattering explosions.

Had the sappers gone up to the wall? Did they have adequate cover?

No. Not yet. One incendiary bomb out of the hundreds, maybe the thousands fired on us by the enemy that night, had unluckily struck one of our vehicles parked by the Anglo-Palestine Bank. It contained explosives and ammunition belonging to the *Etzel* and the *Lehi,* put there in preparation for tonight's operation. Our men were just in time to unload the adjacent jeeps of their precious cargo before they went up in flames but the loss was irreparable.

Time passed agonisingly. Shells exploded all around us but there was no sign of the promised attack.

We began to fear that the whole operation would have to be put off, if not cancelled altogether. Our casualties might even be so heavy as to prevent us taking any part at all, if and when it began. Obviously the enemy knew that we had a concentration of men and equipment there, why else did they persist in shelling us for so long?

And the cease-fire was rapidly approaching.

In spite of all our fears and apprehensions not a word was said. Tense and apprehensive though we were, not one of us dared put into words the suspicion that the night would pass and with it our dream of marching up Mount Zion as victors. In the inferno of exploding shells that surrounded us, each closely followed by another, it became impossible to gauge the distance from the source of fire. "Who knows," we let ourselves hope – "the promised offensive may have started."

We were given an order: "Get ready to charge!"

We spread out, prepared for anything. From the Bible House we were led to Suleiman Road and stood there, our backs to the stone walls of the "Sisters of the St. Vincent" Monastery. We were now able, not only to hear the enemy mortars but also see them hitting their target and exploding. Imagine our consternation when we realized that the enemy was not shooting haphazardly but was receiving exact signals as to where to direct the fire. From time to time a red rocket would be fired on our side, and the place was immediately inundated with mortars. These red rockets were rapidly approaching us and the air was thick with shraphnel everywhere.

A rocket fell into an adjacent empty lot, to be immediately followed by shells, "waltzing" and letting the shrapnel fly in all directions. Another one hit the road just in front of us as we cowered against the wall.

As we had ample protection from the rear, provided by that sturdy wall, I told my friends to take off their steel helmets and cover their foreheads with them, doing so myself.

At that very moment a shell burst about twenty centimeters in front of me. I felt a hard crack in the head. A piece of metal had hit me from beneath the helmet, penetrating the skull above the right eye. There was a heavy flow of blood and I could see nothing in my right eye. I thought it had been thrust out by the haemorrhage. My left eye remained untouched but unable to open. I tried to get up, to ask for help – but I had been hurt in the

308

legs as well. My chest felt scorched and my right hand moved in a queer fashion as if it was paralysed.

I heard sounds of groaning – who could tell how badly others were hurt, probably worse than myself, for I was still upright and they were on the ground... I lay back, waiting for the oderlies to arrive.

Drora, our nurse, asked who needed first aid. Nobody rose or asked for help so I pulled myself up: "I'm wounded!"

It was too dark for Drora to examine me but she saw me standing up, heard me speaking clearly – so she asked if I could cross the road unaided to the First Aid Station in the Ottoman Bank. It was no more than forty meters away – I didn't know if I could make it. But neither was I willing to ask Drora to support me, to expose her to the constant shelling of that segment of road. Yet, if I set out alone, stumbled and fell, I would be endangering not only Drora but other comrades who would be forced to leave their cover in order to bring me in under fire.

"Well, what do you say? Can you make it?"

"I'm not certain."

Guided and supported by Drora I finally reached the First Aid room, walking in complete darkness with one eye blinded and the other refusing to open.

I heard Giora asking: "Who is this?"

No wonder he didn't recognize me, my face bathed in blood. I would have given much at that moment not to have to identify myself, to cause him such a shock. After all, ever since his escape from prison, the three of us, Giora, Dror and I had always fought side by side. Dror had fallen and now I showed up in such a state... In my desire to spare him I tried to make light of things and began humming: "We'll see the enemy bleeding yet... and the light on Zion will shine!" But the croaks that issued from my throat were so bizarre that I gave up the attempt and asked instead: "Giora, why aren't we breaking into the Old City?"

I never heard his reply – it was swallowed up by the sound of an enormous explosion that kept reverberating on and on.

Somebody shouted: "Our sappers have demolished the wall!"

Well, I had finally heard what I had longed to hear! It was music to my ears – only the Messiah's horn could have given me more pleasure. My blood was flowing unremittingly, I could see nothing and the shrapnel splinters were embedded deep in my head. I realized I was badly wounded, might even be dying, but at that moment I was so happy.. a kind of happiness I've never known before.

They bandaged my head, trying to staunch the heavy flow of blood. I could hear my comrades leaving, one by one.

"Good luck! go in peace and return in peace!" I called after them apologising in my heart for having been wounded, for not being able to join them. I prayed for them as I had never prayed before.

I had to be evacuated to hospital, but the road was blocked by barbed wire and concrete so that no ambulance could get through.

Sharon saw to it that I was laid on a stretcher, and sent four fighters to carry me to the ambulance. They carried me through the open street and I prayed that no one would get hurt because of me. Near the Daniel Garden a shell exploded quite close to us and I was hit again on the head. This time the splinter lodged in the skull bone, not penetrating the brain. Amazing luck! I asked my friends if they were all right and begged them to leave me there and save themselves. "Nonsense!" They didn't even try to argue with me.

Finally we reached the ambulance and I was put inside. Just lying there unmoving seemed to slow down the haemorrhage.

I was taken to a temporary branch of the *Hadassah* hospital, located in the buildings of the former English Hospital in Hanevi'im St. When I asked for some water to quench my thirst I was refused, on the grounds that it might harm me. With great gentleness the nurses moistened my dry lips, with me doing my utmost to suck in at least a drop...

"You're in luck," a nurse told me. "Dr. Beller has just come from the United States. We had nobody to treat head wounds before he arrived. Dr. Ashkenazi is the only other neurologist in the country and he's looking after the wounded in Jaffa. A head wound wouldn't have a chance in Jerusalem if it weren't for Dr. Beller, and now he's here he's working day and night, operating all the time without rest and treating each patient as though he were his own son."

While the doctor and his assistants were examining me I gathered from their talk that I should be operated on immediately. It came to me that I was going to die – if not from the splinters in my head then from the operation itself. How could a man survive having his head opened up...?

To die? Yes. I felt I could accept the idea. But then I thought of my poor mother and father – the terrible anguish they would suffer. True, they had five other sons, but I had always known I was their favorite, the one they loved so dearly. Why God, why did you make them love me more than my brothers? I had never wanted it, and now they were going to be hurt where they were most vulnerable.

But I had to resign myself to it. I was no better than my fallen comrades nor were my own kin better than theirs. For every soldier dying in battle there was someone to whom he was the most precious thing in the world.

I must learn not just to resign myself, but to do it gladly. I was doomed to die while still very young, what better way was there to go than for the sake of Jerusalem? And I prayed: "Dear Lord, instead of *Tefillin* on my forehead I pray to you with a piece of shrapnel between my eyes, but this I beg of you: If die I must – let it be so. But please, in your infinite mercy, let me see the salvation of Jerusalem before I close my eyes forever. After that – do as you will with me."

As I lay in my room waiting for the operation and trying to glean some news of what was going on outside, I heard the nurses talking: "They've tried to take the Old City again and failed."

I couldn't believe it, it made no sense. Perhaps I was dreaming.

"Yes. It's all because of the cease-fire."

"But why? Why didn't we go on attacking? The Arabs hadn't even accepted the cease-fire so why did we have to stop at once!!!"

I heard it and decided I was hallucinating with fever.

Two hours later Meir and Saba (Yehuda Leib Schneerson of the *Lehi*), paid me a visit. Meir was very inquiring as to how I felt. I tried to answer calmly. I'd been hurt in the head and lost an eye.

311

Meir stopped me, saying that the doctors thought the eye might still be saved...

"What's with the Old City?" I interrupted him in a loud voice.

"Fine... Fine..." he muttered. His embarrassment made it all too clear to me.

The Old City had remained in the hands of the enemy.

★

Friends came to visit. A few hours ago they had been about to take the Old City. What had happened? Why did they stop?

One of the reasons was that the "cone" given us by the *Hagana* – an explosive device so named because of its peculiar shape – had not been effective in breaking down the walls.

The *Etzel* had managed to penetrate the walls at the New Gate, entered the Old City and cleared a certain area within. But by then they had to call a halt – the time of the cease-fire had arrived – the cease-fire declared by the U.N., which the Arabs had not even taken the trouble to accept. The *Etzel*, ordered to retreat, refused to obey and Shaltiel threatened that he would order the men stationed in Notre Dame to open fire on them. The *Etzel* fighters were thus forced to abandon their bridge-head.

The Old City was not taken that night.

★

With so many wounded there were men whose condition was more critical than mine and I had to wait a long time for my operation. In the meantime my brothers had found out what had happened and began visiting me, one after the other. I made them promise not to tell our parents – there was no reason to worry them before the operation. If I died, they would get an announcement. If not, why destroy their peace of mind?

But Mother felt instinctively that something had happened to her precious son. With four sons fighting on many fronts she suddenly began making inquiries concerning the whereabouts of Zuri. When my brothers came home they had just one answer: "We haven't seen him or heard anything!"

Despairing of my brothers, she went to Mrs. Shalom, who also had two sons in the *Lehi*. As soon as she entered the house Mrs. Shalom asked: "How's Zuri doing?" The poor woman thought that Mother already knew I was wounded. When she realized Mother knew nothing she held her tongue, knowing well that I had lost an eye and my life was in danger, and who was she to give a mother such tidings about her son. Her own son, Benyamin (our comrade Michael) had lost an eye, not far from the actual place I had been hit. But Mother was not to be deterred: "What's happened to Zuri?" she demanded to know.

"He's been hurt lightly in the arm," said Mrs. Shalom. In a panic Mother ran home and told Father to go to the hospital at once: "Our Zuri's been hurt!" Father left at once and, as soon as he saw me, understood everything.

Next time they arrived together.

"Why is your bed so dirty? What's going on here? The whole sheet's covered with blood!"

Poor Mother had no idea my head wound was constantly haemorrhaging.. What luck that she didn't understand.

Sounds of exploding shells again filled the air. When Margalit, my sister came to visit me, she told me that one had burst quite near her. "It was a miracle I wasn't hurt!" she said. "The war, dammit, is going on but for us there is a cease-fire, and the Holy Mount is not in our hands."

I had to wait for 48 hours before my turn came to be operated on, and the barber came to shave off my hair and eyebrows in preparation. Unfortunately for me the barber was a volunteer of much good will but little experience.

Each time he nicked my scalp I felt a searing pain that was almost more than I could bear. By the time he had finished I thought my end had come. Then I was wheeled into the operating room.

"Head operations are done without administering an anaesthetic," said the surgeon. And so it was. My eyes were covered by a towel so that I couldn't see the instruments or what was being done with them, but I felt and heard everything.

At first Dr. Beller opened up my skull, as you open a tin of sardines. Then I heard him saying: "Scissors, please, pincers, gauze..." I could hear the blood vessels beating in my head and the sound of metal splinters being pulled out. There was some hammering and a lancet penetrated my brain. I was in pain, in pain... The local anaesthetic wasn't enough. It hurt so much.

"I will not groan," I told myself. "A *Lehi* man doesn't groan."

My whole body contracted with the pain and the surgeon said: "Tell me when it gets really bad." I did as he told me, and he sprayed some liquid into the skull that seemed to ease the pain a little.

Then the sawing began. As they smoothed the bone through which a hole had been drilled, so that the splinters could be drawn out, I couldn't stop shuddering.

There seemed to be no end to the operation – it went on for hours. Through it all I was wide awake and tried to busy myself with all kinds of thoughts. My head was painful but my thoughts crystal clear. I pondered and ruminated about the mysteries of life and death. Interestingly I no longer felt I was going to die. Did a dying man always feel he was going? How was I to know?

I regarded death as an actual possibility and thought of my friends who had died. What had they felt? Did they realize they were going to die? I remembered my friend Ha'im and was worried by the fact that he had disappeared and that the nation knew nothing of his life or death. There was no tombstone, no grave, no indication of where he was buried.

If I die, I thought, I wanted to be buried in a temporary grave until we liberate the Mount of Olives. And then, when they put me there, I would like them to put up a tombstone for Ha'im next to mine. It would be a good thing, I thought, if Ha'im – Alexander Rubovitch – could find his final rest beside me, just as we had fought next to each other when he was alive.

I should have told this to my friends who had visited me before the operation. Perhaps I could tell the doctor now? No, he was too busy, too concentrated. One mustn't interrupt such delicate work. But if I survived, that would be the first thing I would take care of.

Wavering between life and death it seemed so clear to me that I was face to face with God and he seemed to be waiting to hear my last prayers. Again and again it went through my mind that it

314

wouldn't be fair to ask for life since I was not any better than my friends who had died in battle...

And still the operation went on and on... "When do we finish, Doctor?" "Soon... Soon... Don't worry..."

I had gone into the operating room before sunrise. When I left it – alive – it was after sunset.

I woke up to find myself in room No. 10. When I tried to raise myself a little, I succeeded.

"What's this? Are they bringing healthy people in here now?" joked an injured man in the next bed.

I looked at him with my one eye, full of pity.

"Elida, quiet!" cried one of the nurses.

Elida? Are you Elida? I took a good look at him but failed to recognize him except for the color of his eyes. Was this feeble creature the strong and manly Elida, the same man to whom I had brought a stretcher during the battle for Beit Mazmil?

"I'm Elnakam," I told him. Now it was his turn to be astonished. We had both lost so much blood that we couldn't recognize each other.

After the operation I felt that there was something wrong with my hand, but on examining it the doctor said he couldn't find a thing. Two days later I touched the painful spot and felt some foreign body pressing on the vein of the hand. This time Dr. Beller discovered an incrustation under which lay a splinter which pressed on the major vein, almost cutting it. Again I was taken to the operating room, there to be saved for the second time.

While I lay in hospital, recovering from my injuries, my friends came to visit me. There was Ariella, my darling Kochava, Zamir, Michael and all the others.

One morning, when such a group had assembled, I looked at their faces and asked: "What's happening?"

"Nothing," they replied, avoiding my eyes.

"Don't give me any of that. What are you hiding?"

Bit by bit it all came out. There had been an accident in the camp, an explosion. Five people were killed:

Ariella, so mysterious, so beautiful. Zamir, the devoted and serious group leader. Michael, who lived in my neighbourhood.

Little Uzi, born to old Hillel in the autumn of his days and adopted by all of us. And Kochava. My beloved Kochava to whom I had never revealed what was in my heart.

My wounds healed and I left the hospital, but I wasn't myself. I had lost an eye, and fortunately still had the other. My head was fine but there was no panacea for an aching heart...

★

For nineteen long years I carried the pain with me, day and night, week days and holy days. For me, as for everybody else, there was joy and grief, laughter or anger. I ate and drank, worked hard and raised a family. But deep in my heart there was always the pain, a grief that would not subside. Sometimes, left to myself, I would weep, with or without tears. I wept for Ha'im, for Ben-Zion, for Yankele, for Dror, Uzi and Ariella. And I wept for Kochava, my first love, who had been my dream while living never to be attained, and was now just a memory.

I wept for the fallen, the known and the unknown. There had been so many, yet salvation was still out of reach: a remnant of a country, a taste of independence...

Most of the land, including its heart, Jerusalem, was in the hands of strangers, but my people were indifferent, choosing to disregard this unpalatable fact.

My friends and comrades – had they died in vain? I still lived, but to what purpose?

I remembered my prayer before the operation, pleading to be permitted to hear of the liberation of Jerusalem, even if I were to die immediately afterwards. Was that, perhaps, the reason why I had been allowed to survive? Would I live to see my prayer answered?

Nineteen years went by and it was June 7, 1967. Jerusalem was liberated. That which my comrades and I had failed to achieve was done by our younger brothers. Sinai, Judea, Samaria and the Golan were liberated or was it only a dream?

Then we returned to reality: the land was ours, under our own sovereignty.

But the hour of salvation is still to come. It awaits its own saviours.

316

LIST OF CODE NAMES

Aviram, Yoram – Itzhak Greenberg
Aviram – Meir Kan-Dror
Avramiko – Yoseph Meyuchas
Avner – Tody Pel'i
Achino'am – Sima Assoulin-Solomon
Itamar - Prof. Kalman Perek
Eldad – Yoseph Yagen
Eliezer – Zvi Frank
Ephrat – Sarah Meloumad
Amnon – Ya'akov Erev Cohen
Ariella – Leah Prizant
Arnon – Yonathan Yuval
Arnon – Avraham Levi
Aryeh – Adi Bardanov
Ben-Nun. Amichai – David Gottlieb
Ben-Zion – Moshe Barazani
Ben-Zion – Ben–Zion Yerushalmi
Gavriel – Refael Mamiah
Gid'on – Avraham Danenberg
Jimmy - Rachamin Albalack
Giora - Yehuda Fedder-Bargiora
Dov – Menashe Eichler
Dvorah – Ahuva Gil
Dvorah – Malka Habouba-Levi
Dyll – Avraham Kerilla
Old Danny – Zvi
Finkelstein-Shohami
Dror – Mordechai Ben Uzziahu
Drora – Nitzhia Levi-Ofer
Datan Yifrotz – Yehuda Kan-Dror
Old Hillel – Avraham Karawani
Zamir – David Schneeweiss

Ha'im – Alexander Rubovitch
Hanna – Sarah Hasson
Hanoch – Mordechai Friedman-Gil
Yehoshua, Eli – David Sobol
Yehoshua – Nissim Helber
Yehudit – Batya Barashi-Zaken
Yoav – Rahamim Zilka
Yochanan, Ben-Zion – Benyamin
Gonen (Gonionsky)
Yechezkel, Peretz – Naphtali Cohen
Ya'el – Chaya (Ya'el
Brandwein-Ben Dov)
Yankele – Issachar Huberman
Izhak – Tzalach Mizrachi
Israel – Ephraim Cohen
Israel – Zion Cohen
Issachar – Itzhak Mimran
Kochava – Miriam Fried
Michael – Zion Abougov
Michael – Benyamin Shalom
Michael – Moshe Naor
Nuria – Miriam Barashi-Cohen
Nachshon, Shimshon – Moshe
Hazzan
Uzi – Dov Berman
Amos – Moshe Edelstein
Ophra – Rahel Zelzer
Zephania – Menachem Mor
Shaul – Zion Cohen
Sharon – Meir Golan
Techia – Chaya Mathiovitch
Tamir – Baruch Ephrati
Little Uzi – Assaf Karawani

GLOSSARY

Altelena – Name of Etzel's arms ship destined for Israel and sunk by the Hagana.

Av – The 11th month in the Hebrew Calendar.

Betar – Acronym for Brit Trumpeldor – a National Youth Movement.

"Bevingrad" – Compound in central Jerusalem used by the British Police and Civil Administrative offices heavily fortified by barbed wire and guards. Named after the British Foreign Minister, Ernest Bevin.

Brit Hashmonaim – Religious Youth Movement.

Cheder – Religious early education class.

Cholent – Traditional Jewish food, usually prepared on Friday and kept warm for the Sabbath.

Eretz Israel – Land of Israel.

Etzel – Irgun Zvai Leumi – National Military Underground Organization.

Falafel – Chick peas made into balls and fried.

"Gestapo" – Popular name for the British police armoured cars.

Hagana – Illegal armed force controlled by the Zionist Establishment.

Hagomel – Prayer of thanks after being saved from danger.

Hashomer – An organization of Jewish Guards at the time of Turkish rule.

Hatikva – The Jewish National Anthem.

Havdalla – Prayer said at the end of Shabbath.

Jihad – Moslem Holy War.

Kibbutzim – Collective farms.

Kottel – Western Wall: Remaining wall of the Temple Mount Complex from the destruction of the 2nd Temple.

Kurdim – Jewish immigrants from Kurdistan.

Lehi – Lohamei Herut Israel – Fighters for the Freedom of Israel.

Ma'as – The Deed, an Underground Newspaper printed by Lehi.

Ne'illa – Final Prayer on the Day of Atonement.

Nili – Acronym for Jewish Spy Ring which helped Britain against the Turks in World War I.

Palmach – Hagana Combat Unit trained for Guerilla warfare.

Pitta – Flat round oriental bread.

Shma Israel – "Hear O Israel" A Jewish Prayer.

Shofar – Ram's Horn, blown during specific prayers on Jewish High Holidays.

Shomer Hatzair – Leftist Party, which collaborated with the British.

Tefillin – Philacteries: leather thongs bound on the left arm and a box with a prayer inside, placed on the forehead, used by men during morning prayers.

The Front – A Lehi periodical (He'hazit).

White Paper – British Regulations prohibiting Jewish immigration and limiting purchase of land.

318